LETTERS OF BLOOD

Letters of Blood
and other works in English

Göran Printz-Påhlson

Edited by
Robert Archambeau

Open Book Publishers CIC Ltd.,
40 Devonshire Road, Cambridge, CB1 2BL, United Kingdom
http://www.openbookpublishers.com

© 2011 Robert Archambeau; Foreword © Elinor Shaffer; 'The Overall Wandering of Mirroring Mind': Some Notes on Göran Printz-Påhlson © Lars-Håkan Svensson
© 2011 Ulla Printz-Påhlson on Göran Printz-Påhlson original texts now at the Lund University Library

Some rights are reserved. This book is made available under the Creative Commons Attribution-Non-Commercial-No Derivative Works 2.0 UK: England & Wales License. This license allows for copying any part of the work for personal and non-commercial use, providing author attribution is clearly stated. Details of allowances and restrictions are available at:

http://www.openbookpublishers.com

As with all Open Book Publishers titles, digital material and resources associated with this volume are available from our website:

http://www.openbookpublishers.com/product.php/86

ISBN Hardback: 978-1-906924-57-7
ISBN Paperback: 978-1-906924-56-0
ISBN Digital (pdf): 978-1-906924-58-4
ISBN Digital ebook (epub version): 978-1-906924-59-1
ISBN Digital ebook (mobi version): 978-1-906924-60-7

Cover: Göran Printz-Påhlson (ca. 1950)

Typesetting by www.bookgenie.in

Acknowledgment is made to the Department of Manuscripts and Special Collections of Lund University Library and especially to its head, Birgitta Lindholm, for their kind assistance and to the Swedish Academy for a generous grant towards the cost of preparing the manuscript.

All paper used by Open Book Publishers is SFI (Sustainable Forestry Initiative), PEFC (Programme for the Endorsement of Forest Certification Schemes) and Forest Stewardship Council (FSC) certified

Printed in the United Kingdom and United States by
Lightning Source for Open Book Publishers

For those who knew Printz-Påhlson best

Contents

	Page
Acknowledgements	xi
Contributors	xiii
Foreward: Göran Printz-Påhlson, a Life in and beyond Letters *Elinor Shaffer*	xv
Inbetween: Locating Göran Printz-Påhlson *Robert Archambeau*	xxi
'The Overall Wandering of Mirroring Mind': Some Notes on Göran Printz-Påhlson *Lars-Håkan Svensson*	xxix

The Words of the Tribe: Primitivism, Reductionism, and Materialism in Modern Poetics

Part One: Linguistic Primitivism in Modernism and Romanticism	3
Part Two: Linguistic Reductionism in Poetry Criticism	19
Part Three: The Material Word: From Imagism to New Criticism to Intertextualism	31
Part Four: The Polity of Metaphor and the Purity of Diction	45

Other Prose

Part Five: Style, Irony, Metaphor, and Meaning	59
Part Six: Realism as Negation	67
Part Seven: Historical Drama and Historical Fiction: The Example of Strindberg	79

Part Eight: The Canon of Literary Modernism: A Note on
Abstraction in the Poetry of Erik Lindegren   95

Part Nine: The Tradition of Contemporary Swedish Poetry   109

Part Ten: Kierkegaard the Poet   115

Part Eleven: Surface and Accident: John Ashbery   125

Part Twelve: The Voyages of John Matthias   133

Letters of Blood: Poems

Letters of Blood   141

One

My Interview with I.A. Richards   143

Generation   147

Televisiondreamroutines   149

The Longest-Running Show on Television   150

The Enormous Comics   151

Two

Aelius Lamia: Tankas for Robert Hass   157

Odradek   159

Turing Machine   160

Broendal   161

Two Prose Poems   162

Sir Charles Babbage Returns to Trinity College   163

Man-Made Monster Surreptitiously Regarding Idyllic Scene   164

Joe Hill in Prison   165

Remember the Rosenbergs   166

When Beaumont and Tocqueville First Visited Sing-Sing   167

Three Baroque Arias from Gradiva   168

Three

Comedians   171
Acrobats on the Radio: Letter to Newcomb   175
To John at the Summer Solstice, Before His Return   178

Four

The Green-Ey'd Monster   183
Select Bibliography of Works by Göran Printz-Påhlson 219
A Note on the Text   223

Acknowledgements

Many are the debts I have incurred in the editing of this book, but the greatest debt precedes the actual process of editing, since it dates from my time as a visiting lecturer at Lund University in the late 1990s. It was there that I first met Lars-Håkan Svensson, now of Linköping University, and (briefly) Jesper Svenbro, of the Centre Louis Gernet—poets and scholars who had modelled their careers on their great mentor Göran Printz-Påhlson. Through them came a memorable introduction to Printz-Påhlson's work, and to the man himself. That introduction enriched my own intellectual life, and I cannot repay the debt, except in a small way by dedicating this book to them.

I owe John Matthias of the University of Notre Dame my thanks for sharing his correspondence with Printz-Påhlson, and for his words of wise counsel throughout the process of editing. Thanks are due, too, to Elinor Shaffer of Cambridge University, for her foreword but also for her guidance and forbearance. Rupert Gatti and Alessandra Tosi of Open Book Publishers showed me more patience than I deserved, and I have been helped immensely by the efforts of my assistant at Lake Forest College, Octavio Oliveira de Araujo. The manuscript has benefited from comments by Marcel Inhoff of the University of Bonn, Jean-Luc Garneau and Richard Fisher of Lake Forest College, and Stefan Holander of University College—Finnmark, Norway.

I would be remiss not to thank the organisers and participants of a conference on the work of Printz-Påhlson at Clare Hall, Cambridge, in the summer of 2010. Their questions and comments proved inspiring and invaluable. The Swedish Academy made my presence at that conference possible, for which I offer my gratitude.

Closer to home, let me thank my wife Valerie and my daughter Lila for their encouragement, support, and love during the long, arduous, and happy process of an editor's work.

Contributors

Robert Archambeau is a poet and critic whose books include the study *Laureates and Heretics: Six Careers in American Poetry* (2010) and the poetry collection *Home and Variations* (2004). He has edited several books, including *Word Play Place: Essays on the Poetry of John Matthias* (1998) and *The & Now Awards: The Best Innovative Writing* (2009). His writing has appearing in *Poetry, Boston Review, PN Review, Pleiades, Chicago Review*, and many other journals, and he has received grants and awards from the Academy of American Poets, the Swedish Academy, and other organisations. He has taught at Lund University in Sweden, and is professor of English at Lake Forest College, Illinois.

Elinor Shaffer, FBA, is Senior Fellow of the merged Institute of Germanic & Romance Studies, University of London. She is also Research Director and Series Editor of *The Reception of British and Irish Authors in Europe* (Continuum 2002-). Her publications include *The Fall of Jerusalem: The Mythological School of Biblical Criticism and Secular Literature 1770–1880* (1975), *Erewhons of the Eye: Samuel Butler as Painter, Photographer and Art Critic* (1987). Elinor Shaffer has taught at Berkeley, Cambridge, University of East Anglia, and held Visiting posts at Berlin, Brown, Zurich, and Stanford.

Lars-Håkan Svensson is Professor Emeritus of Language and Culture at Linköping University, Sweden. His main publications are on Renaissance poetry (Samuel Daniel, Edmund Spenser) and contemporary American and Irish poetry. His three interviews with Göran Printz-Påhlson are included in the latter's *När jag var prins utav Arkadien* (1995). He is a critic as well as a translator (among others Aeschylus, Sophocles, Euripides, Sir Philip Sidney, John Matthias, Paul Muldoon, and Les Murray). He lives in Lund.

Foreword: Göran Printz-Påhlson, a Life in and beyond Letters[1]

Elinor Shaffer

The Swedish-born intellectual Göran Printz-Påhlson was known internationally for his modernist criticism and poetry, and his translations of major American, Irish, and English poets into Swedish, as well as of Swedish poets into English. He taught at Harvard, Berkeley and, from 1964 to 1989, in the Scandinavian department of the medieval and modern languages faculty at Cambridge University.

Printz-Påhlson was born into modest circumstances in the town of Hässleholm in southern Sweden. As a student at Lund University he became part of a circle of young writers now known as the Lund group, actively concerned with modernism in poetry and art. He distinguished himself early by his critical work *Solen i spegeln* (*The Sun in the Mirror*, 1958), which was immediately acclaimed in Sweden and has established itself as a major work on modern poetics.

Printz-Påhlson began to publish his own poetry—his first collection appeared in 1956—and worked on a doctorate in Nordic languages at Lund, before moving to Harvard University, where he taught from 1960 to 1962. His time there, with his young family and as part of a lively community, began a long and fruitful engagement with America and American writing, music,

---

1. The above is a slightly expanded version of my obituary of Göran Printz-Påhlson published in *The Guardian*, Monday 6 November 2006 (http://www.guardian.co.uk/news/2006/nov/06/guardianobituaries.booksobituaries)

and mores. In 1963, he moved to the University of California at Berkeley, again teaching his own language, but discovering another American language and world, and exploring the poetry of the west coast in the heyday of the San Francisco movement. At Berkeley he met Thom Gunn, a British poet born in Kent and educated at Cambridge, who like several poets taught at the University, with the backing of Tom Parkinson, an enthusiast for contemporary poetry; Gunn's experimental lifestyle depicted in his poetry of the San Francisco 'scene' was to bring him attention (some shocked at his departure from the 'movement' he had belonged to in Britain) and, later, renown. Poetry readings were a constant feature of the period, set off by Allen Ginsburg's *Howl*, which had been published by Lawrence Ferlinghetti, who ran the City Lights book shop where the Beat poets stayed when they passed through. Ferlinghetti had survived the court case against him for publishing *Howl*, and was vindicated by the verdict: the poem's literary merits outweighed its 'obscenity.' At all the 'readings' the oral, performative element was powerful, and poems were often accompanied by some kind of musical or rhythmic beat. This encounter with America and with a vibrant new poetry scene coloured and animated Printz-Påhlson's lifelong activity of translation of American poets into Swedish, and of Swedish poets into English.

The following year Printz-Påhlson moved to Cambridge, where he taught in the Scandinavian department headed by Elias Bredsdorff, the noted Danish critic, historian, and former resistance fighter. He was elected a fellow of Clare Hall, a newly founded, mixed graduate college, which under its first President, the distinguished physicist Brian Pippard, was an innovative, democratic institution dispensing with high table and chapel. The college absorbed several lecturers in languages with relatively small student numbers, including Norwegian and Russian; it also boasted the only Lecturer in Finno-Ugrian languages in the country. It was then that I met him, as I was a Research Fellow of the College—though we agreed we could just as well have met at Berkeley, where I had held my first teaching post.

While Cambridge was apparently a far cry from Berkeley, there was also a poetry scene in and around Cambridge. Indeed, Donald Davie (who was still at Gonville and Caius College at the time Printz-Påhlson arrived in Cambridge) was promoting American poets there, and the young Jeremy Prynne was beginning his long and intricate correspondence with them. Other poets lived in and around Cambridge, some teaching part-time at the then polytechnic, now known as Anglia Ruskin University. A poetry festival grew up alongside this second University, organized by poet and translator

Richard Burns (now Richard Berengarten), in which Göran was happy to take part. Writers, colleagues, and students who went to learn from him usually stayed to call him friend; his home in the village of Stapleford, and afterwards in a converted pub in Norfolk Street in Cambridge, was a centre of conviviality. The sounds of Thelonious Monk and Ornette Coleman often rang out in his vicinity.

Printz-Påhlson always continued to write his own poetry, if somewhat sparsely; he could link his imaginative places with a light yet learned hand, as in 'Sir Charles Babbage Returns to Trinity College After Having Commissioned the Swedish Mechanic Scheutz to Build a Difference Engine,' and his poems and letters to and from his friends and co-translators form a sub-genre of conversation poem. Moreover, his translations of other poets changed the poetry scene in Sweden, in particular his translations of the great and challengingly idiomatic American poet John Ashbery, whom he had started translating as early as in 1961, and who along with the Black Mountain poets, was also being discovered in Britain by Donald Davie. He also translated the major American poet Robert Lowell into Swedish, a labour of love that took many years to complete. These are permanent acquisitions for Swedish poetry, and for world poetry.

Printz-Påhlson also came to know the local poetry scene in Cambridge, which flourishes somewhat apart from the university. In 1975 he helped the local poet Richard Burns to bring several Swedish poets—Lars Forssell, Lars Gustafsson, Gunnar Harding, and Tomas Tranströmer—to the first Cambridge poetry festival. Later there was a Swedish counterpart: at the Malmö poetry festival in 1989, Printz-Påhlson, Seamus Heaney, John Matthias, and Lars-Håkan Svensson appeared on a panel about 'poetry of place.'

Printz-Påhlson also developed a keen interest in the Irish poets who were so strong a voice in the poetry of the English language. He began to study Gaelic (it was 'very hard,' this accomplished linguist admitted ruefully). One of his most important contributions as a translator into Swedish was a large volume called *Färdväg* (*Itinerary*), which introduced some thirty American, British, and Irish poets whose work exemplified the 'poetry of place' (Heaney pre-eminent among them). The American academic and poet John Matthias, who became his main collaborator in bringing Swedish poetry to English, met Printz-Påhlson in Cambridge in 1973, and returned as a Clare Hall visiting fellow in 1976, when they translated and published *Contemporary Swedish Poetry* (1980), including some of Printz-Påhlson's own.

But Printz-Påhlson was not merely a Scandinavianist, nor an adoptive Americanist, but a comparatist. He joined the editorial board of *Comparative Criticism* (Cambridge University Press, 1979–2004), the journal that I edited for the newly founded British Comparative Literature Association, and he contributed to the journal on Swedish poets. These included in particular Gunnar Ekelöf, in whom W.H. Auden had taken an interest, as he had in Nordic literature generally—a translation of the great poem on a par with *The Waste Land,* 'En Mölna Elegi' ('A Molna Elegy'), appeared in volume one—as well as Erik Lindegren, whom Auden had translated with Leif Sjöberg, he contributed an essay 'The Canon of Literary Modernism: A Note on Abstraction in the Poetry of Erik Lindegren'; and he contributed on Strindberg, 'Historical Drama and Historical Fiction: The Example of Strindberg.' Printz-Påhlson was a leading critic and scholar of Strindberg, whose complexities he explored in essays and lectures throughout his life, in both Swedish and English. His writings on Strindberg are being collected in Sweden; they should also be collected in English. His Lindegren essay is reprinted in the present volume. He also generously allowed part of a wide-ranging dialogue on politics and literature that he had held with Raymond Williams, the radical critic and novelist, and a good friend, to be published in *Comparative Criticism*. The whole of it, as recorded, still deserves to see the light of day. Over the years his 'advice to the editor' never failed to be imaginative, unexpected, and well-grounded. Finally, Printz-Påhlson contributed to a variety of periodicals in the United States, Britain, and Sweden.

As a scholar, critic and, above all, a poet, Printz-Påhlson's range of reference and allusion was extraordinarily wide, but it always homed in on a fine point. The 1980s brought an increasing harvest. He acted as head of the Scandinavian Department from 1982 until his retirement in 1989, three years before the closure of the department together with other small language units, as part of a national reorganisation of university modern language provision that left only five Scandinavian departments in the country (including a new one opened at Edinburgh). This was a source of pain to him, and to all of us. In 1984 he delivered the Ward-Phillips lectures in poetry at the University of Notre Dame, Indiana, on 'The Words of the Tribe: Primitivism, Reductionism and Materialism in Modern Poetics.' Those lectures are brought together and published in the present volume for the first time. His volume of essays, *'När jag var prins utav Arkadien'* ('*When I was Prince of Arcadia*'), appeared in Sweden in 1995;

it has still to be translated into English. His *Collected Poems 1956–83* ('*Säg Minns Du Skeppet Refanut?,*' '*Tell Me, Do You Remember the Ship Refanut?*') published in Sweden in 1983, included his witty but moving brief 'epic' on the Scanian region of Sweden from which he came. He was awarded an honorary doctorate by Lund University in 1987.

Printz-Påhlson's last years, after his return to Sweden in 1998, were however darkened by accident and illness. He is survived by his wife, Ulla, daughter Unn and son Finn, as well as his grandson, Bruno. His posthumous publications, it may be hoped, will carry his work into still wider international circles.

Inbetween: Locating Göran Printz-Påhlson

Robert Archambeau

Shortly after I first met Göran Printz-Påhlson in 1973, he, the British poet Richard Burns and I gave a reading together at Clare Hall, Cambridge, where Printz-Påhlson was a Fellow. We all read from our translations that evening, as well as from our own poems, and Printz-Påhlson amused the audience enormously by reading a poem from *Gradiva* three times—twice in English and once in Swedish. 'When Beaumont and Tocqueville First Visited Sing-Sing' was, in fact, originally written in English. It appears in *Gradiva* translated by Printz-Påhlson himself into Swedish. Discovered there by an American reader of Swedish poetry, it was translated back into English and published in a literary journal. The new English version, obviously enough, was quite different from the first. Printz-Påhlson's reading of the three poems that night formed a comic triptych with an elusive moral. But the adventures of the Beaumont and Tocqueville poem do not end there. A year ago, I picked up Lars Gustafsson's *Forays into Swedish Poetry* and discovered that the one poem chosen from Printz-Påhlson's work to represent him among his Swedish forbears and contemporaries was the ubiquitous 'När Beaumont och Tocqueville först besökte Sing-Sing'—translated back into English for the American edition of the book, this time presumably by Gustafsson. Such are the hazards risked by extraterritorial types who are determined to write memorable work in more than one language.[2]

In his long, ambitious, experimental poem 'The Green Ey'd Monster' (1981), Göran Printz-Påhlson describes two lovers who have ceased to talk to one another, but who go on talking to themselves. 'Every conversation,' writes

---

2. John Matthias, *Reading Old Friends*. Albany: State University of New York Press, 1992, pp. 179–80.

Printz-Påhlson, 'is inbetween these two.' The context in which the passage occurs invites us to see the lovers and their strange (non-)communication as an analogy for the communicative situation of artistic expression, and by extension to see it as an analogy for the relation between a poet and a reader. The reader, like the mumbling lover, imagines but does not address the poet; while the poet addresses, but can only imagine, the reader, absent as she is at the time of composition. What is at stake is intimacy—intimacy and distance. But that is not of primary interest in the present context. More interesting for present purposes is Printz-Påhlson's neologism. 'Inbetween,' he writes, not 'in between.' There is a substance to the state of betweenness for Printz-Påhlson, something demanding a more concrete expression than two prepositions laid side-by-side. John Matthias's anecdote about Printz-Påhlson's position between English and Swedish gives us a clue about why the state of being 'inbetween' carried such weight for Printz-Påhlson, why it required a sturdy, Germanic, compound word. Printz-Påhlson occupied many positions of inbetweenness—between the Swedish and English languages, certainly, but also between poetry and criticism, between the plain style and the vatic, between the Anglo-American and the continental traditions of poetry, criticism, and scholarship, and between the modernist and postmodernist generations. Printz-Påhlson's career was 'extraterritorial' indeed, in both the geographic sense and the sense that word takes on in the philosophy of Gilles Deleuze—as a term for describing things that elude all customary structures and boundaries.

Born in 1931, Printz-Påhlson became known in Sweden both as a poet and a critic while in his twenties, with his first volume of poems appearing in 1957 and his critical study of Swedish literary modernism and its European context, *Solen i spegeln* (*The Sun in the Mirror*) appearing a year later. Printz-Påhlson could have stayed in Sweden and become a national literary figure, but instead left in 1961 for academic posts at Berkeley and Harvard before setting in Cambridge in 1964. In Cambridge he became an associate of Raymond Williams and Frank Kermode and, while continuing to write poetry and criticism in Swedish, he embarked on a career as an English-language poet and critic. In effect, he maintained a half-dozen related careers: as an academic specialist in Scandinavian studies; as a Swedish poet; as a Swedish critic; as an Anglophone poet; as an Anglophone critic; and finally as one of the best translators of English-language poetry into Swedish. He remained prolific until his return to Sweden in 1998, when illness kept him from writing with his prior energy. He died in 2006, leaving us a polyglot literary and critical legacy.

The present volume contains works that Göran Printz-Påhlson wrote in English, along with a few translated items he expressed a wish to see presented in English. It is a selection, not a comprehensive collection, but it does hint at the scope of Printz-Påhlson's achievement as a critic, poet, and scholar in English, an achievement that, on its own, would make for a distinguished career. Of course it gives no real sense of Printz-Påhlson's overall accomplishment, which includes the critical studies *Förtroendekrisen* (Crisis of Confidence) and *Slutna världar öppen rymd* (*Closed Worlds, Open Space*), as well as books of Swedish poetry such as *Resan mellan poesi och poesi* (*The Journey Between Poetry and Poetry*), *Dikter för ett barn i vår tid* (*Poems for a Child of Our Time*), *Gradiva och andra dikter* (*Gradual and Other Poems*), and *Säg minns du skeppet Refanut?* (*Remember the Ship Refanut?*)

While Printz-Påhlson constantly wrote criticism while writing poetry, there were long periods when he lay fallow as a poet. As John Matthias suggests, this may have something to do with the conundrum of the expatriate poet, caught between two languages and two potential audiences, a poet for whom 'the question of whether to write in Swedish or English became sufficiently problematic that the flow of poems in both languages all but ceased.' (Matthias 181) Indeed, even when the poet caught between two languages does write, he runs the risk of not finding his proper audience in either language. When the Swedish poet Jesper Svenbro was asked about Printz-Påhlson's influence on younger Swedish poets, for example, he replied by saying he 'found the absence of [Printz-Påhlson's] influence more significant,' and that it seemed somehow 'easier to be his follower as a Swedish-speaking poet in Thorigny-sur-Marne, France, than in Stockholm'.[3] From Printz-Påhlson to Svenbro—one poet of inbetweenness speaks to another, but just how Printz-Påhlson's work stands in relation to his native and his adoptive communities remains an open question.

Printz-Påhlson certainly understood his conundrum. In fact, the question of the artist who travels and adapts, as opposed to the artist who stays in his place and his local tradition, animates a pair of Printz-Påhlson's poems, 'In the Style of Scott Skinner' and 'Songs of Dock Boggs.' Scott Skinner, a Scottish fiddler who traveled to France and introduced new techniques to the tradition of Scottish folk music, serves as Printz-Påhlson's figure of the

---

3. Jesper Svenbro, 'Thinking Translation,' Paper given at the Göran Printz-Påhlson Memorial Conference (Clare Hall, Cambridge, 28 June 2010).

traveling, adaptive artist. In the poem devoted to him we see the allure of cosmopolitanism, of a broad embrace of the culturally different:

> Two hundred
> thousand wet sea-birds every
> minute serve the mind with writs of constraint
> in *pizzicato* dancehalls all over
> the moody crags. A lone kipper
> is seen to flounder in the volatile traffic
> leaving his ladder, embarking
> for France, land of *cotillions* and plenty

In contrast, the poem devoted to the American bluegrass fiddler Dock Boggs depicts an art born of poverty, provincialism, and the resentment of 'distant authority.' Such art has, however, a certain power born from exactly these circumstances, and the music hits the listener like 'Raw death: a clodhopper shovel/smack in the kisser.' The two fiddler poems offer no conclusion, only a question about the relative merits of two different artistic paths. They are poems in dialogue with one another and, in the tradition of Blake and of Yeats, serve as emblems of the poet's vacillation. If the problem of poetic inbetweenness could never be resolved, it could, at least, be sung.

The condition of the inbetween also manifested itself in Göran Printz-Påhlson's double commitment to the pursuit of poetry and to the pursuit of criticism. He never was, after all, merely a critic who happened to write poetry; nor was he a just a poet who ventured into criticism. He was the true, rare hybrid: the poet-critic. René Wellek gets at the harsh truth about such creatures when he tells us 'the union of the poet and the critic is not always a happy one' and that such a union is 'not necessarily good for either poetry or criticism'[4]. Wellek has in mind T.S. Eliot's statement that the poet-critic always seeks 'to defend the kind of poetry he is writing'[5] — a stance that can all too readily lead to narrowness, unfair judgment, and a blindness to the real, yet alien, virtues of the poet one is reading.

---

4. René Wellek, 'The Poet as Critic, the Critic as Poet, the Poet-Critic,' in *The Poet as Critic*, ed. by Frederick P. W. McDowell (Evanston: Northwestern University Press, 1967), pp. 92–107 (107).
5. T.S. Eliot, *Selected Prose*, ed. Frank Kermode (New York: Mariner, 1975), p. 107.

The poet-critic, in this dim view, is something of a hedgehog, in the sense given to that beast by Isaiah Berlin when he took it as an emblem for the thinker who knows one big thing. Printz-Påhlson, though, escapes the sad fate of the typical poet-critic by virtue of what Berlin might call his foxiness—that is, by virtue of his openness to many things. After meeting Printz-Påhlson, the American poet Michael Anania described him as 'a careening enthusiast,' a term that indicates the all-embracing scope and catholic nature of Printz-Påhlson's interests. As a scholar and critic Printz-Påhlson was a professional comparativist—and what is, after all, a comparativist (at least a good one) but a careening enthusiast, the range of whose sympathies and elective affinities must, by the very nature of the field, be impossibly broad?

In the selection of critical works gathered in this volume, we see three of Printz-Påhlson's main enthusiasms: the examination of the terms of literary criticism; the criticism of classic and contemporary Scandinavian literature; and the study of contemporary American poetry. The essays collected as 'The Words of the Tribe' were originally delivered as the Ward-Phillips lectures in 1984, and take as their subject the terminology of poetics and literary criticism. Printz-Påhlson's concern with the words of the tribe of poets and critics continues in the important essays 'Style, Irony, Metaphor, and Meaning,' and 'Realism as Negation,' which probe the history of critical terminology in a manner similar to that pioneered by Printz-Påhlson's colleague Raymond Williams in the landmark study *Keywords*. In 'Historical Drama and Historical Fiction: The Example of Strindberg,' and 'The Canon of Literary Modernism: A Note on Abstraction in the Poetry of Erik Lindegren,' Printz-Påhlson offers observations on the contexts of Scandinavian writing, and in the essay 'The Tradition of Contemporary Swedish Poetry' he surveys the field of Swedish poetry. 'Kierkegaard the Poet' is an assessment of the great Danish writer, an assessment as important as it is idiosyncratic. Printz-Påhlson's concerns with American poetry are represented by 'Surface and Accident: John Ashbery,' an inquiry into the work of the leading American poet from a perspective of poetic intimacy. Printz-Påhlson's long commitment to the translation of Ashbery allows for a perspective on linguistic particulars that is marginal in most Ashbery criticism. Another kind of intimacy informs a shorter essay, 'The Voyages of John Matthias.' Here, Printz-Påhlson comments on the work of a close friend and collaborator. The piece speaks to Printz-Påhlson's poetic predilections almost as much as it does to Matthias's poetry, which makes it a fitting transition to the selection of Printz-Påhlson's own poetry.

xxvi   Letters of Blood

There is a great degree of overlap between Printz-Påhlson's practice as critic and as poet. Often, for example, he turns to poetry as a form of literary criticism by other means—a phenomenon that accounts for the prevalence of metapoetry in his work—and even, in the case of 'Comedians,' of meta-metapoetry, the poetic exploration of the conditions of writing poetry about poetry. Certain themes, such as that of the meaning of metaphor, recur throughout the critical essays and the poems. But this overlap is always a matter of dialogue, not of doctrine: Printz-Påhlson's poems are never merely illustrations of his critical ideas.

One of the great dialogues to animate Printz-Påhlson's writing is between a plain, discursive style, and a style more mysterious, even impenetrable. The dialogue, present in the margins of many of Printz-Påhlson's essays, is at the center of 'The Words of the Tribe' a version of the Ward-Phillips lectures he gave at Notre Dame in 1985. Here, Printz-Påhlson contrasts two traditions of poetry, one based on a 'vernacular linguistic primitivism' in which 'you posit a model for poetry in a language which is colloquial, contemporary, and non-archaizing.' This is poetry in the tradition of Wordsworth's preface to *Lyrical Ballads*, a tradition of the '*sermo humilis*,' a 'humble and earth-like language.' Printz-Påhlson sees this as a dominant tradition in English-language poetry, not only in Wordsworthian romanticism but also in Anglo-American modernism. It is the tradition, for example, behind the young Ezra Pound's vision of poetic language as a matter of:

> Objectivity and again objectivity, and expression: no hindside-beforeness, no straddled adjectives (as 'addled mosses dank'), no Tennysonian-ness of speech; nothing—that you couldn't, in some circumstance, in the stress of some emotion, actually say. Every literaryism, every bookword, fritters away a scrap of the reader's patience, a scrap of his sense of your sincerity.[6]

Against this colloquial tradition, says Printz-Påhlson, we hear 'the voices of modernist poetry in French or German poetry, from Hölderlin to Celan, Baudelaire to Bonnefoy,' voices that spurn the colloquial in order to 'speak defiantly in another dialect, lofty, vatic, solemn, *sermo sublimis* rather than *sermo humilis*.' For poets in this tradition, 'words are used in poetry not as signs or names, but in *order to name*, in an Adamic act.'[7] It is characteristic of Printz-Påhlson's inbetweenness that he ends the

---

6. Ezra Pound, *The Letters of Ezra Pound, 1907–1941* (London: Faber and Faber, 1951), p. 49.
7. 'The Words of the Tribe,' in Göran Printz-Påhlson, *Letters of Blood*, p. 55.

essay in which he makes these remarks not by taking sides, but by asking questions. Is the vatic, Adamic stance 'to be taken, with the English poet, as an act of social acquiescence in the face of the intractability of language, or with the continental poet, as a defiance of social demands in order to reach the silences behind the words?'[8] When we look to Printz-Påhlson's poetry, we find work that points in both directions. Few poet-critics who have looked as deeply into questions of the ethics and aesthetics of poetic diction have emerged from their inquiries with such broad sympathies. The closest analogue, one imagines, is Donald Davie, and it is perhaps not a coincidence that Printz-Påhlson translated Davie's work.

Davie, of course, was a decade older than Printz-Påhlson, whose generational position points toward another form of the inbetween: the state of transition between old modernist ways of thinking and an emergent postmodernism. Printz-Påhlson's Eliotic sense of tradition, his almost impossibly erudite grasp of 'the mind of Europe,' shows him with one foot firmly placed in modernism. At the same time, his love of popular culture, and his enthusiasm for it as a subject for poetry in works like 'Superman, or: How to Succeed as a Failure' and 'Recollection of Innocence in Experience: or, The Katzenjammer Kids, Middle-Aged, Remembering their Happy Childhood in Africa,' shows that he straddles the gulf between high culture and pop culture in a typically postmodern fashion. In contrast to the great Davie's one extended attempt to understand pop culture—a misguided essay on the Tolkien craze—Printz-Påhlson sincerely embraced the world of pop. As he put it, 'you don't have to be less serious when you write about Superman [...] than when you write about the Rosenbergs.' (Matthias 180) No doubt this sensitivity, this ease with existing inbetween the consecrated and the popular, played a role in making Printz-Påhlson so successful in the apparently impossible task of translating John Ashbery into Swedish.

Inbetween, then, is where we find Printz-Påhlson, even when, as in the present volume, we limit ourselves to work he intended to be read in English. Inbetween is an ambiguous and intriguing space, a place of meetings and exchanges and dialogues and generosity of spirit. No location could be more appropriate.

---

8. 'The Words of the Tribe,' in Göran Printz-Påhlson, *Letters of Blood*, p. 55.

'The Overall Wandering of Mirroring Mind': Some Notes on Göran Printz-Påhlson

Lars-Håkan Svensson

Göran Printz-Påhlson first made a name for himself in Swedish literary life in the early 1950s as a prodigiously learned poet and critic and as the chief theorist of a group of gifted young poets referred to as 'the Lund school' as they were all students at Lund University in southern Sweden. The 'Lund school' was not really a literary movement, however, but simply a circle of friends who happened to share a number of literary interests. Several of them went on to make important individual contributions to Swedish poetry, but at the time they were all associated with the ideas that Printz-Påhlson propagated in his criticism and poems. Under the influence of the tenets and methods of New Criticism, still fairly unknown in Sweden, Printz-Påhlson argued that since all art is fiction and therefore a lie, the best that art can do is to be honest about its ontological status and inscribe this consciousness as deftly as possible into itself. To put it another way: art is art, not reality, and the difference should not be obfuscated. Much of the poetry and criticism that he published during the 1950s was geared to promote this metapoetical programme.

His first publication, *Resan mellan poesi och poesi* (*The Journey Between Poetry and Poetry*, 1955), is a thin pamphlet consisting of six, mostly unrhymed sonnets, whose metacritical bent is suggested by the volume's very title and further brought out by the fact that the last two poems comment on the first two. Metapoetic perspectives also pervade his first full-length collection of poems, *Dikter för ett barn i vår tid* (*Poems for a Child in Our Time*, 1956), which, in addition, shows his skilful treatment of various demanding metrical forms, including the villanella. However, more than anything the collection established him as an accomplished master of irony, almost preternaturally learned and mature for his age. (He was 25 at the time.) The same qualities were discernible in his criticism, much of it first published as articles and book reviews in the local evening paper *Kvällsposten,* and later reworked into the full-scale book chapters of his magisterial critical volume *Solen i spegeln* (*The Sun in the Mirror*, 1958). This study of Swedish modernist poetry, which begins with a long introductory chapter elucidating what Printz-Påhlson sees as a long tradition of metapoetics running from Ovid through Dante to modern practitioners such as Wallace Stevens and Francis Ponge, was immediately recognised as a major critical achievement and remains influential to this day. Even now it is hard to come across a new study of modern Swedish poetry that does not position itself by making reference to the perspectives drawn up by Printz-Påhlson.

The publication of his poems and, especially, *Solen i spegeln* resulted in Printz-Påhlson being seen as one of his generation's most gifted writers. His immediate plans seem to have been to write a doctoral thesis in Nordic languages at Lund—not Swedish or Comparative Literature, as one might have expected. However, this came to nothing. In 1961 Printz-Påhlson moved to America with his young family to teach Scandinavian literature first at Harvard (1961–1962) and, later, at Berkeley (1962–1964). Although he spent comparatively few years in the United States (he left in 1964 in order to take up a position as lecturer in Scandinavian Literature and Language at Cambridge, remaining there until his retirement), there can be no doubt about the deep impact that these three years had on him. He made many friends in the United States and always spoke warmly about the openness he had encountered there, and immersed himself in American literature and culture. Although he claimed to be tone-deaf, he became an addict to bluegrass music; and he wrote articles about, for example, Bob Dylan, Lenny Bruce, and Marshall McLuhan, at a point when they were virtually unknown in Sweden and certainly not recognised as cultural icons. He also wrote about the beginnings of student radicalism at Berkeley well before anyone in Sweden even knew that such a thing existed. All these experiences affected him deeply and can be noticed in the poems in English he began to write at about this time (some of which are included in this volume).

Although it is not easy to exert influence, let alone be a vital force in Swedish cultural life without residing in Stockholm, Printz-Påhlson cut an important and highly respected figure, even during his exile in the United States, In the early 1960s he became a regular contributor to the liberal Stockholm daily *Dagens Nyheter*, which set the agenda for much of the cultural discussion of the day, and he wrote long and learned articles for Sweden's leading literary journal *Bonniers Litterära Magasin* (among them a path-breaking set of articles on Strindberg's narrative technique). Many of the articles produced over these years were later collected in two major volumes of essays published simultaneously in 1971, *Förtroendekrisen* (*The Confidence Crisis*) and *Slutna världar, öppen rymd* (*Closed Worlds, Open Space*), the former showing him to be an astute and well-informed observer of contemporary (not least American) society and politics, the latter demonstrating his familiarity with contemporary fiction and popular culture. He also made a name for himself as a translator. In the mid-50s he had translated William Empson and other modern British poets; he now turned to contemporary Americans such as Robert Lowell and John Ashbery, whom he had discovered at an early stage.

In 1966, Printz-Påhlson published a second volume of poetry, *Gradiva*, a rich collection which, among other things, contains three poems in English, 'Superman,' 'Bringing up Father,' and 'Recollections of Innocence in Experience'—included, so a note tells us, to demonstrate that 'it is not necessary to be less serious in writing about Superman or the Katzenjammer Kids than when writing about the Rosenbergs.' The major part of *Gradiva* consists of two long sections, one consisting of a suite of related poems based on Wilhelm Jensen's novel *Gradiva*, famously analsed by Freud in his 1907 *Dream and Delusion*, the other of two minor suites, 'The Carceri Suite' and 'The Automatons.' *Gradiva*, probably the most ambitious poetry collection published in Sweden during the 1960s, met with considerable critical acclaim, though in retrospect it is easy to see that its prescient treatment of themes such as automata, computers, *doppelgänger*, and so on arrived some fifteen years too early. And when these things came to be on the agenda, their proponents in Sweden were not too eager to remember—or perhaps they were simply unaware—that Printz-Påhlson had written about them long before.

If the tutelary spirits of Printz-Påhlson's early work may be said to have been William Empson and the New Critics, his thought during the 1960s and 1970s was more attuned to the work of Raymond Williams and Frank Kermode (both of whom he knew at Cambridge). It is clear from the articles he wrote during his final year in the United States that he was already interested in the new definition of culture that Williams, Richard, Hoggart, and others were proposing in Britain. One might have expected that his familiarity with these notions would have made him interesting at home, for in the early 1970s, Swedish cultural life underwent a sea-change, political radicalisation intent on dissolving the boundaries between high and popular culture. However, the kind of wide-ranging and comprehensive intellectualism that he represented was not what *Dagens Nyheter* wanted; 'you write in a manner which certainly appeals to readers with a classical education but doesn't reach out to more than a fraction of our heterogeneous readership,' a sub-editor told him in a letter of rejection. Printz-Påhlson's friend, the poet Tomas Tranströmer, found the paper's idea of its readership laughable; 'these culture vultures are beginning to sound like disc jockeys—but they are tragic disc jockeys, for they address an audience that doesn't exist,' he wrote to Printz-Påhlson. Printz-Påhlson's own response appears to have been to consolidate his academic career; to write in English rather than in Swedish, and to resort to silence and cunning—he was of course already in exile.

Fortunately, the Joycean formula served him well. He continued his work as a translator. In 1980 he brought out a volume of *Contemporary Swedish Poetry* translated into English together with John Matthias. In the following year a translation into Swedish of John Matthias's long poem *Bathory & Lermontov* appeared, and in 1984 he published a highly influential volume of translations into Swedish of the work of John Ashbery. And six years later, in 1990, he completed a major volume of translations into Swedish of contemporary English-language poetry, *Färdväg* (*Itinerary*), on which he had been working for several years together with Jan Östergren. This volume features important selections from the work of a number of contemporary Irish poets such as Seamus Heaney, Paul Muldoon, and Derek Mahon, as well as a wide selection of American poets from A.R. Ammons and Elizabeth Bishop to Louise Glück, Robert Hass, John Matthias, James McMichael, John Peck, and Robert Pinsky. The common denominator of the poets included in this anthology is their concern with the poetry of place, expounded in a major essay appended to the volume.

Even more importantly, in 1983 Printz-Påhlson published his collected poems in Swedish, *Säg minns du skeppet Refanut? (Tell Me, Do You Remember the Ship Refanut?)*—the title is a line from a ballad that the poet had heard his grandmother sing. This volume includes a large section of new poems, some of them his very finest achievements. One—a long sequence commemorating his upbringing in southern Sweden—bears witness to his new interest in the poetry of place. To some extent modeled on Hugh McDiarmid's 'A Drunk Man Looks at the Thistle,' it is perhaps Printz-Påhlson's most personal and memorable poem, mixing lyrical passages with wonderfully ironic evocations of regional lore associated with the poet's native landscape of Skåne in southern Sweden. Its subtle and humorous word-play, its exploration of dialectal expressions and its many references to cultural and political phenomena dating from the poet's childhood and youth of course make it sadly unsuitable for translation; however, several other new poems included in this book exist in English versions as well and can be found in this volume.

1995 saw the publication of a final major volume of new essays, *När jag var prins utav Arkadien (When I Was Prince of Arcadia,* 1995) which along with a reprint of *The Sun in the Mirror* (1996) is testimony to Printz-Påhlson's continuing importance as a critic and theorist. The most important of these new essays deal with the role of place and memory in poetry. Some of the inspiration comes from Printz-Påhlson's familiarity with the writings of Seamus Heaney and Jeremy Hooker and the general resurgence of interest in the sense of place in 1970s and 1980s criticism, but his treatment of the topic is inspired by the thought of many other poets, critics, and philosophers; in particular, he relates his sense of place to the notion of 'primitivism' also brought to the fore in his Ward-Phillips lectures and also, with a surprising reference to the beginning of Hegel's *Phänomenologie des Geistes* and to Wordsworth's *Prelude*, discerns another type of mediation of the universal and the individual:

> If the individual must have recourse to what is most singular and primitive in order to discover his character and his fate (the Greek term *ethos* refers us to both directions), the universal and the general is available not only *primarily* in the abode of his childhood but *only* there. The conflict that this generates derives from a world that strikes us as increasingly expansive and open, but in which our deepest affinities, in so far as they are at all maintained, remain at an elementary and primary level in the individual's origin.

* * *

During the last fifteen years of his life, Printz-Påhlson was working on a number of projects. Some were left nearly complete at his death, such as the Ward-Phillips lectures, while others were merely planned—among them a volume tantalisingly entitled *The Invention of Scandinavia*, and another called *The Poem as Process*, a study of the work of John Ashbery, André du Bouchet, Paul Celan, and Göran Sonnevi. He also left a plan for a collection of poems in English. The present volume, which is largely made up of manuscripts now in the care of Lund University Library, is compiled from several of these projects.

The Ward-Phillips lectures entitled 'The Words of the Tribe: Primitivism, Reductionism, and Materialism in Modern Poetics,' constitute Printz-Påhlson's most ambitious effort at developing his views on modern poetics next to *The Sun in the Mirror*; as such, they are also to be related to the ideas set forth in some of the later articles referred to above. It is of course fair to ask if a set of lectures which necessarily cannot make use of recent discussions can be of interest to us today, particularly when one knows that their author was always very keen to refer to, and profit from, the latest developments in the field that he was working in. I think so. As restored and edited by Robert Archambeau, these essays strike me as eminently readable and relevant. They discuss issues which are as much with us today as they were when the original versions were being prepared; they do so very elegantly and with great critical tact; they bring together a vast number of materials not usually discussed in the same text; and they make use of some of the best insights of the structuralist and post-structuralist era while nearly always calling a halt before succumbing to any of the many exaggerations and delusions of this heady period. Their value is enhanced by the editor having very helpfully identified the very diverse sources referred to in them, sending the reader now to Aristotle, now to Sir Peter Medawar, now to John Ashbery.

Much the same may be said about the various individual articles that follow—except that they do not in the same way adhere to Printz-Påhlson's main theoretical concerns but address topics of a more specific nature. Some of them—such as the pieces on Strindberg and Kierkegaard—illustrate Printz-Påhlson's impressive ability to bring his familiarity with the international discussion of such disputed concepts as 'realism,' 'style' and 'irony' to bear on these Scandinavian icons while, in the process, making interesting observations on theoretical discussions too. Other articles included here—such as those on the Swedish modernist poet

Erik Lindegren (on whom he had written memorably in *The Sun in the Mirror*) and 'The Tradition of Contemporary Swedish Poetry'—might be interesting in that they focus attention on aspects of Swedish literature and art usually missed by those who have access only to discussions concentrating on the supposedly major names, whose works are available in translation. The piece on Ashbery—written at a time when Ashbery was not as well-known as he is today but offering perspectives that seem relevant today as well—is interesting also because it gives us a glimpse of Printz-Påhson's practice as a translator.

The second half of the volume consists of a poetry collection, *Letters of Blood*, which naturally invites comparison with the Swedish collected poems. However, while the latter volume is arranged according to a chronological pattern, starting with the most recent poems and going backwards to the oldest ones, the English collection appears to follow a thematic and generic rather than a chronological plan. Of the three sections, one to a large extent reflects the poet's interest in popular culture; another contains poems written or inspired by his early years in the United States and Britain; the third section is devoted to metapoetical topics; and the final section consists of a long poem, *The Green-Ey'd Monster*, which combines several of the concerns of the other sections.

Letters of Blood contains a number of poems that, due to their subject matter and linguistic expression, defy translation into Swedish, while the collected Swedish poems include a number of poems similarly incapable of translation into English. At the same time many of the poems that exist both in Swedish and English raise the question of which came first. The amusing anecdote told by Archambeau about the three versions of the Beaumont and Tocqueville poem likely reflects the complex coming into existence of some of the other poems in section two (written at a time when Printz-Påhlson was beginning to feel confident about writing poetry in English). It is easy to see that the subject matter is common to both the Swedish and English version of the poem and that the execution of individual lines, phrases, and images is adapted to the particular demands and possibilities of the language used—and to the audiences addressed. These poems question our conventional notions of original and translation. In my view, they are all originals, which in its turn suggests that all translations are originals too, not copies. To a Swedish reader, used to thinking of poems such as 'Turingmaskin,' 'Joe Hills sista dagar,' 'Remember the Rosenbergs,' 'Sestina Vertumni' and 'Komiker' as classics of Swedish poetry, it is disconcerting—as well as enriching—to realise that they may have existed in English before the Swedish version was written down, or that the Swedish poem came into being at the same time as an—almost but not quite—identical English poem. The author of the poems would no doubt have been amused at our confusion as to whether we lie or tell the truth when we refer to them as originals and translations.

The Words of the Tribe:

Primitivism, Reductionism, and Materialism in Modern Poetics

Part One: Linguistic Primitivism in Modernism and Romanticism

1

In a little-known lecture of 1942, 'Poetry as Primitive Language,' John Crowe Ransom presents an important program for poetry and poetics. The context of Ransom's remarks—the Avery Hopwood Lecture at the University of Michigan—made it necessary for him to express himself in quite simple terms, as he was talking mainly to undergraduates. It had been just one year after that seminal book of momentous title, *The New Criticism*, appeared, and Ransom set out in his lecture some of the fundamental tenets of the New Critical doctrine, but did so in much plainer language than in his more ambitious essays.

The definition of primitivism offered is not a very helpful one from our perspective, but still of importance for the understanding of a complete body of thought which has had a profound, and often misunderstood, influence on modern poetics. He writes:

> By primitivism I mean an antique or outmoded cast of thought, so that the poetry is likely to seem heroic as compared with contemporary thought, or to seem pastoral, agrarian, medieval, Pre-Raphaelitish, or merely old-fashioned and quaint. After some progress of civilization comes a movement of regress, with poets in charge of it. But I have generally laboured this point in large or philosophical terms, with the result that I seemed to myself profound, but not very pointed, and academically correct, but as a student of poetry, not really close to the topic. (74)

He goes on, adding more disclaimers: 'Today, in your honour, I will talk about the primitive quality that appears in poetry as language. This version of critical theory is brand-new for me, and experimental, since I have not worked it out, but it seems more streamlined and presentable than any other I have hit upon.' (74)

Ransom's definition of primitivism as an 'antique or outmoded cast of thought' leaves a lot to be desired in clarity, and has obviously not benefited from comparison with, say, George Boas and Arthur O. Lovejoy's fundamental distinctions in their 1935 study *Primitivism and Related Ideas in Antiquity;* nor does Ransom seem to take into consideration the quite different insights from Yvor Winters's *Primitivism and Decadence* of 1937. Boas and Lovejoy present a powerful definition of classical primitivism as an enormously influential body of thought, concerned with the historiographical evaluation of primeval times, which are presented as normative for the present-day actions of children and animals, as well as for the pastoral pursuits of innocence, and as forceful models of morality. While the authors do not attempt any definition of 'linguistic primitivism,' their conceptual framework is clearly much more precise than that of Ransom.

Ransom's attempt at determining the area for the criticism of poetry is as little successful: 'literary criticism is not identical with philosophy at large, but it occurs to me that it may well be identical with linguistic [sic].' (74) In the ensuing argument, Ransom defines a primitive language as:

> [...] one whose standard discourse, in trying to be *conceptual* (or rational), is obliged also, and whether or not, to be *imaginal* (or substantival). That is, in trying to make useful formulations about things, relating them by virtue of some common or class property, it is obliged to refer to the many-propertied or substantial things themselves, the things as wholes. Primitive languages are sometimes called *radical* languages: they consist almost wholly in root words, each one denoting a whole thing or whole event. In discourse these roots are jumbled together, and it devolves upon the hearer to figure out the properties in which the things named are related, and by elimination to read into the jumble a consecutive argument. Here is the famous ambiguity of language. You still have it in poetic metaphor, for example, and in all unskilful speech. (75)

This seems to me—and, I think, to any reader with some elementary knowledge of modern linguistics—to be a hopelessly inadequate account of views on so-called primitive languages, an account already outmoded by the time of Ransom's lecture. After Sapir and Whorf on the complications of temporal and other systems in Amerindian languages; after Lévi-Strauss (whether we agree with his methodology or not) and his investigations of the abstract content of myth; after Franz Boas on Kvakiutl metaphor and Bernhard Karlgren on primitive Chinese phonology, it seems impossible to maintain such views at all. Even Wilhelm von Humboldt, writing early in the 19th century, had reached a much more sophisticated standpoint in his observations on the Kawi language.

The idea of a radical language, described by Ransom as consisting 'wholly in root words' (75), is a fiction going back to the very origins of comparative linguistics. In this form, the idea seems parallel to the Pound/Fenollosa hypothesis that, one must insist, addresses itself only to the *written* character in Chinese. It was no doubt of paramount importance for the development of the doctrine of imagism and, as such, conducive to the formation of an implicit theory of language of high modernism (of which more later)

In intimating that poetry in some way is to be, if not identified with, at least derivable from, such a radical primitive language, Ransom has stated one of the most basic tenets of the American version of New Criticism, while at the same time also revealing the fundamental ambivalence of the position. When relating poetry to the shortcomings of primitive languages—ambiguity, for instance—or all 'unskilful speech,' what is implied is a firm distinction between, on one hand, a language that is artless and illogical, *and* somehow poetic in a pristine way and, on the other hand, a perfectly logical natural language which successively gets rid of its ambiguities. This is a distinction Ransom took over from his natural enemies, the logical positivists and the general semanticists, and also a distinction that is recognised by virtually no one today: the basic ambiguities and vagueness of natural languages being fully accepted as ineluctable, and even to some degree extending into the language of mathematics and logic. Furthermore, Ransom seems to be quite unsure of his own pragmatic principles when referring to 'useful formulations' or 'unskilful speech' without clarifying to himself or to his audience to whom or for what purpose these formulations are useful, or which skills are required. Such naivete is indicative of how the later Wittgenstein's arguments on linguistic use (of course not available to Ransom) have been incorporated into our thinking. But to some extent it is also a question of political change, as we see when Ransom exemplifies his primitive language with joking quotes in the homemade pidgin English of an imagined American Indian chief: 'Heap big Indian hunting go, heap big paleface firewater come.' (ibid, 75–76) He contrasts this with the language the chief may have used had he benefited from a college composition course, in which case he would have expressed himself in detailed or pedantic officialese. Ransom very cleverly undercuts the supposed superiority of college-level English, saying 'linguistic precision illuminates the values offered in a bargain.' (ibid, 76) In the decades since Ransom's lecture, history has illuminated such values in a very different way, so that we now would be more inclined to contrast, let us say, a speech by one of the Iroquois orators with a Watergate tape, and not find ourselves convinced of the latter's superiority in logic (although we would have no doubt about the latter's superiority in duplicity). But again, duplicity of intention is not to be identified with excellent logic. Here, events have overtaken primitivism and left it high and dry in the well-intentioned condescension of colonialism.

It was not my intention to conduct a belated polemic against Ransom, whose work I admire, and whose strengths and shortcomings no less a poet than Geoffrey Hill has already examined with exemplary judiciousness. I have chosen Ransom's lecture as a suitable point of departure for this discussion not because it is a good example of his critical ability, but because it shows with great clarity one of the inescapable presuppositions behind the multifarious body of thinking we designate as 'the New Criticism.'

There is no doubt in my mind that the sharply dualist theory of language originating with I.A. Richards and permeating New Criticism is not only linguistically and philosophically outdated and lacking in empirical evidence, but also wholly inadequate in coping with even the most elementary problems of poetics. Concepts like primitivism and pseudo-reference (in Winters), primitivism and ontology (in Ransom), tension (in Tate), paradox (in Cleanth Brooks), and gesture (in Blackmur) all suffer from their secondary nature with regard to logical systems that cannot accommodate the aesthetic principles they embrace, and which have a completely different genealogy. Nonetheless, these concepts have had enormous importance in designating an area of investigation of permanent value for the genealogy of high modernism—indeed diametrically opposed to the locus of logical positivism—an area, situated roughly between technique and philosophy, of which more recent poetical theories of poetics have almost completely lost sight.

2

In the strange meeting of Yeats and Pound in the winter of 1912–1913, the primitivist strain in imagism comes to the fore. The elder and more famous poet was at the receiving end of the younger poet's criticisms and benefited from them. Indeed, he even seems to have relished them. Yeats tells us about the meeting in a letter to Lady Gregory (3 January 1913), a letter that begins with the very down-to-earth experience of persistent diarrhoea:

> My digestion has got rather queer again—a result I think of sitting up late with Ezra and Sturge Moore and some light wine while the talk ran. However the criticism I have got from them has given me new life and I have made that Tara poem a new thing and am writing with a new confidence having got Milton off my back. Ezra is the best critic of the two. He is full of the middle ages and helps me to get back to the definite and the concrete away from modern abstractions. To talk over a poem with him is like getting you to put a sentence in dialect. All becomes clear and natural. Yet in his work he is always uncertain, often very bad though very interesting sometimes. He spoils himself by too many experiments and has more sound principles than taste. (167)

It is quite clear that Yeats was delighted to get led away from 'modern abstractions' to a more authentic experience when working with ancient Irish material for the poem 'The Two Kings' (the Tara poem) and that he appreciated Pound mainly as a medievalist, not as a modern poet. When Pound expatiates on his principles two years later in an oft-quoted letter to Harriet Monroe, he stresses a slightly different conception of linguistic primitivism, although the 'fear of abstraction' is never far away:

> Objectivity and again objectivity, and expression: no hindside-beforeness, no straddled adjectives (as 'addled mosses dank'), no Tennysonian-ness of speech; nothing—that you couldn't, in some circumstance, in the stress of some emotion, actually say. Every literaryism, every bookword, fritters away a scrap of the reader's patience, a scrap of his sense of your sincerity. (49)

This strain of primitivism is distinctive from, although no doubt related to, the primitivism of root languages, which we may be permitted to call *radical* linguistic primitivism. What we designate as *vernacular* linguistic primitivism ('put a sentence into dialect' in Yeats's neat formula) is in its Poundian version hardly distinguishable from a much older and presumably more powerful branch of linguistic primitivism that puts the concrete image before the abstractions of everyday speech, as Hegel noticed in the lecture *Wer denkt abstrakt? (Who Thinks Abstractly?)*.

This imagist linguistic primitivism is of course, *qua* primitivism, dependent on a theory of language that seeks the origin of language—in some *Cratylus*-like fashion—in concrete relations between words and things. There are a number of such theories whose internal relations seem far from obvious.

3

This preliminary mapping of variants of linguistic primitivism has rapidly made the whole picture much more complicated, and it seems imperative that we go back much further in time in order to trace the genealogies of these ideas in modernist poetics. Let us first, however, go back only one step in time, to consider briefly a poet who has been regarded as a harbinger of modernism, but whose poetic ideas clearly had a great deal of independence from mainstream modernism, and who has more recently suffered a noticeable decline in his reputation. I mean Gerald Manley Hopkins.

A decisive moment in the decline of Hopkins's reputation comes with Donald Davie's early essay from 1953's *The Purity of Diction in English Poetry*, 'Hopkins as a Decadent Critic.' Although ostensibly concerned with Hopkins's criticism, this powerful essay is ultimately addressed to the decadence of his poetry. But even if we consult an earlier Kenyon Critics' symposium on Hopkins, which strikes a much more laudatory note (it contains, for instance, the eulogy by Robert Lowell), we shall still find some of the same unease about Hopkins's linguistic primitivism, notably in essays by Austin Warren and Arthur Mizener.

It is easy to make a case for Hopkins's linguistic primitivism, finding it in his preoccupations with techniques from the distant past, with *kenningar* (the old Norse tradition of circumlocution) and alliteration, with Welsh *cynghanned* (harmonic sound arrangement), and even with Duns Scotus's *haecceitas* (quiddity or particularity). All are all tangible archaising devices and can be seen as very much in the tradition of primitivism, according to Ransom's description of 'an antique or outmoded cast of thought.' It is also easy to see that such archaising elements of Hopkins's poetic method are in no way foreign to his contemporaries, although the particular uses of these devices in his poetry were anomalous enough to make the poetry unacceptable to them.

The matter of primitivism constitutes a problem touching not only on Hopkins criticism but also on the reception theory of modernism as a whole. The question to be asked is evidently one of priority: did Hopkins come to his position in philosophical poetics, his 'inscape' theory, through his metrical and linguistic experiments, or did he invent or re-invent his elaborate system of diction and sprung rhythms in order to create an instrument capable of expressing his indomitable desire for the concreteness of the sensual and particular? Harold Whitehall, the metrical expert among the Kenyon Critics, has no doubts on the issue:

> Sprung rhythm, the overstressing devices and a distinctive, if obscure, vocabulary are the interlocking segments of the Hopkins problem. To write sprung rhythm, he was obliged to use alliteration, internal rhyme, and assonance and word repetition. To use these devices, he needed new compounds and syntactic shortcuts. In nothing more metaphysical than this does his breaking down of the barriers of language consist. [...] His verbal innovations exist merely to assure the precise ordering of the musical elements of the line. (354)

Anyone who has read the notebooks of Hopkins, where the obsessive descriptions of particulars are present from the very beginning in simple unaffected prose, may very well be sceptical about such a view. After all, it seems a fitting example of linguistic reductionism—a most peculiar result of the New Critical ideology, in view of its holism in philosophy. The problem, however, remains. I am not proposing a solution to it, as it seems to be a variant of the familiar chicken and egg conundrum, and thus insoluble. But let me remind you of the famous quip attributed to Samuel Butler about evolutionary mechanics, that a chicken is just the means available for an egg to make another egg. This seems as good a description as any of the evolutionary mechanisms in some theories of literary genealogy, where the active creative will or intention of the artist is similarly reduced.

In order to avoid reductionism one is forced to consider the whole gamut of canon formation. It seems inevitable that the discussion of Hopkins's innovation in language and diction must be related to his views on the poetical practices of his contemporaries and immediate forerunners, as much as to the technical devices he found worthy of imitation in ancient poetry.

This is, as could be expected, very much the starting point of Donald Davie's essay. He quotes a letter from the twenty year-old Hopkins to Baillie (10–11 September 1864), where the author outlines a fairly elaborate typology of poetic styles, of which 'the first and highest is poetry proper, the language of inspiration.' (154) This is the voice of the greatest poetry, and Hopkins has very little to say about it. He has more to say about the second type, which he calls Parnassian language, and which he regards as of dubious worth. He exemplifies it with Tennyson, and it seems that doubts about Tennyson had been the first incitement for Hopkins to construct his taxonomical scheme. There is also a sub-species of the Parnassian that he calls Castalian, and identifies with Wordsworth in his less inspirational moments. The third category is the most interesting from our present point of view of linguistic primitivism:

> The third kind is merely the language of verse as distinct from that of prose, Delphic, the tongue of the Sacred *Plain*, I may call it, used in common by poet and poetaster. *Poetry when spoken is spoken in it, but to speak it is not necessarily to speak poetry.* (Ibid, 158) [Second emphasis mine]

Delphic poetry is not exemplified. It seems to me that Hopkins, in his description of the Delphic style, anticipates his much later assertion that poetry 'should be current language heightened, to any degree heightened and unlike itself, but not [...] an obsolete one.' (letter to Bridges, 14 August 1876) (xxxiii) This indeed has a striking resemblance to his last sub-species of the Delphic, the Olympian, which consists of 'the language of strange masculine genius which suddenly, as it were, forces its way into the domain of poetry, without naturally having a right there.' (Ibid, xxxiii)

The idea of the 'tongue of the Sacred *Plain*,' which is not a common language and even less a secular one, but both *sacred* and *plain*, should be compared with Ezra Pound's formula in the letter to Harriet Monroe referred to earlier: 'a fine language departing in no way from speech save by a heightened intensity.' (49)

It is necessary to notice that both Hopkins's and Pound's positions are prompted by their opposition to Tennyson, and to a generalised view of poetic diction associated with Victorian poetry: Yeats's 'abstractions.' While Hopkins and Pound are united regarding Tennyson, in another respect they are opposed, as Davie duly points out, and that is in their views of Milton. For Hopkins, Milton is the supreme example of propriety of language, and Hopkins himself wants to achieve a more 'balanced and Miltonic style.' (235) For Pound, as for Eliot (at least to begin with), Milton is the epitome of idiosyncratic style and the great stumbling block in the development of English poetic diction. How can that be? Given the similarities of their positions on linguistic primitivism it seems hardly possible to believe Hopkins and Pound are speaking of the same poet.

4

Pound never wrote a full account of his views on Milton's poetry, although his comments in *ABC of Reading* on the Latinate syntax of Milton are very pertinent. Milton's 'misdeeds as a poet have been called attention to, as by Mr Ezra Pound, but usually in passing,' T.S. Eliot writes in his first essay on Milton (from 1936), a highly critical but more circumspect and less vitriolic statement than Pound's *obiter dicta*. (258) Eliot concentrates his criticism of Milton on his legacy more than on his practice, but in substance his strictures are the same as Pound's: Milton has created a rhetoric which is 'not necessarily bad in its influence,' but 'bad in relation to the historical life of a language as a whole.' (262) Here Eliot brings in a favourite parallel with Dryden:

> Of the two, I still think Dryden's development the healthier, because it was Dryden who preserved, so far as it was preserved at all, the tradition of *conversational* language in poetry: and I might add that it seems to me easier to get back to healthy language from Dryden than it is to get back to it from Milton. (262)

In his second essay on Milton (from 1947), an essay often regarded as a fairly weak recantation of his earlier criticisms, Eliot in fact reiterates and clarifies his charges against Milton, although tempering them with a much wider and more pragmatic perspective. He now maintains 'the remoteness of Milton's verse from ordinary speech, his invention of his own poetic language, seems to me one of the marks of his greatness.' (ibid, 268) But just prior to that, the strictures seem to remain:

> there are the great poets from whom we can learn negative rules: no poet can teach another to write well, but some great poets can teach others some of the things to avoid. They teach what to avoid, by showing us what great poetry can do without—how *bare* it can be. (268)

This is a concept Davie was to develop in a somewhat different direction, in his idea of the *purity* of English poetical diction. But the norm for Eliot is not a poetic diction, however pure, but a vague notion of something called variously 'prose,' 'ordinary speech,' 'common language,' or the like. Towards the end of his essay, Eliot gives one of his clearest accounts of this version of linguistic primitivism:

> I have on several occasions suggested that the important changes in the idiom of English verse which are represented by the names of Dryden and Wordsworth, may be characterized as successful attempts to escape from a

poetic idiom, which had ceased to have a relation to contemporary speech. This is the sense of Wordsworth's Prefaces. (272)

Indeed it is, and I shall presently follow that trail. But at this point we can safely assign a mode to this kind of primitivism, well known from antiquity in the great inventory of Boas and Lovejoy. But if cyclical primitivism is going to work, it has to be dialectical as well: the historical process has to have enough tension to develop at an even pace. Eliot, philosophically resourceful as always, has some ingenious things to say about this process:

> If every generation of poets made it their task to bring diction up to date with the spoken language, poetry would fail in one of its most important obligations. For poetry should help, not only to refine the language of the time, but to prevent it from changing too rapidly: a development of language at too great a speed would be a development in the sense of a progressive deterioration, and that is our danger today. (273)

These principles, so well-known and so much part of the modernist heritage that we have almost, through familiarity, lost sight of them, have not elicited the same degree of commentary as have other critical concepts central to high modernism in the Pound/Eliot mode, such as dissociation of sensibility, or individual talent, or the objective correlative, or *melopoeia*. This may be because of the vagueness of the model invoked, and the reasonable nature of its implied historicism. Clearly, the conversational model for poetic language cannot be used in any mechanical or even methodical way as a critical tool for censuring poetic diction: it is historically determined as part of the practitioner's art and limited to specific situations when poetic diction is deemed to have deviated too much from a norm which is intuitively or subjectively (in fact poetically) determined. In other historical situations, the opposite principle can be invoked and a formal poetic diction may have to be cultivated and codified.

Pound, although subscribing to a similar kind of primitivism, is much less systematic and relativist in his remarks, and more assertive in relating the deviation from a natural conversational norm to specific linguistic causes. In *ABC of Reading* he blames Milton's unnatural syntax on the inflectional model of Latin: 'the great break in European literary history is the change over from inflected to uninflected language. And a great deal of critical nonsense has been written by people who did not realize the difference.' (50)

There is a passage of Ernest Fenollosa's *The Chinese Written Character as a Medium for Poetry* where the author gives his radically primitivist view of

Aryan etymology, concluding that 'Nature has no grammar.' In his footnote to the passage, Ezra Pound tells us:

> Even Latin, living Latin, had not the network of rules they foist upon unfortunate schoolchildren. These are borrowed sometimes from Greek grammarians, even as I have seen English grammars borrowing oblique cases from Latin grammars. Sometimes they sprang from the grammatising or categorising passion of pedants. Living Latin had only the feel of the cases: the ablative or dative emotion. (50, n.1)

There are obvious grounds for confusion here. It is true that the formal syntax of the classical languages has played an enormous role in forming the poetic diction (and other areas of formalised language) of later times: we can quote the monumental works of Eduard Norden and Einar Löfstedt to this effect. But there is no firm evidence that all cases of syntactical license in poetry are to be regarded as *calqué* on classical models. Moreover, although we can perhaps assume that colloquial Latin was less rigorously free in its word order than the speeches in Livy or Tacitus would make us believe, this does not imply that we can reduce the rules of grammar for that language to 'feel' or 'emotion' (whatever that might mean). Pound here has confused the borrowing of grammatical terms with the actual internalised rules of accidence or syntax employed by the competent speaker.

This situation is today much clarified by recent investigations of case grammar and syntactical typology. Had he had more than a hearsay account of even the contemporary views on these matters, for instance in Sapir or Jespersen, Pound might have been able to avoid this confusion—or perhaps not. It is now becoming abundantly clear that there is a built-in confusion or contradiction in the idea of linguistic primitivism as a doctrine of high modernism. In *radical* linguistic primitivism (of which the Fenollosa/Pound position is a particularly salient example), one posits a primordial form of language made up of root words signifying things or acts in a direct way, and elevates this as a model for poetic language. In *vernacular* linguistic primitivism, one posits a model for poetry in a language that is colloquial, contemporary, and non-archaising. While the first model can lay some claim to absolute validity, the second—if for no other reason because of the fact that colloquial speech changes with the times—has to be relativised and historicised in a cyclical way, in particular at a stage when modernism is in need of gaining some respectability. Eliot and Pound tried to embrace both models in their reckoning with traditional poetic language, which they saw embodied in Miltonic diction in particular. But Pound, being much more of a radical (in this specialised sense if in no other) had to be more violent in his rejection of Milton, as he so easily could have embraced the principle of Latinate syntax, or free word order within metrical constraints, as a form of radical linguistic primitivism. This was of course what Hopkins did, and quite correctly from his premises.

5

When trying to assess the importance of linguistic primitivism for the practice of poetry in high modernism and subsequent literary phases (whether we want to call them postmodern or not) it is imperative to keep in mind the neutral and non-committal nature of the vernacular variety of primitivism. As compared to classical variants of primitivism it is not imbued with any great moral purpose. It is not because of any great vision for the future of mankind that the poet should make his language colloquial: it is a mechanical operation very much like increasing or reducing speed when driving a car. When the poet notices that a formal poetic diction is clogging up the traffic, he steps on the accelerator and makes his language more colloquial; in the next curve he may have to reduce speed and let the language congeal to standard formulae.

Nonetheless, both Pound and Eliot remained on the whole faithful to their principles in their poetic practice. When considering the deletions and emendations prompted by Pound for the most extensive first version of *The Waste Land*, one may be reminded of Yeats's comment on Pound's good principles and deficient taste. Pound evidently had more taste than he got credit for in making Eliot exclude his most abandoned colloquial exercises: 'He do the police in different voices' would have been a far from suitable epitaph on Eliot's poetical talent had he decided to follow a more prolix and polyphiloprogenetive poetic career. As for Pound's conversational cluster technique in *The Cantos*, it is no secret that it has had a most insistent influence on American poetry, noticeably even today, via the legacies of objectivism and projective verse.

The provenance of vernacular linguistic primitivism is obvious, even without Eliot's helpful hint. Nearly all the ideas and also the confusions can be found in the various versions of Wordsworth's prefaces. Since the literature on Wordsworth is so enormous, and the ideas so well known, I shall mention just a few important points. When Ezra Pound writes to Harriet Monroe in favour of a poetic language containing 'nothing that you couldn't *in some circumstance, in the stress of some emotion, actually say,'* (49) he echoes not only Wordsworth's repeated contention that he had been aiming at 'a selection of the language really used [or spoken] by men,' (13) but also his insistence on linking their language with 'the language of extraordinary occasions' (42) and 'language exquisitely fitted for the passion.' (24) And when Pound, earlier in the same letter, argues that 'poetry must be as well written as prose,' (49) he is likewise indebted to the observation of Wordsworth 'that some of the most interesting parts of the best poems will be found to be strictly the language of prose when it is well written.' (19) The relativist and historicist bias to be found in Eliot is also often prefigured in Wordsworth's prefaces, in the rejection of the category of *taste*, particularly in the appendix of 1802, with its historical account of the origin of poetic diction in a perversion of the daring and figurative language or the earliest poets.

Scholars and critics have often emphasised this spirited trans-valuation of 18th century values. In a tightly argued short article, Professor Hans Aarsleff of Princeton has given good evidence for considering an influence in general terms from French thinkers, in particular Condillac, but perhaps also Madame de Staël in her 1800 relativist and historicist account of literature in relation to its social setting, *De la littérature*. One tends to forget that the notion of the primacy of figurative language and its derivation from the passions is an 18th century commonplace, not only to be found in its most eloquent champion, Giambattista Vico, but also in Rousseau, Herder, Hamann, and Monboddo.

Still, the Wordsworthian version has a distinctive flavour of its own in the history of linguistic primitivisms. In one important aspect it differs completely from the otherwise strikingly similar views of Eliot or Pound: it is firmly committed to a social perspective most assuredly stated in its earliest form in the Advertisement of 1798, where Wordsworth says 'the majority of the following poems are to be considered as experiments. They were written chiefly with a view to ascertain how far the language of conversation in the middle and lower classes of society is adapted to the purpose of poetic pleasure.' (1)

In choosing a social class not his own, observable and close at hand certainly, but not relegated to a distant time or land, the poet has to assume the role of spokesman or *translator*, as Wordsworth puts it. We would perhaps today say documentary journalist or anthropologist. The reportorial elements in Wordsworth's poetry may not have been widely noticed, but are in fact both considerable and theoretically essential. More important still, it is from his respect for the social permanence of rustic life that his poetry gathers its strength—a strength not matched in Eliot or Pound, for all their reliance on craftsmanship and for all their considerable (if sometimes confused) social speculation:

> Low and rustic life was generally chosen, because in that condition the essential passions of the heart find a better soil in which they can attain their maturity, are less under restraint, and speak a plainer and more emphatic language; because in that condition of life our elementary feelings co-exist in a state, and consequently, may be more accurately contemplated, and more forcibly communicated; because the manners of rural life germinate from those elementary feelings; and from the necessary character of rural occupations, are more easily comprehended; and are more durable; and lastly, because in that condition the passions of men are incorporated with the beautiful and permanent forms of nature. (14)

This is a powerful statement of mainstream primitivism in social terms with a considerable explanatory force regarding the origin of poetic thought. For beyond Wordsworth's primitivism, and imbuing it with moral purpose, is the whole tradition of the *sermo humilis*: the humble and earth-like language derived ultimately from the Synoptic Gospels and impregnating so much of medieval literature. Erich Auerbach observed this pristine form of linguistic primitivism in his magisterial *Mimesis*, and also wrote the classical essay on *sermo humilis*, which takes as its point of departure the levels of style recognised by St Augustine in his examination of pagan rhetoric. But even beyond that we can listen to the ironic voice of Socrates in Plato's *Phaedrus*, castigating the art of writing and rebuking the speech-writers for their rhetoric: 'In fact, the people in those days, lacking the wisdom of you young people, were content in their simplicity to listen to trees or rocks, provided these told the truth.' (157)

This tradition of linguistic primitivism is one step ahead of other more limited versions, as it does not, in its humbleness or simplicity, invest much trust in writing as an activity, or regard it as a necessity for poetic creation. Thus it is not very highly regarded today. I identify it with Hopkins's despised Delphic of the Sacred *Plain*: 'Poetry when spoken is spoken in it, but to speak it is not necessarily to speak poetry.' (158)

6

Linguistic primitivism has put its distinctive mark on modernist poetry in the whole Anglo-American tradition. When we look at modernism in a wider European setting, we find very little that corresponds to it. The voices of modernist poetry in French or German poetry, from Hölderlin to Celan, Baudelaire to Bonnefoy, speak defiantly in another dialect, lofty, vatic, solemn, *sermo sublimis*, rather than *sermo humilis*. Paul de Man has, in a masterful and pregnant early essay, traced the primary vocabulary of that dialect to its sources in figurative language of great simplicity, 'The Intentional Image in Romantic Poetry.' In this essay he reminds us that whatever the demands of the language, of the social world or the sensual world, or even the ontological primacy of the natural object, words are used in poetry not as signs or names, but in *order to name*, in an Adamic act. He quotes the words of Mallarmé (from his epitaph on Poe) *'donner un sens plus pur aux mots de la tribu.'* (70) Is this to be taken, with the English poet, as an act of social acquiescence in the face of the intractability of language, or with the continental poet, as a defiance of social demands in order to reach the silences behind the words? Those are the questions that will be present for us in further investigations of these problems in this series of essays. Let me conclude here with a quotation from Wordsworth's third 'Essay Upon Epitaphs,' which marvellously comprises both views in two sentences: 'Words are too awful an instrument for good and evil to be trifled with' (129) and 'language, if it do not uphold, and feed, and leave in quiet, like the power of gravitation or the air we breathe, is a counter-spirit, unremittingly, and noiselessly at work to derange, to subvert, to lay waste, to vitiate and to dissolve.' (ibid)

Works Cited

Eliot, T.S. *Selected Prose of T.S. Eliot*. Ed. by Frank Kermode. New York: Harvest, 1975.

Fenellosa, Ernest, and Ezra Pound. *The Chinese Written Character as a Medium for Poetry*, ed. by Huan Saussy, Jonathan Stalling, and Lucas Klein. New York: Fordham University Press, 2008.

Hopkins, Gerard Manley *Poems and Prose*. Ed. by W.H. Gardner. Harmondsworth: Penguin, 1953.

Mallarmé, Stéphane. *Collected Poems and Other Verse*. Ed. and trans. by E.H. Blackmore and A.M. Blackmore. Oxford: Oxford University Press, 2006.

Plato. *Plato's Phaedrus*. Trans. by R. Hackworth. Cambridge: Cambridge University Press, 1972.

Pound, Ezra. *ABC of Reading*. New York: New Directions, 1960.

— *The Letters of Ezra Pound, 1907–1941*. London: Faber and Faber, 1951.

Ransom, John Crowe. 'Poetry as Primitive Language,' in *Speaking of Writing: Selected Hopgood Lectures*. Ed. by Nicholas Delbanco. Ann Arbor: University of Michigan Press, 1990: 73–83.

Whitehall, Harold. 'Sprung Rhythm,' in *The Kenyon Review*. 6.3 (1944): 333–54.

Wordsworth, William. *Wordsworth's Literary Criticism*. Ed. by Nowell C. Smith. London: Frowde, 1905.

Yeats, W.B. 'Letter to Lady Gregory,' in *W.B. Yeats, Man and Poet*. Ed. By A.N. Jeffares. New Haven: Yale University Press, 1949: 167.

Part Two: Linguistic Reductionism in Poetry Criticism

1

Taking my cue from the two quotes from Wordsworth at the end of my first essay—quotes about the dangers of words as instruments for good or evil and about language as a *counterspirit*—I would like to consider another pervasive attitude towards language: the rejection of words as a means of communication and the postulating of a pre-verbal stage of mankind. Such a stage may be imagined as Adamic and set in Eden, or as something brutish, set in the woods where once the Noble Savage ran and communicated without recourse to words. This pre-verbal stage is a commonplace in the Western mystical tradition (and no doubt elsewhere) from Jacob Boehme to Swedenborg. This attitude has been admirably illuminated by Gerald Bruns in his book *Modern Poetry and the Idea of Language*, one of the few investigations of the area that seems to follow a path more or less parallel to my own.

That language can be considered a veil to be lifted or rent asunder in order that man may glimpse a reality behind the words is a notion as old and as un-provable a hypothesis as is its opposite, the idea that words have some special or privileged relation to reality. 'Language was given to us in order to disguise our thoughts' is an old cynical apophthegm, probably coined by Voltaire but popularly attributed to Talleyrand (Edwards 50), who clearly had some experience in the practice of it. The idea was employed by Edward Young, and later by Kierkegaard. In a different, weaker form it can be traced back to Plutarch. The warning that Plato offers to Theaitetos, about the *misológoi*—those who mistrust words—is clearly intended to stave off criticisms from this kind of radically anti-verbal position.

It is not clear whether this anti-verbalism should be referred to as linguistic primitivism, since it involves a negation of language in primitive times or extreme conditions (as in, for example, the ecstasy of the mystic). Is the language of the angels or the animals to be equated with human language? Or, to convert the question into more modern terms, are the analogical extensions of natural language to be taken seriously? Or are they to be regarded as merely metaphorical descriptions of secondary communication systems, organised according to entirely different principles? Once Sigurd (or Siegfried) had slain the dragon Fafnir in the Norse version of the Niebelungen saga, he sat down to roast the dragon's heart over the fire. He burnt a finger when testing the temperature and put it in his mouth. Instantly, he could understand the language of the birds. What dragon do we have to slay, what heart do we have to devour, in order to learn to decipher the cryptic messages of poetry and art? Some believe that we can move beyond the various languages and means of understanding used to interpret poetry, and find the single master-discourse—that we can eat the heart of the dragon.

This vaguely primitivist notion of a more primary language, or pre-language, has another side to it, of equally venerable age. From ancient times, man has tried to decipher the messages inscribed in nature herself, has tried to read the Book of Nature. In particular, starry skies have for millennia fascinated observers who attempted, in order to form higher unities in the seeming chaos, to discern discrete elements (constellations) either to elucidate the physical/historical structure of the universe (cosmology) or to demarcate the influence of heavenly bodies on the individual fates of men (astrology). Like the Book of the World, the script of the stars became an inordinately popular commonplace in Western literature—we see this, for example, in E.R. Curtius's *European Literature and the Latin Middle Ages*, in Gabriel Josipovici's *The World and the Book*, as well as countless quotes from Edward Young, Ralph Waldo Emerson, and the romantic poets.

When Galileo, in his important methodological dialogue '*Sidereus Nuntius*' ('The Messenger from the Stars') brings this ancient metaphor into the focus of his experimental and quantitative methodology, he can claim with enormous authority that he has found the key to the decipherment of this sidereal text in a *language*: in the language of circles and triangles, of numbers and functions, in the abstract languages of geometry and mathematics.

The position reached here by Galileo can perhaps be described as a kind of primitivism, but an ahistorical and firmly methodological or procedural one. It presupposes that every order of the phenomenal world can be ultimately and accurately described, and also predicted, in a language that has been purified of all its contingent qualities. It is a special kind of primitivism, though: Galileo's method is an enormously authoritative statement of *reductionism* in the form of science.

2

In our time 'reductionism' is mainly used as a term of criticism or abuse, so it may be difficult to remember what a powerful idea in the history of Western civilisation the principle of reducibility has been. The idea of a unified science, where every phenomenon could be studied and explained and classified, so that humanistic study and the social sciences could be reduced to biology, biology to chemistry and chemistry to physics in a hierarchical scale, eventually leaving no discernable gaps at all, is one of the most grandiose schemes for the advancement of human knowledge ever conceived. Ever since the mid-19th century, with the all-embracing explanatory aspirations of Comte and Marx, it has been a burning issue in the social sciences, closely connected with the problem of positivism — more so perhaps on the European continent than in the English-speaking world.

Of course the anti-reductionist doctrine, which states that every science or area of knowledge is dependant on its own language and terminology and can explain phenomena only within its boundaries, is as old if not older than reductionism itself. Aristotle makes a very clear and strong case for it in a chapter of the *Posterior Analytics*. Here, one presumes, he is wary of the claims of the Pythagoreans and Plato on behalf of the sciences of mathematics and geometry, claims not reductionist in the modern sense, but which aspired nonetheless to elevate these forms of knowledge to a privileged position in the Greek *paideía* or educational system:

> Nor can a proposition of one science be proved by another science except when the relation is such that the propositions of the one are subordinate to those of the other, as the propositions of optics are subordinate to geometry and those of harmonics to arithmetic. (63)

Although Aristotle's term *episteme* may not exactly correspond to what we mean by a separate science today, the same principle is clearly applicable to any non-reductionist standpoint.

The best statement I know of the problem of reduction, or alternatively, of irreducibility, in the natural sciences from recent times comes is from Sir Peter Medawar's *Induction and Intuition in Scientific Thought*:

> *Reducibility; emergence*: If we choose to see a hierarchical structure in Nature—if societies are composed of individuals, individuals of cells, and cells in their turn of molecules, then it makes sense to ask whether we may not 'interpret' sociology in terms of the biology of individuals or 'reduce' biology to physics and chemistry. This is a living methodological problem, but it does not seem to have been satisfactorily resolved. At first sight the ambition embodied in the idea of *reducibility* seem hopeless of achievement. Each tier of the natural hierarchy makes use of notions peculiar to itself. The ideas of democracy, credit, crime or political constitution are no part of biology, nor shall we expect to find in physics the concepts of memory, infection, sexuality, or fear. No sensible usage can bring the foreign exchange deficit into the biology syllabus, already grievously overcrowded, or nest building into the syllabus of physics. In each plane or tier of the hierarchy new notions or ideas seem to emerge that are inexplicable in the language or with the conceptual resources of the tier below. But if in fact we cannot 'interpret' sociology in terms of biology or biology in terms of physics, how is it that so many of the triumphs of modern science seem to be founded upon a repudiation of the doctrine of irreducibility? There is a problem here to which methodologists can and do make valuable and illuminating contributions. (15–16)

This admirably clear and succinct account is followed by an even longer footnote where Medawar, like Aristotle, uses geometry as a prime example of reductionism.

3

I hope to be excused for such a lengthy opening gambit, but I think these reflections by an eminent scientist are well worth our attention. The importance of Medawar's insights—in particular in the notion of the *emergence* of theoretical concepts—can be brought to bear on the problems of modern poetics on several different levels. Present-day discussions of reductionism have most often been kept within the confines of Althusser's theory of science, which I consider to be one of the weakest links in his often-convincing criticism of empiricism. Althusser's attitude to the separate sciences is conventionalist—like that of the early Foucault—and as his criteria for truth conditions are coherence criteria rather than correspondence criteria, his theory does not seem to be powerful enough to exclude spurious areas of investigation. It cannot cope with the emergence of new science or new sub-fields for science.

Such spurious fields have no doubt emerged in profusion in the area of poetics, both recently and in former times, and one might be able to see a Wordsworthian counter-spirit at work in their language, in order to 'lay waste, vitiate and dissolve.' To lay waste the reader's imagination, to vitiate his judgement and dissolve his patience, that is. As my intentions are not polemical, I shall refrain from engagement in these areas but only address myself to works by scholars whose important contributions are serious and beyond doubt. I will, however, reiterate the point made about irreducibility, by both Aristotle and Medawar—the point about the way notions or ideas or demonstrations of proof are transferable from level to level, but only hierarchically. 'Thus the genus must be the same, either absolutely, or in some respect, if the demonstration is to be transferable [*metabainein*],' Aristotle says. (63) Later he gives an example, brief and to the point, culled from the not too adjacent fields of geometry and poetics: 'Is every circle a figure?—if one draws a circle the answer is obvious. Well, are the epic poems (*epe kuklos*) a circle? Evidently they are not.' (81)

There are some facts about poetry that seem unassailable and incontrovertible, and which have been repeated by generations of poets; for example, that poems are made up of words and not emotions, an idea respected by Eliot and Pound after Valéry.

Eliot would probably have agreed with Michael Riffaterre, the French-American semiotician and stylistic scholar, when he writes in his *Semiotics of Poetry*:

> The language of poetry differs from common linguistic usage—this much the unsophisticated reader senses instinctively. Yet, while it is true that poetry often employs words excluded from common usage and has its own special grammar, even a grammar not valid beyond the narrow compass of a given poem, it may also happen that poetry uses the same words and the same grammar as everyday language. (1)

Dryden, the young Wordsworth, and the youngish Eliot would have been surprised. But Riffaterre goes on to say:

> In all literatures with a long enough history, we observe that poetry keeps swinging back and forth, tending first one way, then the other. The choice

between alternatives is dictated by the evolution of taste and by continually changing aesthetic concepts. But whichever of the two trends prevails, one factor remains constant: poetry expresses concepts and things by indirection. To put it simply, a poem says one thing and means another. (ibid)

The later Eliot would indubitably have agreed with the historicist point made in the beginning of the paragraph, but I am not so sure about the conclusion. Riffaterre describes the poet as someone who says one thing and means another. But there is a much simpler term for that: a liar (*pseudomenos*). So, is poetry a lying activity, perhaps the art of lying? This has been maintained by very respectable people, such as Xenophanes and Plato. But another interpretation of saying one thing and meaning another would be irony, the poet as *ironist*—the first among the Theophrastian characters, and not much better than a liar.

4

Let me return to a previous point before reverting to Riffaterre whose book, I must insist, I find a very substantial contribution to the understanding of one type of poetry. The idea that poetry is a specific and specialised language, and that all the arts are best described as languages, is very widespread at the present time. That the arts are languages has been maintained by Susanne Langer, and from a very different philosophical standpoint by Nelson Goodman and his disciples. Roland Barthes sees the fashion of dress as language, Susan Sontag sees illness as a metaphor, Jacques Lacan sees the subconscious as a language. Examples could easily be multiplied. I shall not ask the question whether this is sound theoretical practice or not; I shall just look at the consequences of some cases closely connected with poetics or the systematic view of poetics in modernism.

I am not here so much concerned about the practical linguistic reductionism of methodology as in *explication de texte* or close reading and the like. Clearly, the poem, *qua* isolated poem, exists on a phenomenological level, a level that is in a very obvious sense linguistic. But in order to maintain that poetry is a specific language *over and above* its linguistic constituents, perhaps a universal language, one needs much more on which to go. Firstly, one needs a separate grammar of some complexity, consisting of, say, one syntactical, one morphological, and one phonological component, each with a separate set of rules—be they phrase structure rules or transformational rules. Furthermore, one needs a lexicon, and in addition one needs separate components for converting prose into poetry and re-converting poetry into prose. Nobody has claimed to have even outlined such an unwieldy grammar with any consistency.

The terminology is familiar to anybody who has attended an elementary course in modern linguistics—the framework I cited was one associated with generative grammar at a fairly early stage of its development. There is no evidence that any of the many rival theories we now have would allow any easier access for a sub-theory of poetic language. However the terminology is also familiar to anybody who has dipped into modern critical theory or poetics where these terms abound, used most often in a loose and completely irresponsible way, together with many other, sometimes completely incompatible terms. It is no secret that the structuralist and poststructuralist methods favoured in recent years have had their most convincing successes in the analysis of narrative—where a respectable terminology has been engendered from within the discipline—but seem very inadequate for the analysis of poetry.

One of the most consistent theoretical accounts of poetic language has been the one given by the Soviet semiotician Jurij Lotman. His sense of the theoretical problems involved in regarding poetry as a language are quite clear, and he has tried to solve these problems by treating the languages of art as secondary modelling systems, that is, as systems which, although modelled on natural languages, at the same time tend to generate further sub-languages. Lotman is far from clear on this point, in spite of his fairly simplistic views on his languages as codes. His translator writes in the preface to the English translation:

> Is literature a language, or cinema, or sculpture? Is a given period or school (Realism, the Baroque) a language? Is a specific genre within these art forms a language? Is a specific text a language? At various points in his work Lotman responds affirmatively to all these questions, and the reader must himself determine what the author means by language in each case. (Vroon, x)

One of Lotman's most interesting points comes in his attempt to integrate a phonological and a semantic component for his grammar of poetic language. In the course of this attempt he comes to regard the poetic *line* as unit of both sound and meaning, as a separate and unique *word*. The view has its venerable antecedents, obviously quite independently, in a passage from Mallarmé's *Crise de vers* (*Crisis of Verse*), where the latter speaks of '*le vers qui de plusieurs vocables refait un mot total, neuf, étranger à la langue et comme incantatoire*' ['the verse that from its constituents makes up a total word, new, strange to the language and like an incantation']. (213)

Yvor Winters quotes Mallarmé's passage in the beginning of *Primitivism and Decadence*, with certain disapproving comments. With his customary shrewdness and consistency, he goes on to say:

> The poem, to be perfect, should likewise be a new word in the same sense, a word of which the line, as we have defined it, is merely a syllable. Such a word is, of course, composed of much more than the sum of its words (as one normally uses the term) and its syntax. It is composed of an almost fluid complex, if the adjective and the noun are not too nearly contradictory, of relationships between words (in the normal sense of the term), a relationship involving rational content, cadences, rhymes, juxtapositions, literary and other connotations, inversions, and so on, almost indefinitely. These relationships, it should be obvious, extend the poet's vocabulary incalculably. (3)

This should be the logical conclusion of Jurij Lotman's position as well, although, sadly, he never descends from high abstraction to make such a conclusion explicit.

This position can indeed be regarded as a first step toward a vocabulary, or lexicon, of poetic utterances, a list of *hapax legomena* or nonce-words that, barring formulaic repetitions and cases of plagiarism, is infinite and, as Winters put it, incalculable. The position could also be regarded as a step towards formulating some morphological rules for the poetic language, or subordinate parts of it, like alliteration, assonance, rhyme, and the like.

5

If we leave the phonological aspect aside (as we have to do for quite respectable 'languages' like logic and mathematics) in an account of poetic language, we can still secure a syntactic component for the grammar, which would order the elements according to certain rules of selection and combination. This is the well-known principle enunciated by Roman Jakobson for his method in poetics, expounded in many ruthlessly multilingual articles.

We all have reason to be grateful that Roman Jakobson, arguably the greatest and most versatile linguist of this century, devoted so much time and energy to questions of poetics. His painstakingly detailed linguistic analyses of poems from many languages unearth many real insights into the workings of language in a poem. But these analyses shed light on the poem by entirely conventional means. In his theoretical statements Jakobson's methodology is as reductionist on the micro-stylistic level as is Lotman on a macro-stylistic level. To maintain that every element in a poem is either opposed to or in parallel with any other element does not give much scope for systematic observation on how, and to what purpose, poets actually work. This is what is ultimately left out of any linguistically reductionist poetics.

I shall not labour this point here any more, but I do wish to emphasise that I find reductionist claims honourable, and see them as partaking of a long tradition of scientific aspirations. I do not believe that linguistic reductionist methods destroy the poetic element, nor that there is a mystical essence in poetry (any more than in any other activity) that cannot be described and analysed. I also believe that advances in textual grammar and pragmatics—what was once known as discourse analysis— will eventually shed much light on the details of poetic composition and appreciation. However, I cannot be convinced that poetry is a *language* in the sense required for this kind of analysis to be successful on a theoretical level. Nor do I think that description can be used in a reductive sense about poetry and the arts.

What, though, about the middle ground between the microscopic and the macroscopic levels? Let us return to Riffaterre. His very impressive ability to read poems in a sensitive way, along with his intimate acquaintance with French poetry and colloquial French, leads to a methodology that is far from absurd, but is nevertheless curiously limiting. His main view of French poetry—a healthy corrective to the idea that French and continental modernism tends towards the lofty, elevated, and prophetic—is that it is in many ways related to riddles, jokes, and conundrums. He uses an elaborate terminology that I am not convinced is always necessary, and which I am not going to reproduce here. Taking a hint from Saussure's anagrams and paragrams, he postulates for his chosen poems the existence of a *hypogram* which is hidden from the reader at first reading, and may consist in a cliché, proverbial phrase, or perhaps most often another previous line in a poem or other text. It is signalled by a certain deviation of language that he calls ungrammatical (in obvious contradiction of current usage in linguistics). He achieves some very impressive results in detailed and revealing poems by

Eluard, Desnos, early Breton, and prose and poetry by Chateaubriand, Hugo, Rimbaud, and Lautréamont. His remarks on the prose poem as a genre are acute (although not, I think, exhaustive) and his explications of Ponge are among the best I have ever read. Still, the model implied for the making of poetry, as opposed to the reading of poetry, is very curious. Riffaterre sees the poem as emerging from a matrix that is 'a minimal and literal sentence,' then transforming into a longer, complex and non-literal periphrasis. Thus his primary category of text-production is expansion, which is a variant of the old *amplificatio* technique: more and more detailed information is added recursively to the matrix until the poem is complete. (19)

The objection that can be immediately raised is that the recursivity of this technique cannot provide any criteria for its completeness or closure: in theory the poem could be amplified *ad infinitum*. And, furthermore, the technique of expansion seems to be contrary to the insistence in modernist poetics on the opposite technique, contraction or concentration, as defended by Pound, for instance in his neat 'dichten = condensare.' (97)

The only important rhetorical category that can be easily handled by ordinary rules of transformation, however, is the transformation of simile to metaphor. This operation, which is part of a general strategy of concentration, has always been regarded as an important step in the conversion of poetic diction of the rhetorical variety to a more unforced and natural language, associated in various instances with romanticism and modernism.

The position of Riffaterre is not the deliberately absurd one of many present-day critics of poetry. He has a firm belief in the accessibility of poetic discourse to rational investigation. Yet his methodology and (perhaps, as importantly) his choice of poems have forced him into an overall view of poetry that is curiously antipathetic towards the claims of romantic and modernist poets of the last two centuries. In spite of his strictly objective and scientific attitude, he seems to be feeding his theory with definitions that are persuasive, but favour a specific kind of poetry seen from a limited point of view. Here we can see how linguistic reductionism, however legitimate from a certain point of view, can result in the trivialisation of poetry by reducing it to a game or a conundrum. There is evidence that this idea of ludic poetry is a serious contender for a conspicuous place in postmodernist poetics: I am thinking, for example, of the so-called 'Martian School' of British poetry.

6

It would be demonstratively unfair to include Leo Spitzer, with his truly modest attitude towards his life-long service to philology (beautifully expressed in the Princeton lecture of 1948, 'Linguistics and Literary History') among the linguistic reductionists. He shows himself to be, in this statement of hermeneutic principles, a sworn enemy of reductionism. I will, however, mention him here because I want to refer, however briefly, to his favourite example of fickleness and unstableness, in the words conundrum, quandary, *'calembour,' 'calembredaine,'* etc., which are all derived from similar roots. In this connexion he makes a most ingenious excursion into 'Cratylisme'—in Genette's mimological sense: 'Thus we must conclude that the instability is also connected with a semantic content: a word meaning 'whim,' 'pun' easily behaves whimsically—just as in all languages throughout the world, the words for 'butterfly' present a kaleidoscopic instability.' (7) Spitzer takes this as a hint of the instability that threatens the work of art, and he concludes:

> The reason that the clues to understanding can not be mechanically transferred from one work of art to another lies in the fact of artistic expressivity itself. [...] To overcome the impression of an arbitrary association in the work of art, the reader must seek to place himself in the creative center of the artist himself—and re-create the artistic organism. (28)

This activating element in art and poetry, and the problems involved in applying organic models to it, will be, with the benevolent blessing of Spitzer, a *leitmotif* for my next two essays.

Works Cited

Aristotle. *Posterior Analytics*. Trans. by Hugh Tredennick. Cambridge, MA: Harvard University Press, 1930, II.

Curtius, E.R. *European Literature and the Latin Middle Ages*. Trans. by W.R. Trask. London: Routledge, 1953.

Edwards, H. Sutherland. 'Historic Phrases,' *MacMillan's Magazine*, 35 (1876–1877): 48–54.

Galilei, Galileo. *Sidereus Nuntius*. Trans. by Albert van Helden. Chicago: University of Chicago Press, 1989.

Josipovici, Gabriel. *The World and the Book*. Basingstoke: Macmillan, 1971.

Mallarmé, Stéphane. *Oeuvres complètes*, 2 vols. Paris: Pleiade, 1945, II.

Medawar, Sir Peter. *Induction and Intuition in Scientific Thought*. Philadelphia: American Philosophical Society, 1969.

Pound, Ezra. *ABC of Reading*. New York: New Directions: 1960.

Riffaterre, Michael. *Semiotics of Poetry*. Bloomington, Indiana: Indiana University Press, 1978.

Spitzer, Leo. *Linguistics and Literary History: Essays in Stylistics*. New York: Russell and Russell, 1948.

Vroon, Ronald. 'Preface' to Jurij Lotman, *The Structure of the Artistic Text*. Trans. by Ronald Vroon. Ann Arbor: University of Michigan Press, 1977.

Winters, Yvor. *Primitivism and Decadence: A Study of American Experimental Poetry* New York: Haskell House, 1969.

Part Three: The Material Word: From Imagism to New Criticism to Intertextualism

1

If words were things, pigs undoubtedly would have wings.

In the philosophical history of Western thought, materialism and idealism have been the two main attitudes towards things. The first one says, *simpliciter*, that things are the only entities that exist, the second one, perhaps surprisingly, maintains they do not exist at all. Both views have, traditionally, had some difficulties in coping with words.

Jorge Luis Borges, the Argentinean poet and creator of parables, described a non-existent world in his early *ficción* 'Tlön, Uqbar, Orbis Tertius.' The story describes with great accuracy a world that is not only fictional in the ordinary sense of being invented by an author, but is also imaginary on its own fictional level. It may indeed have been created by a secret society over the centuries. The knowledge of Tlön is fragmentary and derived from the eleventh volume of a mysterious encyclopaedia, but some facts emerge with remarkable clarity. 'The nations of this planet are congenitally idealist,' writes Borges. (8) The languages of the southern hemisphere consist exclusively of verbs and have no nouns, while in the northern 'the prime unit is not the verb but the monosyllabic adjective.' (ibid, 8–9) Borges continues:

> The literature of this hemisphere [...] abounds in ideal objects, which are convoked and dissolved in a moment, according to poetic needs. At times

they are determined by mere simultaneity. There are objects composed of two terms, one of visual and another of auditory character: the color of the rising sun and the faraway cry of a bird. [...] These second-degree objects can be combined with others; through the use of certain abbreviations, the process is practically infinite. There are famous poems made up of one enormous word. This word forms a *poetic object* created by the author. The fact that noone believes in the reality of nouns paradoxically causes their number to unending. (ibid, 9)

This staunchly anti-reductionist Borgesian world takes a dim view of scientific enquiry:

Every mental state is irreducible: the mere fact of naming it—*id est*, of classifying it—implies a falsification. From which it can be deduced that there are no sciences on Tlön, not even reasoning. The paradoxical truth is that they do exist, and in almost uncountable number. (ibid, 10)

The menacing ending of Borges's fable, which intimates that this transparent fictional world will gradually become a substitute for the real world and take over its history, its languages, and its arts, points to the dangers of such uncontrollable idealism. But beyond the description of idealism in language, there is another subtext or anti-text here present that Borges surely has had in mind when creating the pale and haunting idealism of Tlön. That is the materialist philosophy professed by the academicians of Lagado, in the third voyage of Jonathan Swift's *Gulliver's Travels*, where the reducibility of language to thing is taken for granted:

The other [project] was a scheme for entirely abolishing all words whatsoever; and this was urged as a great advantage in point of health as well as brevity. For it is plain that every word we speak is in some degree a diminution of our lungs by corrosion, and consequently contributes to the shortening of our lives. An expedient was therefore offered, that since words are only names for *things*, it would be more convenient for all men to carry about them such *things* as were necessary to express the particular business they are to discourse on. And this invention would certainly have taken place, to the great ease as well as health of the subject, if the women in conjunction with the vulgar and illiterate had not threatened to raise a rebellion, unless they might be allowed the liberty to speak with their tongues, after the manner of their forefathers; such constant irreconcilable enemies to science are the common people. However, many of the most learned and wise adhere to the new scheme of expressing themselves by *things*, which hath only this inconvenience attending it, that if a man's business be very great, and of various kinds, he must be obliged in proportion to carry a greater bundle of *things* upon his back, unless he can afford one or two strong servants to attend him. I have often beheld two of those sages almost sinking under the weight of their packs, like peddlers among us; who when they met in the streets would lay down their loads, open their sacks and hold conversation for an hour together, then put up their implements, help each other to resume their burthens, and take their leave. (213)

Both views—of course in their fictional presentation they are hardly devoid of satiric or facetious intention—reduce language to an absurd state. In the materialist version every word is an individual thing, and as such all abstraction or generalisation is impossible. In the idealist version, the intimate state of psychology makes every connection equivalent to every other connection: 'In other words, they do not conceive that the spatial persists in time [...] this monism or complete idealism invalidates all science.' (Borges 9)

2

In order to avoid such absurd reductions of language as these, people have resorted to various strategies, most often historicist or organicist in their origins:

> Is *thinking* impossible without arbitrary signs? And—how far is the word 'arbitrary' a misnomer? Are not words etc. parts and germinations of the Plant? And what is the law of their Growth?—In something of this order I would endeavour to destroy the old antithesis *Words* and *Things*, elevating, as it were, words into Things, and living Things too. (156)

Thus Coleridge in an oft-quoted letter to Godwin, which serves as ingress to the important chapter on *energeia* in Gerald Bruns's book *Modern Poetry and the Idea of Language*. Bruns, after quoting Coleridge, writes: 'I came round to the term 'energy' by design, partly as a way of avoiding what may seem like an obvious point, that Coleridge's theory of language is organic in character.' (44) The organicist mode of explanation of language is, of course, far from self-evident or self-explanatory.

Ever since Aristotle, who invented a biological blueprint for the other sciences and arts, one has to contend with this model in two very different versions, depending on whether the model is taken from one or another of the two branches of biology, morphology, and taxonomy. Morphology is concerned with the interrelations and functions of the different parts of the individual animal or plant, taxonomy with the interrelations of genera and species in the order of animals and plants. It was not until the historicised evolutionary hypothesis of Darwin (and his forerunners) that a fully integrated system of biology could be achieved, where morphology would be linked as a gradual changing mechanism of morphologically determined organs in defining the emergence of new species.

Organicist metaphors thus fall into two categories, each quite distinctive. One can have a model morphological model, as in the quotation from Coleridge above, where individual words are likened to the flowers and leaves of the plant as living and organically out-folding entities—a metaphor much favoured by the romantics. Alternately, one can see the various types of linguistic or literary activities as species of taxonomy or nomenclature, with sets of similar objects grouped together in such a way that classificatory or historical contiguities are preserved. This type of taxonomic organicist model has obviously been enormously strengthened by the success of Darwinian ideas in the 19th century. Aristotle himself, in his *Poetics* for instance, had a strong taxonomic bent to his organicism, and it is to him that we still owe the basic demarcations of the genres of literature, such a tragedy, comedy, and the like. This model is very much alive in our time, as can be seen from Northrop Frye's strongly generic critical system, or in the critical practice of the Chicago Neo-Aristotelians.

3

It may be true, as Donald Davie maintains, that Ezra Pound did not play a very important role in the formation of imagism and that, conversely, its theoretical importance for his own development has been exaggerated. Nevertheless, Pound's imagism is still a very convenient point of departure for the discussion of the place of language in modernism.

In 'A Few Don'ts' Pound offers us the classical definition of an image: 'An image is that which presents an intellectual and emotional complex in an instant of time.' (95) The definition seems cautious to the extent of limited usefulness. In the book on Gaudier-Brzeska, he gives a different definition: 'the image is the word beyond formulated language.' (88) This is more in keeping with the tradition of nominalist mysticism from the Middle Ages, which often seems to have played a decisive role in T.E. Hulme's formulations of his imagistic theory.

Pound's insistence on the distinction between image and idea may contain the first hints in the direction of what Eliot later termed the dissociation of sensibility with its background in Rémy de Gourmont and French materialism. But even more important for understanding the problem are Pound's remarks in 'How to Read' about the *function* of the critic and poet, in society and in his relation to language: 'the individual cannot think and communicate his thought, the governor and legislator cannot act effectively or frame his laws, without words, and the solidity and validity of these words is in the care of the damned and despised *literati.*' (21)

The image or vortex is important here, as it serves to restore the relations of language to reality. I would like to emphasise the role of medieval literature here, which Pound returned to in 'How to Read':

> It is not only a question of rhetoric, of loose expression, but also of the loose use of individual words. What the Renaissance gained in direct examination of natural phenomena, it in part lost in losing the feel and desire for exact descriptive terms. I mean that the medieval mind had little but words to deal with, as it was more careful in its definitions and verbiage. (2)

Here Ezra Pound links his version of the dissociation of sensibility with the advances of the natural sciences in the Renaissance, perhaps somewhat surprisingly in light of the scientism he displays in other contexts.

To return to the definition of the image: when we read 'an image is an intellectual and emotional complex in an instant of time' what is noticeable is the addendum 'an instant of time.' Donald Davie has made, in his first book on Pound, *Ezra Pound: Poet as Sculptor*, an interesting string of suggestions about the relation between sequentiality and permanence in *The Cantos* and, using a distinction derived from the contemporary theories of Adrian Stokes about sculpture, made another distinction between the activities of the carving of stone and the moulding of plaster:

> But the carving of stone and moulding of plaster (or of clay, so as later to make a bronze casting) are very different operations, and profoundly different because the artist's way with his material represents in miniature his way of dealing with the whole material world. (154)

It is true that Pound's imagism is of a different character from the Bergsonian intuitionism of, for instance, T.E. Hulme. Following the sculptural metaphor through the later *Cantos*, Davie manages to make more sense of Pound's aesthetic principles than any earlier critic; in seeing the poet's quest as a quest to unravel the *forma* underneath the phenomenal or historical world, Davie reveals Pound as an extreme idealist (albeit of a rather special immanentist kind) rather than as an academician from Lagado, carrying round all his words and definitions in the form of substantial images that have to be multiplied *ad infinitum*. The understanding of Pound as a Lagadan poet had provoked an objection from Yvor Winters in *The Function of Criticism*:

> Pound, early in his career, adopted the inversion derived from Locke by the associationists: since all ideas arise from sensory impressions, all ideas can be expressed in terms of sensory impressions. But of course they cannot be: when we attempt this method, what we get is sensory impressions alone, and we have no way of knowing whether we have had any ideas or not. (47)

Whereas Locke's question, as echoed by Swift, was whether it was possible to abstract from the world of sense-impressions at all, the question of the imagist poet is, in fact, the opposite: whether one can, at least in poetry, as putatively in primordial language, recreate sense experience in words.

Davie goes on to say in his effective rebuttal of Winters: 'for this state, of not knowing whether we have had ideas or not, may be precisely the state of mind that Pound aimed to produce—and for good reasons.' (218) As I see it, this is an argument from indeterminacy that has been very influential in apologies for modernism. As long as the images are there, creating epiphanies for the readers, we are not served by questions whether they convey ideas or not; the *ruling* idea can be calmly deduced: the intention to create a state of indecision in the reader's mind as to whether ideas are being conveyed or not. This view has been constitutive for much postmodernist theory.

There is not much need to pursue the background linguistic theory of what is loosely termed imagism any further: the special problems have been very adequately dealt with by Donald Davie in an earlier book, *Articulate Energy*, which contains a profound and sympathetic refutation of Ernest Fenollosa; and by Hugh Kenner, who gives the authoritative account of the historical idea context in a few chapters of *The Pound Era*. Instead, I want to pursue two issues connected with imagism: first, the sequential nature of poetry and second, the question of sculpture as the master metaphor.

As Borges realised so clearly, the consequences of a boundless idealism would be a literature of infinite variety and nuance. As he said, 'there are famous poems made up of one enormous word. This word forms a *poetic object* created by the author.' (9) As we can see, this is a description of the poem of imagism, unlimited by reality. But also in no need of sequentiality or time. It is simultaneous, plastic, and freed from logic and syntax. The poem becomes one enormous unique word, as Mallarmé might have wished. But this word-poem is, in its idealist framework, removed from its space-time and, in its totality only interpretable in terms of the poet's complete experience. This experience also includes the making of the poem, which is clearly an event in space and time. As its elements are ordered only by accidents of simultaneity and contiguity, it has no beginning and no end and should ideally be circular in shape, like *Finnegans Wake.*

Sculpture—rather than painting, which can easily be made sequential and serial, since it is two-dimensional—seems to offer a natural analogue to poems like these. But the question is, *what* kind of sculptural activity? In the idealist framework, it must be moulding rather than carving, since carving presupposes an empirical availability of the underlying material. Carving claims an immanentist version of idealism, *in rebus* rather than *ante res*.

Such an extrapolation from Borges's fiction may seem a futile exercise. It would no doubt be counter-intuitive for most people to try to maintain that any poem that is a poem of our world and not a Tlön-poem could be interpreted in such terms. Nonetheless, there are very considerable traces of such views in the doctrines of imagism and, perhaps, even more so in its postmodern successors like projectivism.

4

We are now in a better position to understand some of the problems we have encountered before. When John Crowe Ransom, in 'Poetry as Primitive Language,' referred to the metaphorical properties of language (which he called imaginal or substantival) in such a way as to make it clear that his view of the materiality of language was of a separate and concomitant phenomenon:

> Does your metaphorical word refer to the single property which makes it logically fit for the argument, or does it also evoke an image and refer to the independent substance? Homer was fond of the 'wine-dark' sea, and used the locution again and again; ostensibly he meant a shade of color, but incidentally his readers and singers were sure to receive a fleeting image of the substantial and very good thing named wine. (75)

It is not to be denied that visual imagery of great vividness may accompany novel words or word collocations (which of course the floating formulae of Homeric poetry were *not*), or that in the Homeric example a thirsty *rhapsodos* might have used an *epitheton ornans* of this kind to refer to the substance itself as a fitting reward for his efforts—but surely in that case he would use some gesture or sign language to indicate his plea. As a theory of the metaphoric and figurative properties of language it is, to say the least, crude. Aristotle had a much more advanced idea of metaphor, when he said in the *Poetics* that it was the foremost of the tropes, as it indicates a true sense of similarity.

A theory of mental images as a concomitant to figurative expressions obviously cannot explain the appropriateness of figurative expressions as a function of language: it cannot but emphasize the anomalous and perhaps extraneous nature of figurative language. As a literary theory it has been critically dealt with by Donald Davie in *Articulate Energy* and by Rosamond Tuve; its antecedents have been traced in short books by Frank Kermode and Nick Furbank. We can recognize it as a variant of the Academy of Lagado theory of language, where all sorts of objects are, if not carried around for conversation, at least conjured up, as so many jacks-in boxes, when ever the word appears. However, in spite of its crudeness and obvious explanatory weaknesses—or perhaps because of these drawbacks—it has been a very popular and pervasive theory.

In his important concluding essay from *The New Criticism*, Ransom has given a much more worked-out version of his views, taking its starting point in Charles Morris' recently published monograph on semiotics, from the *Encyclopaedia of Unified Science*. He calls it 'Wanted: An Ontological Critic.'

The ontological commitment of criticism is, according to Ransom (and it is a slightly odd use of the term) a commitment to finding out what is essential or constitutive for poetry, its poeticity, one might say. Ransom links it with two tendencies in language, one towards determinate meaning and one towards indeterminate meaning. They correspond roughly to his two categories of logical and primitive language, but here he is more eager to consider rhythmical or metrical constraints on discourse as the main reason for the poetical disfiguration (or figuration) of language. When semantic/logical and metric/phonetic constraints are perfectly matched or balanced, the result is great poetry. The idea is that these constraints force language into certain patterns recognizable as poetic patterns, but very little reasoning is offered to show exactly how this is done.

It is understandable that the theories of language available to Ransom fell short of his ambitions. He was eager to resist the positivist social semiotics of Charles Morris and equally eager to dissociate himself from the psychologism of the early I.A. Richards. But even so, one is sometimes surprised at the quaintness of his arguments. He seems to believe that the reason one does not find mathematical formulae in poetic discourse is because the *metric* constraints somehow take liberties with logical values. It is, of course, perfectly possible to say: 'two plus two equal four' in both verse and prose, and Tom Lehrer has written a song called 'New Maths,' which may not be great poetry but certainly is verse and still contains quite complicated mathematical computations without invalidating their correctness. The reason why so few mathematical textbooks are written in verse is quite simply that the form is not needed for their purpose.

There is a problem with the theory of language underlying New Criticism—and I would limit the term to the inner cenacle of Ransom, Tate, Penn Warren, Winters and Brooks, perhaps Wimsatt, but not Burke and Blackmur, and I would also exclude the transatlantic pedagogues Richards and Empson, whose ideas are of a completely different origin. The problem is not so much that the theory is inadequate to deal with poetry (no other theory seems to have been able to do much better) but that it is inadequate in dealing with its 'counter spirit,' ordinary language. In assimilating willy-nilly the standpoints of their adversaries, like Charles Morris or early Richards, the New Critics came up with a very confused view of ordinary discourse, which was seen by necessity to be both logical and referential. Murray Krieger was perhaps the first to point out this discrepancy in a very astute chapter of his book, where he makes the justified observation that there is no more than a contingent relationship between these two properties. A statement can be referential and still not be logical: as in 'snow is white, because grass is green,' and it can be logical without being referential: as in 'all men are mortal, the present king of France is a man, the present king of France is mortal.' As Krieger ingeniously remarks:

> ...if the logical problem is properly seen as separate from the semantic problem, then indeed the foundations of the prose-poetry distinction based on referentiality, upon which modern criticism is built, are seriously shaken. For then the term of prose discourse are seen also deriving their meanings from a controlling context, in this case a logical context. They are no longer free to point uninhibitedly any more than are the terms of poetic discourse which are contained by a unique, formal context. (147)

This mistakenly exclusive view of contextualism, which is in fact the opposite of the imagist view of language as a repository of discreet units of experience, created problems with critical terminology that are still with us. But there are—and it may be easier to see this now than when Krieger wrote his book — further and wider implications of the New Critical ideology to be considered. The New Critics were apologists for poetry, no doubt, and they had to fight their battles on several fronts at once, against the historicism of the established scholars of literary studies, and against the scientism of their contemporaries in American social sciences, anthropology and linguistics. In this respect they were staunch anti-reductionists, eager to establish an independent domain for the study of poetry literature. I think this is the ambition that makes Ransom raise his rather peculiar claims for the ontology of the work of art. As several of them were practising poets, they had a strong and wholly beneficent interest in integrating the study of, and writing of, poetry in the academic curricula, which has had, after all, an unsuspected degree of success in American educational life.

René Wellek has, in his essay 'Poet, Critic, Poet-Critic,' levelled serious charges against both Ransom and Tate for their anti-intellectualist positions regarding criticism, which are no doubt well deserved, but seem to stem from a curiously aggressive stance on Wellek's part as regarding poets in relation to their *métier*. The eclectic and confused nature of Ransom's theoretical position is pointed out and summarized with Wellek's customary superb skill, and Tate's occasional priestly posturing receives some well-earned censure. But the main charge is that the poet-critic, having a vested interest in the poetry business, tends to be unfair to his colleagues. This presupposes that the scholar-critic is not equally likely to be influenced in his judgements by extraneous or ideological concerns, which seems optimistic, if not naive.

In spite of their partisan and sometimes passionate nature, the ideas of the New Critics were in the long run successful, but mostly only insofar as they were taken up and institutionalized by a second generation of scholars/critics/philosophers. Central concepts would be defended by Susanne Langer, by Austin Warren, or by René Wellek. But this process certainly changed some of the fundamental ideas that had been the cornerstone of the original New Critical outlook. In exchange for the rather unintended Hegelianism of Ransom or the scholastic *bricolage* of Tate, you get an austere Kantian idealism with some roots in Cassirer and Croce.

There is yet another aspect of the original New Critics which has been, by and large, misunderstood. It is their commitment to conservative ideologies. In the case of Tate, Ransom, and Penn Warren, a commitment to Southern Agrarianism. This is clearly an unremittingly and most unashamedly primitivist ideology. But in the dualist conception of the world of discourse they were paying tribute to, it pertained only to their realm of poetry, not to their criticism. Their theory of language was an organicist one, modelling itself (mainly in morphological analogues, not in generic ones as in the case of the Neo-Aristotelians or Northrop Frye) on the growth of the individual organism. Ransom, in his essay 'The Concrete Universal: Observations on the Understanding of Poetry' is also here most open and articulate:

> Suppose we say that the poem is an organism. Then it has a physiology. We will figure its organs, and to me it seems satisfactory if we say they are three: the head, the heart, the feet. In this organism the organs work all at the same time, but the peculiarity of the joint production is that it still consists of the several products of the organs working individually. (560)

This is a very uncomfortable model for primitivist modes of thought and was no doubt the reason for some of the wilder flights of fancy and changes of direction in Ransom's critical thinking. His ideal for a critical language was not a poetic language, the language of texture or of the mixed world, where images vie with ideas—but what he called logic, a reasoned discourse which takes its model not as we might expect from the abstract languages of logic and mathematics, but from the pragmatic and mundane discourse of technical science, business, law and advertising:

> An advanced language is one in which the standard discourse is perfect or nearly perfect conceptually, and the imaginal or substantival range of meaning has all but disappeared. At this stage language conquers its involuntary ambiguity. It becomes fit for big business, technical science and all other forms of thinking. ('Poetry as Primitive Language' 76)

In spite of his early agrarian opposition to big business, it is noticeable how much Ransom's critical language is derived from the world of business and advertising. Suffice it here to cite a couple of stray titles of essays: 'Criticism Inc.,' and 'Wanted: An Ontological Critic.' I consider 'Criticism as Pure Speculation 'an equivocal case. This brisk matter-of-fact tone, which to some lesser extent influenced also the other New Critics such as Winters and Blackmur—and which perhaps had something to do with Eliot's fastidiousness and offhand neatness of distinction in his criticism—is very typical of its period. It is in any case altogether different from Pound's belligerent but also pedagogically benevolent colloquialism.

The rhetoric of critical language is in itself a critical area worth studying, but few people, with the honourable exception of Kenneth Burke, have taken the trouble. The New Criticism became, and on the whole quite quickly and efficiently, a part of the scholarly establishment it had started out opposing, and some of the strategies used for this purpose were at variance with basic tenets of its philosophy. When it had spent its energy as an active force and was ready to depart from the scene of the American critical debate, it was no longer the jargon of the boardroom or the advertising agency that offered itself for emulation, but the language of the computer and the electronic engineering sciences. The dreams of the Material Word were put paid to in the Electronic Village. There are cases when the Marxian doctrine—that an era's ruling classes produce its ruling ideas—takes on a special significance.

5

The principles of intertextualism were very clearly formed by Eliot in the first section of his essay from 1919, 'Tradition and the Individual Talent,' and very little has been added to these principles in subsequent discussion. Indeed, the principles have gained the acceptance that they deserve (that is: they are almost universally recognized). It is very difficult to argue against the view that all texts, when interpreted by a community of readers and scholars interact and establish relations, in particular as one is employed in a *métier* (as Eliot terms it) which has its main objective in comparing texts—it is little like arguing against the multiplication tables or Newton's law of gravity. The question of language enters into the argument on this level only as a presupposition, and a necessary one, in that it is the public nature of language that makes intertextualism an inescapable condition. Had all poems in some Tlön-like world been written in private and unique languages, one might have been able to find arguments for a wholly individual interpretation of artistic texts.

There are of course always questions of demarcation and evaluation that, in this case, characteristically involve the business of canon-formation. Fortunately, neither this thorny problem, nor the problem of the attitude of the individual author is part of our present topic. Whether you approach the question of intertextualism from the point of view of an idealist or a materialist conception of language is inessential, as long as you remember the fundamentally contextual nature of language. Structurally, if not substantially, intertextualism—even in its infancy—is dependent on a theory of language that is relational in a wide sense, that is, that allows for a wider net of relations outside the grammatical and syntactical categories.

It is doubtful that either Eliot or Ransom, had read Marx and Engels' momentous remarks on language in *The German Ideology*, which had not been printed when Eliot's essay appeared, and which hardly would have figured on Ransom's reading list in German philosophy. Still, the general drift of the Marxian arguments would have been quite familiar to both Eliot and Ransom.

We have so far been using the term 'materialism' in a general way without taking into consideration the very specialized sense that the term has acquired in a context representing a very important body of thought in this world. I am thinking of the conjunctions 'historical materialism' and 'dialectical materialism' as used in Marxian literature for almost a century and a half. Even in its earliest form, the language theory of historical materialism, as expressed in *The German Ideology*, is strongly relational, and neatly avoids the old dichotomy of material or ideal language by identifying language with consciousness, with a practical intercourse of men reaching back to their tribal existence. The similarity to the all-embracing claims of intertextualism is striking and more than accidental: if there is a true begetter of these, it is to found in the claims for a world literature without limits, dreamed of by Marx and Engels in their early years.

Let me end, as in my first lecture, with two quotations about language, one from the beginning and the other one from near the end of that voluminous, loose, and baggy monster of a book, *The German Ideology*. The first:

> Language is as old as consciousness, language *is* practical consciousness that exist also for other men, and for that reason alone it really exists for me personally as well; language, like consciousness, only rises from the need, the necessity, of intercourse with other men. (51)

And the second, striking a more critical note in its attack on the philosophers' abstractions of language from our normal language:

> The philosophers would only have to dissolve their language into the ordinary language, from which it is abstracted, to recognize it as the distorted language of the actual world, and to realize that neither thoughts nor language in themselves form a realm of their own, that they are only *manifestations* of actual life. (118)

My next essay will concern itself with the question of how these abstractions function in models of actual languages, in poems and poetics, in prose and thesciences, and also with how these models re-enact the 'intercourse with other men' in the real world.

Works Cited

Borges, Jorge Luis. 'Tlön, Uqbar, Orbis Tertius.' *Labyrinths: Selected Stories and Other Writings*. New York: New Directions, 2007: 3–18.

Bruns, Gerald. *Modern Poetry and the Idea of Language*. New Haven: Yale University Press, 1974.

Coleridge, Samuel Taylor. *Unpublished Letters of Samuel Taylor Coleridge*. Vol. 1. Ed. by Earl Leslie Griggs. London: Constable, 1932.

Davie, Donald. *Ezra Pound: The Poet as Sculptor*. London: Routledge and Kegan Paul, 1965.

Krieger, Murray. *The New Apologists for Poetry*. Minneapolis: University of Minnesota Press, 1956.

Marx, Karl, and Friedrich Engels. *The German Ideology: Part One with Selections from Parts Two and Three*. New York: International Publishers, 1970.

Pound, Ezra. 'A Few Don'ts by an *Imagiste*.' *Modernism: An Anthology*. Ed. by Lawrence S. Rainey. Oxford: Wiley-Blackwell, 2005: 95.

—. *Gaudier-Brzeska: A Memoir*. New York: New Directions, 1970.

—. 'How to Read.' *The Literary Essays of Ezra Pound*. New York: New Directions, 1968: 15–40.

Ransom, John Crowe. 'The Concrete Universal: Observations on the Understanding of Poetry.' *The Kenyon Review*. Vol. 16 (1954): 554–64.

—. 'Poetry as Primitive Language.' *Speaking of Writing: Selected Hopgood Lectures*. Ed. Nicholas Delbanco. Ann Arbor: University of Michigan Press, 1990.

Swift, Jonathan. *Gulliver's Travels and Other Writings*. New York: Bantam, 1984.

Winters, Yvor. *The Function of Criticism*. Denver: Swallow, 1957.

Part Four: The Polity of Metaphor and the Purity of Diction

1

This being the last essay in this series on the 'Words of the Tribe,' I feel obliged to bring as many threads of argument as possible, if not to an end, at least to some kind of tangled visibility. Before I start to summarize, however, I would like to pursue further a question I touched on earlier. This is the question of the single-word reduction of a poem, or of the poetic line, as we have encountered it in Mallarmé, in Winters, in Borges and in Riffaterre. It seems to be a central if somewhat submerged tenet of modernism, and has not elicited as much commentary as could have been expected. The possible consequences of such an idea have very wide ramifications. One can isolate two possible permutations of such a view.

Firstly, one can see this word formation in a non-reductionist way, as cancellation of normal word boundary-markers under restriction of supra-segmental constraints on rhythm and prosody. Whether or not this occurs in poetry is to some extent an empirical question and can be elucidated by investigations of, say, readings of poems, especially readings by the poets themselves. More important, though, are the resulting theoretical implications as to the communicative aspects of poetry. If the line, or the whole poem, is to be regarded as one word, it is not a word that can be understood in the normal way, as a function of some semantic relationship or as an entry in a dictionary or lexicon. It must rather be treated as a very indeterminate entity, comprising all of its separate sub-words. As such it does not mean anything but itself (which makes it a name: hence the insistence of the romantics and their modern followers, like de Man and Octavio Paz, on naming in poetry).

It may have been ideas of this kind that inspired the mysterious hints from Coleridge and Poe about how a poem would be better if only generally, and not completely, understood. These hints, of course, immediately beg the question of what it means to say that a poem is understood. If it only means that the reader infers that it has been the poet's intention to create a poem that is not intelligible, then we have a situation that involves a kind of understanding, but of a meagre and unrewarding kind. If it means a fuller and more integrated mode of grasping its content, then a one-word-theory of poetry clearly needs to presuppose the existence of some extra-linguistic faculty of intuition or the like. Many such theories have been available ever since Kant made his influential distinction between *vernunft* and *verstand*, between theoretical and practical reason. Bergsonian intuitionism is only one of many formulations of this dualism. In any case, adherents of the non-reducible one-word-doctrine for the poem are sure to find antecedents for their dualist interpretations in romantic and modernist theories. Mallarmé, whose copious pronouncements on these matters are significant but also very difficult to understand—and thus preferably to be avoided—did, no doubt, consider poetry as part of a wider non-semantic context, with music and ballet as its nearest relatives. The question that remains is, as with all dualism, a question of ontology.

A second possibility is to regard the poem not as one word in itself, but as reducible to one word, or a phrase stating its message or prose meaning. If, ontologically, the first permutation gravitated towards Cartesian or Kantian dualism, this second permutation has a strange historical pedigree in the powerful conventional, and at one time uncontroversial, views that poetic discourse can be generated from plain discourse through a number of rhetorical devices, devices at least vaguely enumerable in an informal way. Favoured for centuries by the rhetorical manuals—which one should remember, as is not often the case, were written as much for the benefit of forensic and public oratory as for poetics—this view has had a long period of decline, but seems, as in the quoted case of Riffaterre, to have been recently reclaimed as a sophisticated theory. It is an emphatically rationalist and reductionist conception which allows full reflexivity and transitivity in its operations. In the versions we have encountered in Winters and in Riffaterre, it promises both reducibility to a logical statement, and reversibility—so that, starting from these, you may generate, through the rules of *amplificatio*, the poem from its nucleus, guided by the restrictions imposed by genre expectations. The problematical character of this activity becomes obvious when we are confronted with historical development or genre shifts: arguments have to be found to make the genre restrictions universal and eternal. As with the first permutation of the idea of the word-poem, one has to find a faculty of the human mind tuned to such restrictions, but otherwise unknowable.

2

It seems that we have come to a dead end, or at least to some instruction reading: 'go back to square one!' But I would like to point out that these somewhat claustrophobic constructions are not unlike the larger models of human knowledge that have dominated the last three centuries of Western philosophy. Even empirical and scientific knowledge has had to rely on explanations in terms of correspondence criteria (as related to things), or in terms of coherence criteria (relating to internal consistency).

In a more limited and perhaps more fruitful sense, one can see these constructions as parallel to more recent schools of thought, like structuralism, or transformational generative grammar in linguistics. The problematic place of difference and identity in the first permutation of the word-poem theory, having to work on a genetically determined identical text on two separate levels, but relinquishing the problem of identity to a larger categorical framework, reinforces the hermeneutic circle of understanding. In the second permutation, formalized operations of substitution or equivalence within the text seem to preclude any rapprochement to mimetic structure. The *amplificatio* technique only allows for more and more exhibits to be displayed but, if we are allowed to develop the forensic parallel, no court-room confessions, no culprit suddenly bursting into court, shouting: 'I did it! I did it!' It is to be noticed that it is the rationalist version of the theory that supplies the strongest prohibitions on direct imports from empirical reality.

3

We would perhaps be well advised to transfer attention from the most hypothetical case of the one-word poem to one of the features which would figure as exhibit A in most of the trials of poetic language we could envisage. This is a *metaphor* in its more extended sense of the essential and formative element in figurative language.

Recent years have seen a great swelling of the literature on metaphor, but not all of these studies add much to the clarification or re-interpretation of the actual mechanisms at work. The expectations of demarcation and elucidation of metaphor within the framework of linguistic syntactical analysis, which were strong in the early history of transformational generative grammar, have remained unfulfilled. This has to do with the attempts to create a hierarchy for different levels of grammaticalness, attempts that had to be abandoned at a fairly early stage, together with analytic criteria and classification of natural specifics in the lexicon. Noam Chomsky himself always showed a healthy scepticism towards these developments: he remarked as early as *Aspects of the Theory of Syntax* that he thought that linguistic theory was unlikely to be able to handle metaphoric extensions, or stylistic variations, as long as reliable criteria for paraphrase are not forthcoming. In more recent years, literary theorists and philosophers of all camps have taken over the struggle to bring the concept of metaphor into some intellectual respectability.

It is easy to see that metaphor falls as easily as the one-word poem theory into one of the two grooves we noticed at the beginning of this lecture; it can either be regarded as an ornamental amplification of the argument of the text, or as an organic excrescence on the linguistic utterance, providing a bridge to a perhaps unknowable reality. The two main theories of metaphor that have been most popular in recent years, the comparison theory and the interaction theory, fall neatly, although perhaps not snugly, into these two grooves.

The main problem with metaphor as a functional element of language is its submerged character. It has been a commonplace at least since German romanticism to insist on the ability of language to absorb metaphors in its active structure. It does not feel right to regard such sunken or petrified metaphors as irrevocably dead: as long as metaphor is a living, functional force in language, as long as it is generative, a dead metaphor can always be re-activated. It is reactivated, though, at perhaps too great a cost: remember the Victorian habit of putting skirt on chair-legs in the name of modesty.

It is surely time to apply some *amplificatio* technique to this rather arid reasoning. But let me first refresh our memory about *mimesis*, which stands in a hidden but important relation to metaphor: I'll recap the most elementary argument from book ten of Plato's *Republic*: If an artisan makes a bed, he fashions it after some model, or idea, or form: it is an imitation of this form. If a painter paints a picture of the bed, it is thus an imitation of an imitation, an imitation to the second degree. This was one of Plato's many arguments against mimetic art. A comparison-based idea of metaphor can be seen as a mimesis argument. When the artisan has constructed the bed, he wants a name for the four supports underneath it and looks out the window and sees a ram grazing in his field. 'Eureka,' he says, 'just like my bed, four supports, one in each corner: I'll call them *legs*.' 'How clever you are,' says his wife, 'what a brilliant metaphor: just think of applying a word like "leg" which refers flesh-and-blood to a wooden thing like a support under a bed.' But perhaps not—perhaps our artisan and inventor of metaphors has not invented a subcategory of 'legs made of wood instead of flesh-and-blood' but just extended the category of legs to include both wooden and flesh-and-blood objects. 'Listen,' he says to his wife, 'I was even cleverer than you thought: through an act of abstraction, I extended the category of legs to include both wooden and flesh-and-blood objects.' 'Didn't I say you were clever,' she says. 'What do you want for dinner?' 'I wouldn't mind having a leg of mutton,' he says, eying the ram outside. When they sit down at the table, he says 'And *what* is this?' And she says, 'Just a leg of the old settee we threw out last spring cleaning. If you are so clever with your abstractions you can always categorize it again.'

A leg of mutton is no philosophical argument, as little as the stone Dr Johnson kicked, in order to refute Bishop Berkeley. What I mean is, metaphor is no category mistake, as has often been maintained by the comparison school of thought, nor can it be called a sort-crossing or a type-crossing. Metaphor cannot be handled with classificatory arguments; if I say: 'A whale is a fish,' the answer is not: 'What a brilliant metaphor!' but is instead: 'You are wrong, a whale is not a fish; it is a mammal.' And it does not help saying 'Of course I know a whale is a mammal, but I meant it as a metaphor: if you consider the *tertium comparationis*, all the ways a whale resembles a fish: it lives in water all its life; it has fin-like flukes; it cannot live for long on dry land: wouldn't you agree that I have created a marvellous metaphor according to Aristotle, managed to discern the similar in the dissimilar, and shown myself to be a superior mind?' The answer is still: 'The whale is not a fish.'

Why is this so? In one sense it is defendable to say that we do not know. In another sense we know very well. If we say: 'Man is a wolf' the answer is not 'No, man is not a wolf,' but: 'Oh, yes, *homo hominis lupus*, brilliant idea!' The problem is not that we don't know what metaphorical use of language is, we know that fairly well; the problem is that we don't know what *literal* language is like. If we say that a painting is blue, that is a literal statement. It we say that it is sad, that is not normally a metaphorical statement but just means that it expresses sadness; if we say that a man is feeling sad (although we might find it difficult to prove it) it just means literally that; if we say a man is feeling blue, it means the same thing, but metaphorically. Or consider another example. When we go to a bar in the United States and ask for a cocktail—a Martini, say—we invariably encounter the question: 'And how do you like it? Straight up or on the rocks?' If we take this as referring to our own position when imbibing our drink: whether we want to stand up straight or go outside to sit on some heap of stones, we are just mistaken, and not about the metaphorical meanings but about the *literal* meanings of words. This goes to show that the meaning of words is rigorously restricted by the extraneous conditions, whether they are metaphorical or not, which should not come as a surprise. But that gives the interaction theory—treating the tension between tenor and vehicle, or focus and context, or focus and theme—as many difficulties to contend with as the comparison theory.

Metaphor in the sense we use the term in poetics, that is, informally, a novel and rapid interconnecting of different spheres of meaning, is probably a comparatively rare phenomenon in conversation and common speech, in contrast to *mentions* of metaphors or clichés of the type we have just exemplified.

A true metaphor in this sense has always to be announced in some way, to be foregrounded. But this is very rarely done in conversation where the received metaphors from a standard stock of phrases, often from domestic usage or from the animal kingdom, dominate: 'He is a pig!' 'She is a mouse!' 'What a mess!' Monroe C. Beardsley's connotative or intentional theory of metaphor is eminently applicable to these cases. But poetic metaphor is only ostensibly of this type. When Hamlet swears his companions to silence, he hears the ghost intone underground: '*Swear!*' he instantly replies: 'Well said, old mole! Cans't work i' the earth so fast?' (1199) This does not invoke any secondary connotations from the stock of standard views of moles, nor does he here compare his father's ghost to a little blind furry animal with shovel-like paws, nor, even less likely, does he replace him for ornamental purposes with such an animal, nor conjure up a mental image of one. He just refers to the habit of moles to travel underground, and in such a way that it will elicit a response in the expectations raised for the whole situation, for the action of the play and its main character.

Metaphor in this sense is always self-conscious in that it brings attention to itself with irony. It is the most self-conscious of the tropes. But the operation invoked is one of generalization from reality, or from fictional reality, not the presentation of reality. It is a kind of abstraction, like generalizations of national charter, such as: 'Scots are parsimonious' or, to stick closer to Hamlet: 'Danes are drunkards.' 'Mole' implies a statement: 'Corpses underground should be still and not travel around like moles.' It is not reducible to such a statement, though, nor could it be replaced with such a statement.

4

Substitution criteria are clearly helpless to establish demarcation lines between what is metaphorical and what is literal, and they also fail to generate metaphorical utterances from literal ones. One way out—and it has proved with time to be very popular—is to turn the whole question upside down and historicize it. Giambattista Vico tried this in his *Scienza nuova* (*The New Science*) of 1725, the first treatise to assert that figurative language preceded literal language in human history. He believed that in the historic time of the *gentes*, or tribes, language (in its pre-articulate state) could be derived from the poetic logic of the four master tropes: metaphor, metonymy, synecdoche and irony:

> The heroic language was a language of similes, images and comparisons, born of the lack of genera and species, which are necessary for the proper definition of things, and hence born of a necessity of nature common to entire peoples. (262)

Vico's influence has been deeply felt in Western thought on very different levels, but in contrast to many of his followers, he was no primitivist, not even in the cyclical sense implied in his philosophy of *ricorso*. He believed that mankind could benefit from progress, and that the powers of abstraction which he saw at work in articulate language were more beneficial than the forces of primitive language. Homer was both the recorder of dissolute mores of a heroic age, and a founder of the virtues of the Greek city-state, of its polity or civility, favourite expressions of approbation with him. It is from this I have derived one of the terms of my title 'Polity of Metaphor.' As a term, 'polity' is more pliable and accommodating than 'policy,' and it lacks the Machiavellian or cunning connotation of the latter.

Not that cunning is goes needed. Metaphor is activated only when it is made self-conscious or foregrounded. That also means that it has to be made conscious of its own history and its own conditions. Hamlet's mole metaphor belongs to the *sermo humilis*, not only because it stems from the everyday sphere of experience, but also because it belongs to *humus*, to the earth, just like corpses, and thus reinforces the hidden, illicit ways language has to travel. 'Cans't work i' the earth so fast?' is, among other things, an address to the facility with language Hamlet exhibits on many occasions.

Such a view of metaphor has had some difficulties in gaining ground: it was, I think, systematically used for the first time in a remarkable book by William Empson, *The Structure of Complex Words*, which has hardly been added to or surpassed in the years since its publication. The view is also quite close to the basic insights of a book by Paul Ricoeur, *The Rule of Metaphor* (where the original French title, *La métaphore vive* retains the organicist bias).

The Viconian concept of the *gentes* or tribes in their barbaric splendour has travelled a long way through the anthropologizing theories of the origins of civilization in the eighteenth and nineteenth centuries. It can be strongly felt in the Marxian view of language as an emanation of social consciousness. Moreover, it ended up on the tombstone of Edgar Allen Poe, in that line of Mallarmé: *'donner un sens plus pur aux mots de la tribu'* ['to give a purer sense to the words of the tribe']. (70) The line that offers a truly Viconian vision of the power of abstraction of the poetic imagination, a power that would lead Mallarmé to the ultimate abstraction in the shape of the white sheet of paper.

5

At this point it may be appropriate to recapitulate briefly the main themes and the main concerns of our investigation. My search has been for the road of transit—as Coleridge reminds us, this is the true meaning of *methodos* in Greek—between ideas in the maze of poetic theories. I found one such road of transit in primitivism of language, which threatens to overwhelm the clarity of statement in poetry with the richness of particulars of matter. I found another in reductionism that threatens to reduce the tangible to arid formulae. But these dangers are only there when the roads or methods are abused, as Ezra Pound remarked in a short early essay (being in a more serene and less excitable state than usual):

> A return to origins invigorates because it is a return to nature and reason. The man who returns to origins does so because he wishes to behave in the eternally sensible manner. (92)

The recourse the poet has to the world of abstract science is, as Wordsworth and Coleridge often testified, a real and not an imagined source of strength. I leave the assertion to Wordsworth in *The Prelude*, in his praise of geometry:

> Mighty is the charm
> Of those abstractions to a mind beset
> With images, and haunted by itself;
> And specially delightful unto me
> Was that clear Synthesis built up aloft
> So gracefully, even then when it appear'd
> No more than as a plaything, or a toy
> Embodied to the sense, not what it is
> In verity, an independent world
> Created out of pure Intelligence. (179)

Earlier in *The Prelude* Wordsworth had related a dream of a friend (presumably Coleridge) about an Arab of the Bedouin Tribes, encountered in the desert. With true dream-logic, the Arab is described as carrying two things, a stone and a shell, being at the same thing alternatively Euclid's *Elements* and a book of all poetry, an ode of human passions. The lodestone of pure intelligence and the haunting voice of mankind are the two guiding principles or *archai* in the poet's search. But the phantom is at the same time Don Quixote in search of the unattainable and irrevocable. At least part of him is. He is a semi-Quixote.

The search for abstraction in the messages of mankind gives a suitable ending to these essays, which have been looking for roads of transit between levels that may be incompatible. But before ending, let me add a couple of further examples or *paradeigma* (as Vico was quick to point out, in the Greco-Roman city-state polity, these meant 'punishments') drawn from contemporary or near-contemporary poetry's insights into the basic dialectics of abstractions.

The purification or *katharmos* needed for both poetic language and mathematical abstraction—and clearly they have been parallel *methodoi* for most of our history—is indicated from as far back as Quintilian, in the dialectics of abstract and concrete. Modernist poetics has made the transfer from abstract generalization to concrete detail the only privileged one. This is not the view of the poets, though, in particular not of Wallace Stevens, for whom abstraction was necessary part of the supreme fiction. Consider these lines from 'A Primitive like an Orb':

> Here, then, is an abstraction given head,
>
> A giant on the horizon, given arms,
>
> A massive body and long legs, stretched out,
>
> A definition with an illustration, not
>
> Too exactly labelled, a large among the smalls
>
> Of it, a close, parental magnitude,
>
> At the centre on the horizon, concentrum, grave
>
> And prodigious person, patron of origins. (443)

This giant, this 'definition with an illustration, not too exactly labelled' can be recognized in one of the stage-managed asides in John Ashbery's 'The Skaters,' where the poet comments on the progress and nature of his long poem:

> This, thus, is a portion of the subject of this poem
>
> Which is in the form of falling snow:
>
> That is, the individual flakes are not essential to the
>
> > importance of the whole's becoming so much of a truism
>
> That their importance is again called in question, to be
>
> > denied further out, and again and again like this.
>
> Hence, neither the importance of the individual flake,
>
> Nor the importance of the whole impression of the storm,
>
> > if it has any, is what it is,
>
> But the rhythm of the series of repeated jumps, from
>
> > abstract into positive and back to a slightly less
> >
> > diluted abstract. (152)

That the dialectical movement is more important than the individual elements or *stoicheiai*, seems a lesson straight out of Plato. But the movement does not end there: as if to answer Ashbery's somewhat coy caveats, Robert Hass replies in his prose poem 'The Beginning of September,' a work endangered by ferocious sensual and appetitive implosion:

> Words
>
> are abstract, but *words are abstract*
>
> is a dance, car crash, heart's delight.
>
> It's the design dumb hunger
>
> has upon the world.' (38)

For me there remains only to quote the first three lines of the last stanza of the Stevens poem:

> That's it. The lover writes, the believer hears,
>
> The poet mumbles and the painter sees,
>
> Each one, his fated eccentricity. (443)

If some hearers are now believers, at least in the possibility of poetry and poetics, this Semi-Quixote is satisfied. Satisfied to have mumbled, to the end, his fated eccentricities.

Works Cited

Ashbery, John. *Collected Poems 1956–1987*. Ed. Mark Ford. New York: Library of America, 2008.

Hass, Robert. *Praise*. New York: Ecco, 1979.

Mallarmé, Stéphane. *Collected Poems and Other Verse*. Ed. and trans. by E.H. Blackmore and A.M. Blackmore. Oxford: Oxford University Press, 2006.

Pound, Ezra. 'The Tradition.' *Literary Essays of Ezra Pound*. New York: New Directions, 1968: 91–93.

Shakespeare, William. *The Riverside Shakespeare*. Vol. 2. Ed. G. Blakemore Evans. Boston: Houghton Mifflin, 1997.

Stevens, Wallace. *The Collected Poems of Wallace Stevens*. New York: Vintage, 1990.

Vico, Giambattista. *The New Science of Giambattista Vico*. Trans. by Thomas Goddard Bergin and Max Harold Fisch. New York: Anchor, 1961.

Wordsworth, William. *The Prelude, or, the Growth of the Poet's Mind*. Ed. Ernest de Sélincourt. Oxford: Oxford University Press, 1953.

Other Prose

Part Five: Style, Irony, Metaphor, and Meaning

'Style' is very much a nineteenth century term, not that it can be deemed to have been unknown before or after that momentous period, but rather that it seems, at that particular time, to usurp the areas of other, presumably more technical terms as the century moves along. In the second half of the century it becomes a cover-term, not only for the technicalities of the arts and literature, but also for the many skills required for the mastery of those technicalities, and even the *verve*, the *panache* that goes into that mastery and eventually colours the life-style and character of the artists themselves. This is in accord with the origin of the word, as the name of an implement in the art of writing and calligraphy, and describes very accurately its connections with the characteristic mixture of the crudely scientific and the elegantly decadent that seems to set its stamp on the period. When the *stylus*, like pen or pencil, is finally abandoned by the litterateurs of the following century for the typewriter and the word processor, there is suddenly much less cause for worrying about style in the sense of the individuation of language (or of brush-strokes) How the automation of various skills of composition and spelling, with the help of mechanical spell-checks and thesauri, will eventually affect the skills of writing in our time, is far from clear, but without any doubt it will be of paramount importance for any predictions of cultural development.

1

The terms that were the predecessors of 'style,' or at least its rivals, terms like 'diction' and 'taste,' had a much more rigorously definable range of meaning, which made them quite unpopular with the romantics. One is reminded of

Wordsworth and Coleridge's concerted attacks on these eighteenth century concepts.

'Diction' very forcibly retains the classical demarcations between different styles appropriate to different genres and even different areas of subject matter or social occupations. As there were, in traditional Aristotelian aesthetics, three major genres, the epic, the dramatic and the lyric, there had to be likewise three major dictions or styles: the elevated, the plain and the medial (terms and definitions could, of course, vary a great deal).

The distinctions could also be illustrated in various ways. A very popular scheme from the Middle Ages was the *Rota Virgiliana*—the Wheel of Virgil—in which the three major genres of Virgil's literary production were highlighted as models for the three levels of diction. The language of the medial diction is the sweet bucolic language of his *Eclogues*. The diction of the *arator* or ploughman is the one found in his *Georgics*, and the elevated or sublime diction of the soldier or lord is the one to be found in the Roman national epic, the *Aeneid*. As far back as classical antiquity, however, there had been attempts to add to this too meagre scheme of things: in Demetrius Phalereus' treatise *On Style* (*De elocutione*), for example, the most widespread handbook of style known from late classical times, there are *four* levels of diction: the medial being split in two: the elegant (*glaphyrós*) and the forcible or terrifying (*deinós*).

Whatever the divisions, this taxonomy of diction eventually came to seem inadequate as a measure of style: even before Buffon minted the phrase that the '*style est l'homme même*,' (11) we may find examples of the use of 'style'—Demetrius had used the term 'character' in order to denote his four categories of diction—which point in the direction of individuation for marking individual idiosyncrasies of language (or art). 'Character' is, in etymology and use, closely akin to 'style,' as its primary meaning is a sharp stylus and the incised mark it makes (*charactêros*). The Aristotelian term *êthos*, which is normally translated 'character as habitual manner or disposition,' has a very different use and provenance.

Demetrius's recommendations of the use of 'forcible' style (with Demosthenes as a prime example) is certainly to be descried in one of the most influential investigations of style from the mid-nineteenth century: Herbert Spencer's long essay of 1852, 'The Philosophy of Style,' which is now largely forgotten but was read and quoted far into this century by, for instance, the Swedish modernist Pär Lagerkvist, who refers to it constantly and admiringly in his early manifesto of 1913, *Ordkonst och bildkonst* (*Verbal Art and Visual Art*).

The dynamic/mechanical conception of language Spencer adheres to, and his uniform argument from a general concept of progress, now seem wide off the mark. How can we find rational arguments for his view that Saxon words are more primitive and forceful than Latin ones, or that the word order of English (with the adjective preceding the noun) is more natural than, say, the word order of French? This relegates the entire essay to that context of evolutionary thought that we somewhat inaccurately refer to as Darwinist, the same context to which we must relegate the curious defence of the linguistic and symbolic abilities of brute animals and mute infants in Samuel Butler's lecture from 1890, 'Thought and Language.' Still, Spencer's version of language is very persistent as his model of style is resolutely anti-taxonomic and in favour of individual and intuitionist criteria of values. Curiously, he seems in the end to fear the too forceful individuation of language and appears to want to end with the ideal of a style adaptable to any mode and character of expression.

Spencer's prescriptions, and to some extent also his prejudices, are followed in their anti-taxonomic bias by most subsequent writers on style (with some notable exceptions, such as Gerard Manley Hopkins). Spencer echoes through Remy de Gourmont and John Middleton Murray (especially in his lectures at Brasenose 1921, which resemble almost embarrassingly resemble Spencer even in their title), and continue to echo through Leo Spitzer, Barthes, and Riffaterre's earlier pronouncements. These views are admirably contrasted, sometimes to mutual detriment, in Gérard Genette's essay '*Style et signification*' ('Style and Meaning'), no doubt one of the most significant contributions to the study of style for some years.

Remy de Gourmont's series of articles '*Les funérailles du style,*' ('The Funerals of Style'), later the book *Le problème du style* (*The Problem of Style*), were occasional works, as he himself points out, in refutation of a quite conventional and soon forgotten book by Albalat. It served to codify, however, the opposition of the conventionalities of nineteenth century style in identifying the ornamental view of language and metaphor as a bourgeois aberration. Gourmont's importance as a mediator between symbolism and naturalism has not yet had its proper recognition, nor has his view of style as '*une spécialisation de la sensibilité*' ['a specialty of sensibility'], and of art as '*l'exercice spontané et ingénu d'un talent naturel*' ['the spontaneous, ingenious exercise of a natural talent']. (32) For Gourmont's intellectual version of primitivism—soon to be absorbed by his admirers among the modernists and imagists, Eliot, Pound and T.E. Hulme among them—bridges the seemingly contrary movements of symbolism and naturalism. His dissociation-of-ideas theory is echoed far into later decades, and I would maintain that latter day deconstruction owes much to his crisp and refractory iconoclasms to his theories. In spite of his natural bias, his book is a deconstruction of the often-repeated naturalist definition of style attributed to Buffon, immodest perhaps in its belief in the intellect: '*Le signe de l'homme dans l'œuvre intellectuelle, c'est la pensée. La pensée est l'homme même. Le style est la pensée meme*' ['The sign of man in intellectual work is thought. Thought is man himself. Style is thought itself']. (673)

The more specialised approach to style that has been engendered by developments in modern linguistics is, in its scientific bias, clearly indebted to the Spencerian model of language and style, not least the once-vigorous branch of statistical stylistics. Its problem has been that, as it takes the definition of style to be the deviation from a linguistic norm, it also has to leave the question of the wider definitions of style unanswered (or circular, as Genette points out with great ingenuity, when he argues that style is simply what is studied in stylistics). Serious attempts at widening not only the definitions, but also the applications, of the concept of style as in Georges-Gilles Granger's *Philosophie du style* (*Philosophy of Style*) have hardly had the attention they deserve. The impasse has led to some intemperate attacks on the subject itself, most prominently by Stanley Fish. The analysts of deviance are content with treating a very small subset of sentences within poetic discourse, sentences that are in no way typical of poetry and imaginative fiction at large.

2

Recent years have seen a great swelling of the literature on metaphor, in books, in symposia, and in periodicals—but not all of these studies add much to the clarification or reinterpretation of the actual mechanisms at work in metaphor. The expectations of demarcation and elucidation of metaphor within the framework of linguistic syntactical analysis, which were strong in the early history of transformational generative grammar, have remained unfulfilled. This has to do with the attempts to create a hierarchy for different levels of grammaticalness, which had to be abandoned at a fairly early stage, together with analyticity criteria and classification of natural *specifica* in the lexicon—in itself a very instructive little chapter in the intellectual history of language study. Chomsky himself always showed a healthy scepticism towards these developments: he remarked as early as *Aspects of the Theory of Syntax* that he thought linguistic theory was unlikely to be able to handle metaphoric extensions, or stylistic variations, as long as 'reliable criteria for paraphrase are not forthcoming.' (42) In more recent years, literary theorists and philosophers of all camps have taken over the struggle to bring the concept of metaphor into some intellectual respectability.

It is easy to see that metaphor falls into one of the two grooves we could notice in de Gourmont's account of style; it can either be regarded the way nineteenth century rhetorical theory insisted, as an ornamental amplification of the argument of the text; or in accord with esoteric romantic theory, as an organic outgrowth of the linguistic utterance, providing a bridge to a perhaps unknowable reality. The two main theories of metaphor which have been most popular in recent years, the 'comparison' theory and the 'interaction' theory, fall neatly, although perhaps not too snugly, into these two categories.

The main problem with metaphor as a functional element of language is its submerged character. It has been a commonplace at least since German romanticism to insist on the ability of language to absorb metaphors in its active structure. It does not feel right to regard such sunken or petrified metaphors as irrevocably dead: as long as metaphor is a living, functional force in language, as long as it is begetting or generative, a dead metaphor can always be reactivated. But this comes at some cost, perhaps often at too great a cost, if you remember the Victorian habit of putting skirts on chair-legs in the name of modesty.

3

Irony is one of the master tropes recognized by Giambattista Vico in his *Scienza nuova* (*The New Science*):

> Irony certainly could not have begun until the period of reflection, because it is fashioned of falsehood by dint of a reflection which wears a mask of truth. Here emerges a great principle of human institutions, confirming the origin of poetry disclosed in this work that since the first men of the gentile world had the simplicity of children, who are truthful by nature, the first fables could not feign anything false; they must therefore have been, as they have been defined above, true narrations. (90)

The ironist is, in a sense, not concerned with style at all, only with truth. Already Theophrastus, in his *Characters*, defined the ironist as a liar and a pretender. More recently, Richard Rorty has tried to provide the ironist with a formidable task in reconstituting a moral philosophy on a relativist basis, building a 'final vocabulary' sceptical of all previous ones. 'The generic task of the ironist is the one Coleridge recommended to the great and original poet,' says Rorty, 'to create the taste by which he will be judged.' (97) The task seems to me most inauspicious and surprisingly similar to the homespun existentialism that Norman Mailer expounded some decades ago (and dependent, too, on criteria of style plainly redolent of the more murky backwaters of American pragmatism). It is sobering to consider the peculiarities of all schemes of irony, in that they are, to a greater degree than other forms of troping, dependent on tacit understanding, or complicity. Nobody has said it more elegantly than the late Paul Grice:

> While I may without any inappropriateness prefix the employment of a metaphor with *to speak metaphorically*, there would be something very strange about saying, *to speak ironically, he is a splendid fellow*. To be ironical is, among other things, to pretend (as the etymology suggests), and while one wants the pretence to be recognized as such, to announce it as a pretence would be to spoil the effect. (54)

4

The title of this essay vaguely reverberates with echoes of an 1822 play by a minor German romantic writer, Christian Dietrich Grabbe: *Scherz, ironie, satire und tiefere bedeutung* (*Joke, Irony, Satire, and Deeper Meaning*), which was rediscovered by André Breton and claimed as a forerunner of surrealism. The play is a fairly gross and grotesque concoction of various motifs from melodrama and folklore. The devil is caught in a cage, enticed there by sixteen rubber sheaths—at this time a fairly new commodity—and from there proclaims a worldview now fairly close to postmodernist orthodoxy of the French letter variety: that is, the world is a cheap romance novel from a lending library, now being perused by a pretty lady, while Hell is the ironic part of the book. In this the play seems even to resort to parody of its own ironic stance. The author is bold enough to advertise this fact in the short preface, where he says that the play derides itself (*verspottet sich selbst*) and thus is impervious to further criticism.

The concept of romantic irony, as introduced by Friedrich Schlegel, is no doubt central to the formation of subsequent modernist claims, and the archetype of the *ironist* is now, as it was then, Hamlet. As ironist, however, he could not proclaim his irony, or advertise it: the *fabula* itself, in the first place (and we must with Vico accept it as in some sense true and consistent) would prohibit it, insofar that such an admission would be catastrophic to his mission, if that is to be identified with feigning madness in order to find out the truth. Taken as a description of the poet's predicament, irony is a fatal trap, a catch-22, rather than an instrument for recovering value from experience.

We can recognize this as the predicament of many of the clowns in literature, from Shakespeare to Beckett — and in that way Hamlet is a clown, even if he does belong to a higher social order. But it is the plain-spoken clown Lavatch, 'a shrewd knave and unhappy,' (108) in *All's Well That Ends Well* (again a title not without prospects of irony) who gives the clue when speaking to the untrustworthy and cowardly Parolles of his 'similes of comfort' when abusing him. Immediately before, Lavatch has deliberately misconstrued Parolles' the figural expressions (as 'high-falutin' as his name indicates) which prompts Parolles to say:

> Nay, you need not stop your nose, sir. I spake but by a metaphor.
> Clown: Indeed, sir, if your metaphor stink I will stop my nose, or against any man's metaphor. (113)

Speaking the truth is a dangerous game, and sometimes involves less than pleasant odours. In Grabbe's play, the unfortunate clown Gottliebchen, less articulate and more abused than Lavatch, receives many a flea in his ear before he is asked by the schoolmaster to shut his mouth, preferably with his hand, because that looks more allegorical and poetic. But that *allegoresis* — so dear to our postmodernists and deconstructors — must be resisted.

The vigorous detroping of the clown we find so frequently in Beckett, often with the same scatological odour as in Grabbe, is an inversion that is as powerful as irony, as elegant as abstraction. We also find it, if with more fragrance, in Wallace Stevens' harmonious world, where the first requirement of the supreme fiction is that it must be abstract: 'We seek/ The poem of pure reality, untouched/by hope or deviation, straight to the word.' This statement has its even more succinct corollary, untouched by the deviations of style, insisting that the deeper meaning sought is the plainest meaning of all: 'So sense exceeds all metaphor.' (471)

Hell, as in Grabbe's play, or in William Empson's poem 'This Last Pain,' is of the party of irony, as powerfully negated and exposed as fiction: 'Imagine then.../ What couldn't possibly be there/ And learn a style from a despair.'(32)

Works Cited

Chomsky, Noam. *Cartesian Linguistics: A Chapter in the History of Rationalist Thought.* New York: Harper and Row, 1966.

Empson, William. *Collected Poems.* New York: Houghton Mifflin, 1949.

Gourmont, Remy de. 'Les funérailles du style,' *Mercure de France.* Serie Moderne, vol. 43 (1902): 5–35, 329–369, 640–673.

Grice, H. Paul . *Studies in the Way of Words.* Cambridge, Massachusetts: Harvard University Press, 1989.

Leclerc, Georges-Louis, Comte de Buffon. 'Discours sur le style,' *Histoire naturelle, générale et particulière: supplément,* vol. 4. Paris: L'Imprimerie Royale 1777: 1–20.

Rorty, Richard. *Contingency, Irony, and Solidarity.* Cambridge: Cambridge University Press, 1989.

Shakespeare, William. *All's Well That Ends Well.* Ed. John L. Lowes. New York: Macmillan, 1912.

Stevens, Wallace. *The Collected Poems of Wallace Stevens.* New York: Vintage, 1990.

Vico, Giambattista. *The New Science of Giambattista Vico.* Trans. by Thomas Goddard Bergin and Max Harold Fisch. New York: Anchor, 1961.

Part Six: Realism as Negation

Ever since the publication of 'On Realism and Art,' that authoritative and succinct analysis of the vicissitudes of meaning in the term 'realism' by Roman Jakobson (1921, in Czech), its interpreters—although to no such extent its users, alas—have shown commendable caution in ascribing to it any coalescence between its broader philosophic and everyday usages on one hand and its purely theoretical usages in the other. We have now many times been sternly admonished to restrict the term's prescribed meaning to a conventional context, as a designation of a literary or artistic movement or group or mode in the nineteenth century, to abandon all foolish hope of finding any permanent mimetic criteria for the term, and to content ourselves with family likenesses in the references of the term. Even Professor Wellek, who is always on his guard against such 'extreme nominalism' fully as much as against vacuous metaphysics, is, on the whole, hesitant about supplying tangible criteria for realism in his *Concepts of Criticism*. There is, even more surprisingly, no reference here to Jakobson's famous article, in spite of their erstwhile although temporary sharing of the same language, nor is there any listing of it in Wellek & Warren's *Theory of Literature*.

If this be true of the Western world, even represented by such *emigré* eminences as Jakobson and Wellek, it is not so within the Central European Marxist tradition. There the focus of the discussion of realism has been sharply and unashamedly aimed at *mimesis*. The whole Brecht-Lukács debate is firmly anchored in a general view of human reality that is impermeable to formal criteria. '*Realismus ist keine Formsache,*' ['realism is not a matter of formality' Brecht writes, '*man kann nicht die Form von einem einzelnen Realisten (oder einer begrenzten Anzahl von Realisten) nehmen und sie die realistische Form nennen. Das ist unrealistisch*' ['one cannot take the form of individual materialists and call it realistic form. That is unrealistic']. (41) In *Discriminations* Wellek states, with some satisfaction one may guess, that he has counted the instances of the phrase *'wiederspiegelung der wirklichkeit'* ['reflection of reality'] in the first volume of Lukács's *Aesthetics* and found that it appears 1032 times. (92)

As it is, the essay by Jakobson seems to have had little direct influence, its relativistic bias apart. Relativism is of course a main tenet of the essay, but there are also others, more easily overlooked. They have hardly been perceived, either by the nominalists or the mimeticists. Not even in that chic penumbra of intellectual *catch-as-catch-can* which is present-day *structuralisme* have they made any noticeable impact, doubtless because of the general aversion to realism in that movement (the only exception seems to be Gérard Genette, in *Figures*).

A parallel observation can be made regarding Erich Auerbach, whose monumental *Mimesis* is, sometimes surprisingly, taken wholly as a magnificent brief for relativism. Thus Harry Levin: 'when Professor Auerbach finds no formula for the presentation of actuality *(dargestellte wirklichkeit)* in different languages at different epochs, he impressively documents our need for assuming a relativistic point of view. (69)

Far be it from me to rock, as it were, the relativistic boat. Let us just look at some usages of the term that, although open to nominalist strictures, seem to throw some light on historical and psychological connections.

1

It does not appear necessary, in order to maintain an historical awareness and terminological accuracy, to ban from one's vocabulary all usages that seem derived from quotidian experience. Raymond Williams argued precisely this very convincingly in his discussion of tragedy as a natural mode of experience in *Modern Tragedy*. It would instead seem plausible to assume that the specialized usage takes its strength from various everyday usages. When the politician, the legislator, etc. talks about realism, isn't he then referring to well-definable qualities of a hard-nosed, level headed, no-nonsense kind? So Thurman Arnold speaking from the experiences of the New Deal: 'Realism, effective as it is as a method of political attack, or as a way of making people question ideas which they had formerly considered as established truths, ordinarily winds up by merely making the world look unpleasant.' (6) The cost of level headedness is an unpleasant world, at least in the eye of the beholder; its reward, presumably, some kind of moral integrity. In this quasi-philosophical sense, the word is in the English language clearly of an Emersonian pedigree (as citations in the

Oxford English Dictionary make clear). And the source beyond is as obviously Schiller and Goethe. In their intense correspondence of the summer of 1796, the two German writers discuss at great length the recently published *Apprenticeship of Wilhelm Meister*. Speaking, with his customary critical acumen, of two of the heroines of the book. Schiller says: '*Natalie und Therese sind beide Realistinnen; aber bei Theresen zeigt sich auch die Beschränkung des Realism (sic), bei Natalien nur der Gehalt derselben*' ['Natalie and Therese are both realistic, but Therese shows the limits of realism, Natalie its content']. (137) It is (I take it) not altogether surprising to find that the female sex has claims to seniority in realism; it is at least altogether fitting that the first realists appear in a Gothic fiction like *Wilhelm Meister* and not in real life!

Schiller continues his criticism the following week and is still keen on reading the novel in the categories realism vs. idealism in their relationship to Nature, a framework familiar from '*Über naive und sentimentalische dichtung*' ('On Naïve and Sentimental Poetry'). He criticizes—with ample praise for details—the 'machinery' of Gothic plots and counterplots which he sees as extraneous to the moral fable and goes on to comment on the hero of the novel:

> *Dass er nun, unter der schönen und heitern Führung der Natur (durch Felix) von dem Idealischen zum Reellen, von einem vagen Streben zum Handeln und zur Erkenntnis des Wirklichen übergeht, ohne doch dasjenige dabei einzubüssen, was in jenem ersten strebenden Zustand Reales war..., dieses nenne ich die Krise seines Lebens, das Ende seiner Lehrjahre, und dazu scheinen sich mir alle Anstalten in dem Werk auf das vollkommenste zu vereinigen.* (147)
>
> ['The fact that he passes under the beautiful, happy guidance of nature (through Felix) from the ideal to the real, from a striving to act to a recognition of what is real, without losing that which was initially real... I call this the crisis of his life, the end of his apprenticeship, and I think all the devices of the work unite perfectly to this end.']

Goethe, not without some hidden amusement one may assume, replies that he is well aware of the creaking of the Gothic machinery in the novel, adapting Schiller's philosophical term for his literary purposes:

> *Der Fehler, den Sie mit recht bemerken, kommt aus meiner innersten Natur, aus einem gewissen realistischen Tic, durch den ich meine Existenz, meine Handlungen, meine Schriften den Menschen aus den Augen zu rücken behaglich finde.* (149)
>
> ['The error, which you are right to notice, comes from my inner nature, from a certain realistic tic, which makes me want to hide my existence, my actions, my writings from others.']

In the phrase 'realistic tic' we can, I would venture, observe at close quarters an important semantic shift; Goethe has evoked what Keats would have called the negative capability of the word and is now able to invest it with specific technical content, referring it to his unwillingness, in the name of verisimilitude, to accept the full consequences of the overriding silliness of contemporary literary conventions. Schiller is also happy to accept it thus and remarks in his reply: '*Das, was Sie Ihren realistischen Tic nennen, sollen Sie dabei gar nicht verleugnen*' ['You are by no means to deny what you call your realistic tic']. (151)

There is here a rare opportunity to witness the genesis of new meaning in this unique dialogue. Professor Wellek dates the birth of the new meaning to a letter from Schiller to Goethe two years later, 27 April 1798, with a much less dramatic shift. (226)

The following dialogue is fully as interesting and entertaining, but I refrain from making any claims for its originality:

> 'My dear fellow,' said Sherlock Holmes, as we sat on either side of the fire in his lodgings at Baker Street, 'life is infinitely stranger than anything which the mind of man could invent. We would not dare to conceive the things which are really mere commonplaces of existence. If we could fly out of that window hand in hand, hover over this great city, gently remove the roofs, and peep in at the queer things which are going on, the strange coincidences, the plannings, the cross-purposes, the wonderful chains of events, working through generations, and leading to the most *outré* results, it would make all fiction with its conventionalities and foreseen conclusions most stale and unprofitable.'
>
> 'And yet I am not convinced of it,' I answered. 'The cases which come to light in the papers are, as a rule, bald enough, and vulgar enough. We have in our police reports realism pushed to its extreme limits, and yet the result is, it must be confessed, neither fascinating nor artistic.'
>
> 'A certain selection and discretion must be used in producing a realistic effect,' remarked Holmes. 'This is wanting in the police report, where more stress is laid perhaps upon the platitudes of the magistrate than upon the details, which to an observer contain the vital essence of the whole matter. Depend upon it there is nothing so unnatural as the commonplace.' (190)

This passage, first published in 1891, shows the full weight of the intervening discussions of realism and naturalism, the other differences between the respective pairs of distinguished interlocutors notwithstanding. The rhetoric of naturalism is ingeniously invoked, although the mythical situation is of some antiquity: it derives from *Le diable boiteux* (*The Lame Devil*), a proto-naturalistic fable of the demon who plays peeping Tom to the complacencies of the bourgeois world, removing the roofs of houses to feast his eyes on the unsavoury spectacle – which also vastly fascinated Strindberg.

As the original *tranche de vie,* this exactly prefigures naturalism's interest in the seamy side of life, the lower depths of human existence. But here the moral fervor of the literature of indignation has been displaced in favor of the more decadent search for strangeness. The habitual objection to art as being lacking in verisimilitude is thus not brushed aside but met with the argument that life itself is as quaint if not more so. The emphasis is on 'selection and discretion' but even more on specification the living details against the dead commonplaces. Sir Arthur would probably agree with the Elizabethan dramatists who according to T.S. Eliot professed an 'impure art': 'The aim of the Elizabethans was to attain complete realism without surrendering any of the advantages which as artists they observed in unrealistic conventions.' (116)

Let us summarize the similarities and differences with the dialogue of almost a hundred years earlier. Both have a psychological point of departure in realism as a negative activity, in Goethe's case a refusal to conform wholly with the conventions of Gothic fiction; in the case of Sherlock Holmes a similar wish to break through the barriers of convention and take the lid off the phenomena. What has been added in the latter is the insistence on 'selection' and the absolute value invested in 'detail.' In the first instance, he is but echoing another naturalist commonplace, implied in itself in the metaphor of 'cutting' in 'the slice of life,' which was authoritatively expressed by Henry James in the 'Preface' to *Roderick Hudson*: 'Really, universally, relations stop nowhere, and the exquisite problem of the artist is eternally but to draw, by a geometry of his own, the circle within which they shall happily *appear* to do so.' (5)

While as to the second, the obsession of realism is with detail, not infrequently inessential or gratuitous detail. This is interestingly stressed by Roman Jakobson, who refers to it under the heading of his characteristic D as a 'condensation of the narrative by means of images based on contiguity.' (43) Too little attention has been given to this element in Jakobson's presentation of realism, which he later expanded into his theory of figurative language and aphasia. It is a genuine observation of a concomitant characteristic of realism, which is contingent as to both the conventional and mimetic concepts of realism, i.e. there is no necessary entailment between richness in detail and veracity, or consequently, between richness in detail and verisimilitude. It is nevertheless a well corroborated observation that realism — like some other movements — tends to favor discourse on what is known as a high level of redundancy: it is tempting to refer to this as the Principle of Redundancy (abbr. PR).

2

Terms like 'realism' become difficult to handle not only because of any inherent ambiguity in their meaning but also – more importantly – because they command the assent of their users and imprecate the condemnation of the opposite. Terms which evoke persuasive definitions of this type might be called *protreptic* or hortatory. 'Realism,' however, has a wider range of hortatory appeal than most terms: it is rare to find creative artists or writers seriously maintaining that their art is in no way in correspondence with reality. This is often realized even among the enemies of realism. So Robbe-Grillet:

> *Tous les écrivains pensent être réalistes. Aucun jamais ne se prétend abstrait, illusioniste, chimérique, fantaisiste, faussaire... Le realisme n'est pas une théorie, définie sans ambiguité, qui permettrait d'opposer certains romanciers aux autres: c'est au contraire un drapeau sous lequel se range l'immense majorité sinon l'ensemble– des romanciers d'aujourd'hui.* (171)
>
> ['All writers think of being realistic. No one ever calls himself abstract, illusionary, chimerical, whimsical, or a forger... Realism is not a theory, clear and unambiguous, which would allow us to oppose some novelists to others. It is on the contrary under which gather the vast majority, if not all, of today's novelists.']

Attacks on realism are most often launched in the name of some greater claim for realism. Therefore it seems that Strindberg is quite justified in observing, late in his life in *Tal till svenska nationen* (*Speeches to the Swedish Nation*), that there was something snobbish and effete in the attack on '*skomakarrealism*' ['shoemaker realism']: '*Och på ett gammaldags junkeraktigt sätt begagnades namnet på ett aktat yrke som skällsord*' ['and in a clunky, old-fashioned way use the name of a respected profession as a slur']. (84)

For that very reason, it seems to me that there is something artificial and specious about the polarity of *creatio* and *mimesis*. The heterocosmic view of the created work as a self-contained world in its own right, is rarely construed as autotelic but most often as just-mimetic, like the monad of yore, mirroring the whole universe within its confines. The Christian and Platonizing dominance over the whole Western tradition has ensured a privileged position for anagogical and hermeneutical modes of thought. Every narrative is always in readiness to be interpreted as something else: the only authority to which appeal can be made is the intention of its creator. But nature and history are also there waiting to be interpreted, to give up their hieroglyphical keys, to display their signatures. Even a refusal to interpret is in fact a kind of interpretation, a statement of the impenetrability of the world. Hence the strange marriage of realism and symbolism in modern art: the epiphanies of authenticity in a contingent world. The more ardently the artist believes in the order of a transcendent world, the more is he willing to wax fanatical in his devotion to the reproduction of the imperfectibilities of this one. So Dostoevsky is—as Sven Linnér has documented so convincingly—always presenting his art as a realistic one, and the ageing Strindberg regards himself as the naturalist of spiritual experience.

A. D. Nuttall has demonstrated in *A Common Sky: Philosophy and the Literary Imagination* how a problem of greatest philosophical importance—the objective existence of the world—has dominated also the literary imagination for a long time. But this problem is seen almost exclusively from the viewpoint of British empiricism. There is a counterpart within the tradition of existentialist thought, the tradition that is the bearer of what Adorno used to call 'the jargon of authenticity.' Realism in a more philosophical sense is no doubt the problem child of this uncomfortable union. Adorno says in his late work, *Negative dialektik*:

> The historic innervation of realism as a mode of mental conduct is not foreign to the philosophy of Being. Realism seeks to breach the walls which thought has built around itself, to pierce the interjected layer of subjective positions that have become a second nature. (78)

This is well put and gives, in fact, the first intimation of a more than contingent relationship between realism as a mode of experience and realism as a technique. The impenetrable, viscous nature of phenomena, as they appear to the existential observer—when Roquentin contemplates the root of the tree in *La nausée* for instance—seeks a technical counterpart in the rich, impenetrable texture of the language of realism, in short in the Principle of Redundancy.

3

That literature as a totality evolves according to complicated patterns that can best be discussed in dialectical terms is hardly any longer a controversial statement. None but the most inveterate positivist or old-fashioned evolutionist can seriously maintain that atomistic or organicist models are in any way useful for descriptive or explanatory purposes. But exactly how a dialectical evolutionary theory works in detail is much less often, if ever, discussed. This is in itself understandable as it involves the thorny technicalities of Hegelian dialectics.

Negation is a key phrase in the system of logic of Hegel who defines the dialectical movement as the Negation of a Negation. It is also an important, although extremely obscure, concept in the later metapsychological speculations of Freud; his short essay on *'Die Verneinung'* (*'Denial'*) discusses problems central to the formation of a reality principle. Negation and contradiction have a long history—from Marx to Mao—in the development of dialectical materialism. None of these often extremely technical questions can be discussed here.

In a quite general sense, however, it is obvious that the negative aspect of literary development seems at least as important as the positive one. This is quite striking when you contemplate direct or indirect influence, as does Anna Balakian:

> It is interesting to note that very often the influences of authors of the same nationality and language are negative influences, the result of reactions, for generations often tend to be rivals of each other and in the name of individualism reject in the work of their elders what they consider to be the conventions of the past. (29)

A most elaborate theory of negative influence in poetry has been proposed by Harold Bloom, in a number of books of which *The Anxiety of Influence, A Map of Misreading* and *Poetry and Repression* are the most important ones. Bloom, who is heavily indebted to Freudian theory but also to present-day luminaries like Derrida and Lacan, is able to discern what he calls six 'revisionary ratios' in the psychological dependence of the 'ephebe' on the 'strong poet' in a semi-mythological confrontation known as the 'primal scene of instruction.' These ratios span the gap from *clinamen*, the swerving of atomic particles according to Lucretius, to *apophrades*, the return of the dead, which refers, somewhat surprisingly, to the influence of a younger poet on an older and dead one. A relevant example from Scandinavian literature would be the strange intrusion of Birger Sjöberg's tone and vocabulary in the third stanza of Fredmans Epistel 81, 'Märk hur vår skugga' ['Note how our Shadow']. More recently, the visionary and theological aspirations of Harold Bloom's work have become more obvious, and his interest in the Kabbalah and the kabbalist Isaac Luria has caused him to introduce further terms of more general nature like *zinzum* being the first step in a kabbalistic dialectic series, signifying the divine contraction before the creation.

Bloom's speculations are easily dismissed as poetic ravings; they are quite blatantly controversial. Göran Hermerén in his book *Influence in Art and Literature* manages to do so with the help of some elementary logic chopping. There is a hilarious but ultimately depressing primal scene of destruction in the confrontation of the extreme positivist and the extreme visionary. It seems unnecessary. Harold Bloom may sometimes go overboard in terminological frenzy, but he is an extremely learned and sensitive reader of poetry with a strong and passionate interest in the continuity of the poetic tradition. Unfortunately, his theory is very much confined to poetry and to romantic and post-romantic poetry in particular; it is not easily transferred to prose or the concept of realism or a more historical political context of dialectics but is squarely set on the Freudian-Nietzschean stage that Bloom occupies with such panache. Without any doubt some of his main observations have a general application.

4

Strindberg provides a prime example of the anxiety of influence; he is, of course, as he declared himself time and again basically a product—positively or negatively—of romanticism. Most of his comments on his relationship to his literary heroes, be they Zola or Dickens, Goethe or Balzac, are of great interest in this connection. In a late article from *Tal till svenska nationen* (*Speeches to the Swedish Nation*) he constructs his 'map of misprision' for C.J.L. Almqvist. He calls it *'Urtjuva,'* using an ancient Swedish legal term:

> Den som stulit annans boskap, men uppgiver sig ha hittat den, åligger att göra sig *'urtjuva'* genom lysningsvittnen eller ed. Uttrycket är gott och kunde användas på de litterära kombandit-bolagen i vår nutid, då begreppen om den litterära äganderätten blivit så försvagade av okunnighet, ondska och dålig smak, att rätte ägaren stämplas som tjuv av tjuven. (107)
>
> ['Whoever steals another man's cattle but pretends to have found it, is by law forced to make an 'urtjuva' in front of witnesses or by oath. This expression is a good one and may well be applied to the literary bandit-publishers of our time, for our notion of literary property is so weakened by ignorance, evil and bad taste that the righteous owner shall be denounced as a thief by the thief.']

Strindberg protests his innocence too much and must ultimately be condemned by the court of misprision: his misreadings of the poems of Atterbom and Heidenstam in *Tal* can be seen as something less than creative misunderstandings in Bloom's sense. But the general dialectical point made is broader than in any case Bloom has analyzed, as it is subsumed under the perennial confrontation of vacuous romanticism vs. detailed realism, of hazy poetry vs. level-headed prose. This is emphasized in the quotation from Tegnér Strindberg has appended to his discussion and condemnation of Atterbom, 'pekoral-poesiens anor.' ['twaddle-poetry tradition']. It is the same quotation which 28 years earlier concluded his polemical discussion '*Om realism. Några synpunkter,*' ['Realism: Some Comments'] first published in *Ur dagens krönika 2*, 1882: 'Jag älskar prosan, livets verklighet/urformationen utav tingens väsen' ['I love the prose, the reality of life/ur-formation out of the essence of things']. (*Samlade skrifter*, vol. 17, 199)

In that same early essay Strindberg attempted a definition of realism which is an interesting version of the Principle of Redundancy:

Realism kallas den riktning inom alla konstområden, då framställaren söker att göra det åsyftade intrycket, det vill säga giva illusion, genom att utföra de viktigaste av den mångfald detaljer varav bilden är sammansatt. (191)

['Realism is that tendency internal to all areas of art wherein the creator attempts to create the intended impression, i.e. create an illusion, by way of chiseling out the most essential of the manifold of details of which the image is composed.']

But Strindberg goes on to explain his views in such a way as to emphasize mainly the correct division in genus and species (now as much as 28 years later aiming evidently at Atterbom):

Författaren till dessa synpunkter kan, då han läser i ett gammaldags poem om en ros och en fjäril, icke se dessa abstrakta släktbegrepp; hans öga våndas innan det får välja ut arten.

Denna bild kan således icke heller klargöra symbolen, det inre, andliga, 'det obeständiga i kärleken,' ty där sensationen är otydlig blir tanken slapp.

När nu de ungas hjärnor blivit genom tränering annorlunda beskaffade än de gamles, så skall ett olösligt missförstånd uppstå. (193)

['When reading an old-fashioned poem about a rose and a butterfly, the author of these opinions finds himself unable to grasp such abstract generic concepts; his eye agonizes even before selecting the species.

This image will thus also be powerless to clarify the symbol, the innermost, the spiritual, 'the evanescent within love,' for wherever the sensation is vague thought grows flaccid.

Since the brains of the youth have now become differently formed by training than those of the old people, an insoluble misunderstanding shall arise.']

Strindberg is quite aware that it is the poets who arrange our misunderstandings and that it is always a new poem that is the meaning of another poem, two Bloomian theses he has absorbed, *par apophrade* no doubt. He is, as it were, advocating a climb down the tree of classification, a realism which is popularly known as 'scientific,' but in fact ultimately derived from Plato's conception of *diairesis* or division. This becomes the picture of the descent of realism as Strindberg's career illustrates it, where the principle of redundancy, rigidly adhered to, at long last resolves itself in the absurdities of quotidian minutiae. The true heir to this original Strindbergian misprision is no doubt that latter-day master of philosophical PR, Samuel Beckett. It strikes me that this view of the misprized realist is very much like the oddly attired man the eponymous hero of his novel *Watt* encounters on Westminster Bridge:

> It was blowing heavily. It was also snowing heavily. I nodded heavily. In vain. Securing me with one hand, he removed from the other with his mouth two pairs of leather gauntlets, unwound his heavy woolen muffler, unbuttoned successively and flung aside his great coat, jerkin, coat, two Waistcoats, shirt, outer and inner vests, coaxed from a washleather fob hanging in company with a crucifix I imagine from his neck a gunmetal half-hunter, sprang open its case, held it to his eyes (night was falling), recovered in a series of converse operations his original form, said, Seventeen minutes past five exactly, as God is my witness, remember me to your wife (I never had one) let go my arm, raised his hat and hastened away. A moment later Big Ben (is that the name?) struck six. (36)

Groping for exactness we come up with the absurd. May that also be a warning to the literary critic—in that his misprisions of the complexities of terms may easily obfuscate the obvious.

Works Cited

Adorno, Theodor. *Negative Dialectics*. London: Allen Lane, 1973.

Arnold, Thurman. *The Symbols of Government*. New Haven: Yale University Press, 1937.

Balakian, Anna. 'Influence and Literary Fortune.' *Yearbook of Comparative and General Literature*. 1962: 143–152.

Beckett, Samuel. *Watt*. New York: Grove, 1959.

Brecht, Bertolt. *Über realismus*. Frankfurt: Suhrkamp, 1971.

Doyle, Sir Arthur Conan. *The Complete Sherlock Holmes*. Ed. Christopher Morley. New York: Doubleday, 1960.

Eliot, T.S. *Selected Essays*. London: Faber, 1951.

Jakobson, Roman. 'Realism in Art.' *Readings in Russian Poetics*. Ed. Ladislaw Matejka and Krystyna Pomorska. Cambridge, Massachusetts: Harvard, 1971: 38–46.

James, Henry. *The Art of the Novel*. New York: Scribner, 1953.

Levin, Harry. *Contexts of Criticism*. New York: Scribner, 1963.

Matthias, John. *Reading Old Friends*. Albany: State University of New York Press, 1992.

Robbe-Grillet, Alain. *Pour un nouveau roman*. Paris: Editions de Minuit, 1963.

Schiller, Freidrich von, and Johann Wolfgang von Goethe. *Briefwechsel zwischen Schiller und Goethe*. Vol. 1. Stuttgart: Cottafchen, 1881.

Strindberg, August. *Samlade skrifter*. Vol. 17. Stockholm: Bonniers, 1919.

—. *Tal till svenska nationen samt andra tidningsartiklar 1910–1912*. Stockholm: Bonniers, 1919.

Wellek, René. *Discriminations*. New Haven: Yale University Press, 1970.

Part Seven: Historical Drama and Historical Fiction: The Example of Strindberg

1

In attempting to place the refraction point of these generic terms in as precise a way as possible, one finds there is only one canonical critical text to consider, the second chapter of György Lukács's *The Historical Novel*, first published in Russian in 1937, entitled 'Historical Novel and Historical Drama.' There he gives consideration to the particular circumstances, delineated in the first chapter, which led to the emergence of the historical novel of romanticism, notably his prime example and paradigm, the novels of Sir Walter Scott, and notices that these circumstances are in no way relevant to the historical drama, which already at the time had a long and venerable history:

> Even quite apart from French classicism and the bulk of Spanish drama, it is obvious that both Shakespeare and a number of his contemporaries produced real and important historical dramas e.g. Marlowe's *Edward II*, Ford's *Perkin Warbeck* etc. In addition there comes, at the end of the eighteenth

century, the second great flowering of historical drama in the early work and the Weimar period of Goethe and Schiller. All these dramas are not only of an incomparably higher artistic order than the so-called precursors of the classical historical novel, but are also historical in quite a different, deep and genuine sense. (Lukács, *The Historical Novel*, 89)

This difference would come as a surprise to no one even moderately well acquainted with the history of the drama in modern times. What is new and refreshing is Lukács's conception of historical drama as a genre, a conception engendered by his dialectical method: he sees it exclusively in its relationship to the historical novel, which is, after all, the subject of his investigation. As he is describing and defining a *new* genre, the novel set in the more or less distant past, he feels, quite rightly, no obligation to describe a genre that has existed for more than two-thousand years—however one chooses to interpret the elements of historicity in Greek tragedy.[9] What he is obliged to do is to establish demarcation lines between genres of contrasting natures, and, as he is a Marxist, to explain them in terms of dialectical materialism, that is, as a reflection, or *Widerspieglung*, of historical conflicts between social classes.

Lukács explains those conflicts for the historical novel in a way that has become a model of its kind for dialectical literary analysis at its most successful. In his first chapter, he outlines the emergence of the historical novel of romanticism and establishes a pivotal role for this kind of novel as practiced by Walter Scott: a broad-canvas painting of an age riddled by conflicts of historical importance, the portrayal of colorful historical characters as set pieces of the novel, not presented in depth or in the process of development, but seen entirely through the eyes of a 'mediating' hero who is himself distanced from the conflict in question, either by origin or circumstances, while nevertheless profiting from the experience in individual terms. *Waverley* (1814) established the mold for this type of novel, for a long time to come and in an exemplary and authoritative way, not only, as Lukács adumbrates for the 'classical' historical novel of the nineteenth century, by Cooper, Stendhal, and Balzac, even Tolstoy, but also for the exotic 'adventure' novel of later times, by Melville, Conrad, even Graham Greene.[10]

---

9. For the social-mythical interpretation of Greek tragedy, see, in particular, Vernant.
10. The generous definition of *'roman d'aventure,'* proposed by Jacques Rivière (235–81) as early as 1913, has hardly had the critical follow-up it deserves.

The 'form' of this novel, if one invokes a slightly earlier formulation from Lukács's pre-Marxist period,[11] is utterly different from the 'form' of the historical drama, with its much longer and more prestigious pedigree, and can be encapsulated in neat oppositions, which I here rather freely summarize:

(1) The historical novel is slow-moving and accommodating to detailed observation—the historical drama instead concentrates on 'dramatic' momentous events.
(2) The hero of the historical novel is 'unheroic' and 'middling ': a mediator—the hero of historical drama is tragical/heroic.
(3) The historical novel represents the life and viewpoints of the Common Man: it is *democratic*—historical drama represents the life and viewpoints of monarchs and political leaders: it is *aristocratic*.
(4) As the novel continues to develop during the romantic age, we can notice a certain tendency toward conflation of the two genres, a progressive 'dramatization' of the novel and a similar 'novelization' of the drama. Lukács (125) is more perceptive and more insistent on the latter—which he brilliantly exemplifies with Ibsen's *Rosmersholm* (1886)—than on the former.

It is a great pity that Lukács never comments on Strindberg's historical plays—or Ibsen's for that matter—in this long and teemingly rich chapter, but, as Strindberg never wrote a major historical novel and the historical *novel* after all is the main concern of Lukács's investigation, it is perhaps not altogether surprising. The almost scientific rigor of Lukács's theory—a very rare thing in aesthetic theorizing—is, however, highlighted by the fact that we can, in applying the contrastive formula of Lukács's observations to Strindberg's historical fiction and drama, satisfactorily predict their contrasting natures.

I assume the general observations of György Lukács's study of historical drama and historical fiction to be accepted by almost everybody as simple truths. In a way, this acceptance seems to have precluded

---

11. See the essay 'Metaphysik der tragödie' in Lukács, *Die seele* (325–73); and *Entwicklungsgeschichte*. According to Stanley Mitchell, in an introduction to a translation of a central chapter of the latter work, one can regard *The Historical Novel* (orig., 1937) as a Marxist reformulation of this work and the later, intermediary, and more Hegelian *Die theorie des romans* (1916).

further investigation of the subject. Historical fiction, which has seen an unprecedented period of flowering on many levels in the period since the first publication of Lukács's book, has inspired in the same period very few major critical studies (one of the worthy exceptions being a book on the American historical novel [Henderson]) as compared to other subgenres of the novel, like the novel of fantasy and science fiction or the novel of manners, while drama criticism has moved away—again with some honorable exceptions (Lindenberger)—from a concern with a temporal theme. There are reasons, however, for pleading for a reopening of the case: we can, while acknowledging the insights of Lukács's pioneering work, explore inroads into the subject matter that might have been closed to Lukács because of his adherence to a simple *Widerspieglungs*-theory and an orthodox *diamat* methodology. Such an explanation could be made with the help of the unorthodoxy of a Walter Benjamin or a Peter Szondi (in this particular case following closely in Benjamin's footsteps) and with the observations of the origin of the novel by the maverick Soviet critic/philosopher M. M. Bakhtin, whose original, if somewhat loosely organized, work has become generally available to us only in the last decade.[12]

2

Strindberg never wrote a major historical novel, as I remarked before, but his life-long interest in Balzac (which has elicited a great deal of discussion) and in Walter Scott (which was shared by many of his contemporaries, not least, Gustaf Fröding) is well attested.[13]

On the other hand, Strindberg left a monumental legacy in the twelve major plays on Swedish history—if we follow Walter Johnson's masterly study *Strindberg and the Historical Drama* (1963), establishing the *canon* or measuring rod—which may be the only matching sequence to Shakespeare's ten canonical plays on English history that any Western country has to show. In addition, he wrote plays with themes from Swedish

---

12. See Holquist and Clark for the background of Bakhtin and the Bakhtin Circle and a first introduction to the now extremely complex and controversial issue of authorship within that circle. Some of Bakhtin's most challenging remarks on the novel are to be found in the late (and undisputed) fragmentary essays (see Bakhtin, *Speech Genres*, 132-58).
13. Strindberg's relationship to Balzac is too complicated to survey in a note: the book by Jan Myrdal entitled *Strindberg och Balzac* is unfortunately in no way an attempt to unravel these complications, but just a reprint of his previous articles on the two authors. Strindberg has attested that, late in his life, he still kept on rereading Walter Scott.

history, most notably *Mäster Olof*, in (at least) two versions (1872, 1875–76) and the attempted series of dramas on world history of which only four plays were ever completed. More importantly still, he created the series of short fiction collected in *Svenska öden och äventyr* (1882–91; *Swedish Destinies and Adventures*), which is probably without counterpart in any national literature and represents one of the most convincing and startling innovations of a literary form that Strindberg ever produced and which he, furthermore, followed with two volumes in the new century—one, *Historiska miniatyrer* (1905; *Historical Miniatures*), containing short stories on subjects from world history, the other, *Hövdingaminnen* (1906; *Chieftain Memories*), with Swedish settings. To this work can be added non-fictional accounts of a wide variety of historical topics, studies of world history ('Världshistoriens mystik,' 1903; 'The Mysticism of World History'), his histories of the Swedish people and of Stockholm, painstakingly detailed studies on orientalism, etc. The range and import of Strindberg's historical interests are indeed awe-inspiring.

If for the time being we limit ourselves to the drama and fiction, we shall find ourselves able to confirm Lukács's observations on the two forms as valid, at least as regards the 'canonical' series on Swedish history. The short stories of *Svenska öden* are detailed in their observations and fairly slow-moving (as in point 1); their heroes are of the people: there are very few, if any, characters drawn from textbook history (point 2); and the viewpoint is aggressively and unabashedly populist (point 3). While, on the other hand, the major dramas of Swedish kings are 'dramatically' concentrated to momentous historical events (point 1), they have larger-than-life heroes of the tragic mold at their centers (point 2) and are thus unhindered in expressing the viewpoints of the leaders of the people. There are some apparent exceptions to this; the stories of *Svenska öden* gradually change character during the years of publication, and late tales like 'Tschandala' or 'The Man of Straw' can perhaps be regarded as quite conventional and weak examples of short historical novels in the traditional mold. In *Hövdingaminnen* we have, as the title indicates and as already John Landquist pointed out, an open concern with the leaders of men.[14]

In the dramas, owing to the traditional requirement of the form, we also find occasional expressions of the viewpoint of the common man, but it can

---

14. *Hövdingaminnen* was the intended title of the book, but the publisher convinced Strindberg that *Nya svenska öden* ('New Swedish Destinies') would invoke the popular success of the earlier books. Landquist reinstated the original title.

be regarded as inherited from the very structure of classical drama in which the chorus is invited to mouth a commonsense view of tragic incidents.

The later historical tales, however, do not at all conform to the quoted requirements but are quite blatantly written with a different and more varied conception of the historical narrative in mind. On the whole, there is in Strindberg's work a striking confirmation of Lukács's observation of certain structural necessities in the distinction between the two traditional forms. There is no mystery in this, no prescience claimed: Strindberg is aware of the traditional requirements of the two 'forms,' which had been shaped by a poetics of the novel emerging in German romanticism and finding expression in the theories of Goethe, Friedrich Schlegel, and Hegel, the same theories that surely had helped to form Lukács's intellectual development. Hegel insists on the priority of action and conflict in tragedy in contrast to the passive subjectivity in prose and lyric poetry. Schlegel regarded the modern novel, the emerging novel of romanticism, as constituting a unique genre (*eine Gattung für sich*) to be further subdivided into differentiated genres according to historical contingencies (Szondi, 'Friedrich Schlegel'). But Goethe, in the long discussion between Serlo and Wilhelm in the fifth book, seventh chapter of the *Lehrjahre* (1795–96), manages, even before the modern novel has come of age, to state the salient distinctions (Lukács never quotes this celebrated passage in his second chapter):

> In the novel, as in the drama, we see human nature and action. The difference between these genres does not lie simply in their outward form... In the novel, opinions and occurrences are above all to be presented: in the drama, characters and actions. The novel must move slowly, and the views of the main character must, in one way or another, obstruct the unravelling of the whole.
>
> The drama must speed, and the character of the hero must drive on towards the issue, and only meet obstructions. The hero of the novel must be passive, or at least not highly effectual; we demand of the dramatic hero impact and deeds. Grandison, Clarissa, Pamela, the Vicar of Wakefield, even Tom Jones, if not passive yet retarding characters [*retardierende Personen*], and all occurrences are in a sense molded upon their dispositions. In the drama, the hero moulds nothing upon himself, everything resists him, and he clears and shifts hindrances out of his way, or else succumbs to them.

(Goethe 28; trans. Pascal 22)

Retardierende Personen: it is certainly a striking description, imbued with almost literal significance, of Strindberg's 'heroes' in the historical short fiction: Sten Ulvfot from 'Odlad frukt' (1882; 'Cultivated Fruit'), the Öland peasants in 'Nya vapen' (1883; 'New Weapons'), Kristian in 'En ovälkommen' (1882; 'An Unwelcome'): if they are apt to *reculer*, it is not so much *pour mieux sauter* as in order to opt out of their former existence, or even of life itself. The new weapons acquired by the oppressed Öland peasants, in the wonderfully sardonic story of that name, are called *flykt* ('running away'), as the peasants remind the justice of the peace when faced with a Russian invasion.

But is the reverse proposition as obviously true of Strindberg's historical drama, are the dramatic heroes to be seen as *per se* prominent and prone to action? They are so by virtue of their offices as kings (or Queen) of Sweden in turbulent times, but hardly always in other ways. We need to look at the problem from another angle and invoke other authorities, in order to give more weight to the question.

As far as historical fiction goes, there is another distinction to be considered, namely, that between historical novel and historical tale or short story—a distinction in which formal criteria break down and disappear. It is the received wisdom of the practitioners of the art,[15] that the short story as a separate genre did not break off from the novel or the cyclical collection of tales, until the mid-nineteenth century and that it was, as a popular genre, reinforced by various discursive modes, not least the ethnographical or investigative essay (Beachcroft, ch. 7), that it achieved its character and independence from he amorphous mass of legends, fairy tales, anecdotal histories, ghost stories, and so forth that flooded the popular literature in earlier times.

As an early theorist of the short story, Edgar Allan Poe can be said to have attempted a *rapprochement* of the historical tale to something we can term anecdotal history. The young Henry James, whose suspicions of the historical romance were considerable, attempted to do the opposite; in a review article for *The Nation* (15 Aug. 1867) on some indifferent historical romances, he makes some worthwhile comments on the incompatibilities of the historical and the literary imagination. He is, however, willing to

---

15. It is striking how much the theory of the short story has been directed by practicing short-story writers; in addition to Poe and James, one can note studies by H. E. Bates (1941) and Sean O'Faolain (1948), both entitled *The Short Story*, and Frank O'Connor, *The Lonely Voice: A Study of the Short Story* (1964).

make an exception of Balzac, whom he calls 'a historical novelist inasmuch as he was the historian of contemporary manners.' In adumbrating Lukács's distinction between 'real' and 'imaginary' historical figures, he is led to a further dissociation of historical fact from literary imagination and adduces as example: 'George Eliot's 'Romola'... [,] a very beautiful story, but... [one] quite worthless, to our mind, as a picture of life in the fifteenth century.'

Much the same could perhaps be said for at least a certain number of Strindberg's historical tales in *Svenska öden och äventyr*, in which the veneer of historical detail sometimes wears very thin, as Fredrik Böök and many more have pointed out. The prime example is possibly 'En häxa' ('A Witch') from 1891, which was transposed from the first half of his contemporary novella 'Schleichwege' (or 'Genvägar'), with very few changes, just adding a few touches of local and temporal color, but nonetheless with quite convincing results, in spite of considerable occurrences of what James would call 'moral anachronisms.' Towards the turn of the century, in the expert hands of Strindberg and others, this type of tale becomes a *bravura* showpiece, which in Scandinavian literature was to culminate in Johannes V. Jensen's intensely atmospheric historical novel *Kongens fald* (1900–01; *The Fall of the King*) and early short stories. It is what the Russian Formalists might call *sjuzhet* without the fabula: it will ultimately resemble, as I think Poe and James could foresee from their mutually opposed standpoints, a certain type of popular history much more than it resembles the traditional historical drama.

3

So far, we have approached the problem of historical drama vs. historical novel in an entirely conventional way, that is, through genre distinctions, which are themselves historical and transitory. The organic models, which have determined our thinking of genre development and genre change, since romanticism, no doubt, but most emphatically since Brunetière, have encouraged modes of describing these phenomena in terms of growth, branching out, withering and dying. In fact, genre changes seem to develop in many different ways, not least in reviving dead genres or in conflating adjacent genres or collapsing differentiated, but cognate, genres.

The question is whether these genre distinctions are as fundamental and immutable as distinctions between media? A television screen can be used for written texts, as indeed it is today by most of us in the shape of the word processor, but it does not become a book, as little as the 'speaking books' (in Swedish, *talböcker*) for blind people are books. New media may engender new genres, but they are still bound by the modes of representation—oral, written or acted. There are no printed dumb-shows, no radio mimes, no oral calligraphy.

Clearly, much of the distinctiveness of these modes has to do with basic relations of time and space. The oral representations is sequential in time, the written is not. The acted representation is both sequential in time and bound to a particular observable locus in space. Technological innovations, like video recording, may affect boundary changes a little, through repeating and scanning devices, but some fundamental distinctions are certain to remain. A film is still bound to have, in spite of all cutting or scrambling devices available, 'a beginning, a middle, and an end,' although, as the now quite truistic witticism goes, 'not necessarily in that order.'

The unity of time and space, the *chronotope*—to use Bakhtin's term (*The Dialogic Imagination* 84–248), in an essay that I have found helpful, but perhaps less sharply focused than most of his other work—is not a discovery of our time. Shakespeare knew it well and uses it for showing up its incompatibility with real time and space, not least in historical drama, as in *Henry V*, where he has the Prologue address his audience with the question,

> can this cockpit hold
> The vasty fields of France? or may we cram
> Within this wooden O the very casques
> That did affright the air at Agincourt? (lines 11–13)

and prompt them to 'make imaginary puissance' just in order to affect 'turning the accomplishments of many years,/ into an Hour-glass.' (lines 25, 30–31)

That the cockpit—or, variously, the Wooden O of the Shakespearean stage—cannot be identified with the world will not come as a great surprise to most, except to the rough prospectors of Dawson City, or wherever, who with the help of their sixguns tried to dissuade Othello from strangling his wife. The spatial disparity is unique for acted representation, but both narrative and drama share the temporal disparity. It can be described and labeled in various ways: *Erzählzeit versus erzählte zeit* (Günther Müller); *temps de l'enoncé and temps de l'enonciation* (Benveniste, Gerard Genette); and *Aktzeit versus Textzeit* (Harald Weinrich). These various proposals in all their intricacies have been judiciously presented by Paul Ricoeur in the second volume of his truly monumental investigation *Temps et récit* (passim, 121 n.l). Inexorably, the discussion leads back, as does indeed the discussion of the origin of genre distinctions, to Plato's and Aristotle's interwoven interpretations of *mimesis*, or imitation, and *diegesis*, or 'pure' narration (which I have commented on in a different context; see Printz-Påhlson, 'Det Episka'). This seems to be the only way to make sense of Bakhtin's chronotope and the seemingly arbitrary definitions he introduces.

But let us return to the fourth set of distinctions, culled from Lukács's observations on the historical novel and historical drama: the dramatization of the novel and the novelization of the drama, which can be observed towards the end of the nineteenth century. There is no mystery about the first: it is well attested in the practice of important novelists like Henry James, Conrad, and Joyce, who deliberately curb authorial comment in the direction of the dramatic; it was elevated into critical dogma by the New Critics. The second point is more controversial and also more difficult to unravel. The tendency towards what is known as 'epic' theatre can hardly be called novelistic in any stricter sense.

Still, it is hardly controversial to say that all drama contains a modicum of narrative, or, if you want, pure narration or diegesis. This element is what, ever since Aristotle, we are used to calling 'plot' (*mythos*). It means that the drama can be translated into a narrative. Strindberg did exactly that with 'Herr Bengts Hustru' ('Sir Bengt's Wife'), the play that he 'translated' into a short story.

Now we are ready to see what constitutes the unique character of the historical drama *qua* history: it is the underlying narrative or Mythos already exists. The author of the historical drama is allowed a certain freedom in selecting his material, but in the case of the canonical plays on actual historical characters he has to face the preconceptions of his audience or his readers. He might challenge such preconceptions, but he cannot disregard them. He cannot write about Gustavus Adolphus and suppress all references to the Thirty Years' War. He cannot have Queen Christina marry her cousin Charles and live happily ever after.

Or, again let us look at the problem from another angle. The acted representation is, in spite of its tangible presence, an ascetic art: it spurns the sources of information over and above the plot, which is fundamentally unraveled by means of dialogue. Consequently, normal, everyday drama is one of the most demanding of genres, in the sense that it requires an immense effort on part of the spectator, who is faced with a handful of strangers who go about their business in complete disregard of him. Neither is he allowed to put questions to them about their background, intentions, and so on; nor can he, as the reader of a novel, skip a chapter, leaf through to the ending of the book, or go back to the beginning. The spectator is lost unless he is a trained theatre-goer: he is forced to remember very intricate things about people he has never heard of and does not care tuppence about. This is a frightening experience: no wonder a prospector from Dawson City would reach for his gun when he saw the big black feller throttle his little bride.

Here the historical drama of the canonical type is a godsend, and we, in our sophistication, can easily forget the most important single fact about it. It is presumably as the Greek tragedy might have been to the Athenians—about people we know. And every Swedish child knows his Charles XII: he has seen the portrait of him as King of Spades on the most popular deck of painted cards in Sweden (cf. Staffan Björck's brilliant comments on the social content of playing cards: 174–80), or on the once immensely widespread *Kungatavlan* ('The Pictorial Succession of Kings'), which used to adorn every other privy in Sweden. There is every reason to take Strindberg's idea of the theatre, in the preface to 'Miss Julie,' as a Biblia Pauperum in dead earnest.

4

If you, as a playwright, want to impart background information in your play, there are principally two different ways you can go about it:

(1) You can add information over and above the dialogue, in stage directions, program notes, prefaces, and so forth. This is the *Nebentext*, which Egil Törnquist has studied in some Strindberg plays ('Strindbergs bitext' 102) with fascinating results.

(2) You can impart background information to the audience through the dialogue itself, which tends to strain the bounds of probability in many cases of contemporary drama. This is the *exposé* that Strindberg sometimes castigates in his *Öppna brev till Intima teatern* (1909; *Open Letter to the Intimate Theater*). But it is obvious that this is much more acceptable in historical drama of the canonical type, as the monarchs, politicians, and leaders of men, who make up the central characters, are quite likely to express themselves in long-winded discourses on the obvious, the most splendid example is the long *ekphrasis*, or interpretation of the portraits of the whole Folkung family, which King Magnus addresses to Queen Blanche at the beginning of Act V of *Folkungasagan* (1899; *The Saga of the Folkungs*). The

tone is here indistinguishable from the tone of Strindberg's essay 'Världshistoriens mystik' and clearly emanates from the notorious Green Sack. (Printz-Påhlson, 'Allegories')

Strindberg is in this way also able to add to the characterization of Magnus, ingenuous and voluble as he is. The garrulous Magnus can be allowed to offer this piece of self-analysis (or rather analysis of the drama he happens to be part of: he ends his monologue with, 'Detta är folkungasagan' ('This is The Saga of the Folkungs'), which would have been utterly inappropriate in the taciturn Charles XII. But the exposé goes much further than Magnus can possibly know: it establishes the mode or mechanism governing the whole sequence of plays on Swedish history.

It is, I believe, this mode, which has often been called panoramic, since its wide-lens perspective seems to embrace so much more than the individual fates and characters. It may be that Birgitta Steene uses the word in a more technical sense when she denies the panoramic character of the later history plays in an early and pioneering study: 'Thus Strindberg's historical cycle broke into fragments—although in one sense he had already completed its pattern in *The Saga of the Folkungs* and his individual historical plays gradually lost their panoramic perspective.' (Steene, *Strindberg: A Collection* 136)

It seems to me that, insofar as a certain kind of continuity is established—and Strindberg was willing to go to great length to fill in the gaps in his narrative *fabula*, at least up to *Carl XII*, which establishes the *katastrophé* or peripeteia—that the panoramic perspective is retained or even intensified in the later plays, that is, if the whole cycle is read diachronically and not synchronically.[16] This perspective is perhaps most obvious in *Carl XII*, with its silent protagonist, its constant proleptic hints of things to come (in the truculent characters of Gyllenborg and Horn, for example), and the final withdrawal of judgment on the king's character. It is the Swedish nation,

---

16. In emphasizing the predominantly and uniquely psychological nature of Strindberg's history plays, Herbert Lindenberger also denies the panoramic aspect: there is no 'larger, controlling myth,' as in Shakespeare, for instance (Lindenberger 122). He is quite correct in seeing the plays of the Damascus cycle as Strindberg's only completed 'panoramic' dramatic sequence, in that they 'transfer the historical vision of most earlier panoramic plays to a wholly psychological realm while at the same time retaining their vastness and their imaginative grandeur.' (88) I have tried to suggest a link in my analysis of *Damascus III*. (Printz-Påhlson, 'Allegories' 228–31) The explanation must surely reside in the Hegelian framework of *Verletzung* and *Kollision*, which Lindenberger himself points to in a footnote (171, n. 68). As Strindberg is busy with the *Aufhebung* of the national myth—with, as we might say today, deconstructing it—he is the more likely to let the historical pageant take on a deliberately theatrical, or unreal, character.

the Swedish people, who are the agonists of this tragedy, not the king. The master narrative, which runs through the whole series of plays, is here exposed as being the destiny of a nation. And this master narrative is as much in evidence in the later short fiction, hence the shifting character of the stories in *Hövdingaminnen*, even if they only occasionally touch upon the same subject matter as the plays.

5

History in modern times has been given many names, most of them abusive. 'History is bunk,' said Henry Ford. 'History is a nightmare from which I am trying to awake,' is the neat summary of Stephen Dedalus in *Ulysses* (1922). In 'Little Gidding' (1943), one of the major meditations on history in our time, T. S. Eliot seems to want it both ways: 'History may be servitude,/ History may be freedom.' (III, 13–14)

Strindberg's view of history, or in this case Swedish manifest destiny, is equally reductive. In *Carl XII*, it is hammered in metaphorically, in images of disease and bankruptcy and of death (as it had been already in the short story sharing its chronotope, 'Vid likvakan i tistedalen' ('At the Wake in Tistedalen'), from *Svenska Öden*.

There is, however, a reversed exposure of the Swedish national myth embedded in the history plays, one that uses a chronotype of a very different nature. This reversed exposure occurs in the short satirical folktale 'Gullhjälmarne i Ålleberg.' ('The Gold Helmets of Ålleberg'), which is included in *Sagor* (1903; *Tales* 102–10). It is one of the most delightful and witty of Strindberg's late tales, to be set next to his early satire on Swedish history, 'De lycksaliges ö' (1890; 'The Island of the Blessed') which used to be included in school anthologies and must have bemused countless generations of Swedish schoolchildren.

The story resolutely identifies its chronotope as folkloristic, and its time as *adventure time*.[17] The soldier Anders Kask from Västergötland, who is on temporary duty in Stockholm, is trying to gate-crash at 'Skansen,' at the time at its very height of nationalist grandeur. Trying to find an entrance from the rear, he is approached by several talking animals—a squirrel, a snake and a hedgehog—that offer their help. At last, with the

---

17. The expression is Bakhtin's (*Dialogic Imagination* 81), but it could also be identified with his 'folkloric chronotope.' I have had to disregard his fine distinctions.

help of a pixie, he finds the entrance to the mountain and is introduced to the giant, who presents himself as Giant Svensk. After having passed some traditional tests, he is taken to see the Gold Helmets, who have been moved from their original habitat, near his birthplace in Västergötland. They turn out to be, not surprisingly, the past kings of Sweden, asleep in the mountain, waiting to be called to the rescue when Sweden is in danger. So far, Strindberg has been using a number of well-known folktale and legendary motifs and struck a whimsical parodic note that is pleasantly obscure. The rest is pure satire: the Giant Svensk is to give account to the Gold Helmets on the present state of Sweden, which is far from encouraging, as one might expect. The folkloristic models are numerous. The idea of the ancient king returning to the country in its hour of greatest need is extremely widespread—Arthur in Avalon or Frederick Barbarossa in the mountain. The animal helpers can be easily recognized as a favorite folktale motif—Propp's celebrated category F[18] (Propp 57)—and the knights in the mountain are known from various regions of Sweden. At least two more specific sources need to be identified: the story of the giant Gjelle, which was collected by Nicolovius in his famous work on folk life (109 ff.), and the most widespread and influential of Swedish eighteenth-century political ballads, that of Sinclair (*Sinclairvisan*), written by Anders Odel (Hörnström). The wayward Scanian giant Gjelle, who asks mundane questions about his native Gislöf, and the Swedish martyr Major Malcolm Sinclair, who rouses the sleeping twelve kings in the mountain, provide the ideal subtexts for Strindberg's satire. Swedish history, heroic/tragic as it is to Strindberg, is also encapsulated in the spurious and factitious nationalism of Skansen. And, as if the verbal send-up were not enough, the soldier Kask, like the very casques that did affright the air at Agincourt, is sent up, literally, in the modern turbolift to Skansen, from where he can witness Gustaf Vasa entering with his Dalecarlia following; whether it is the customary midsummer pageant or the real happening is not stated. But the inference to be drawn may be that there is hardly any difference. In adventure time the imaginary puissances are as great as the real ones, for as Eliot reminded us in the hour of a modern Agincourt (1942):[10] 'history is a pattern/of timeless moments.' (V, 21–22)

---

18. As to the Shakespearean element in British wartime propaganda in those years, see the exemplary article by Graham Holdemess, in which he attacks the ideological foundations of the traditional interpretation, exemplified in Tillyard.

But, whereas Eliot's etiolated vision finally succumbs to bland pieties of the moment, the jaunty irreverence of Strindberg's soldier seems ready to join the carnivalesque pageantry of Shakespeare's company: 'Admit me Chorus to this history;/Who prologue-like your humble patience pray.' (*King Henry the Fifth*, Prologue, lines 32–33)

Works Cited

Bakhtin, M. M. *The Dialogic Imagination: Four Essays.* Ed. by Michael Holquist. Trans. by C. Emerson and M. Holquist. Austin: University of Texas Press, 1980.

—. *Speech Genres and Other Late Essays.* Ed. by C. Emerson and Michael Holquist. Trans. by Verne McGee. Austin: University of Texas Press, 1986.

Beachcroft, T. O. *The Modest Art: A Survey of the Short Story in English.* London: Oxford University Press, 1968.

Benjamin, Walter. *Die ursprung des Deutschen trauerspiels.* Frankfurt: Suhrkamp, 1963.

Björck, Staffan. *Löjliga familjerna.* Stockholm: Aldus, 1964.

Böök, Fredrik. *En litteraturvetenskaplig analys av tre noveller ur Svenska öden och äventyr.* Modersmålslärarnas Förening 3. 3rd. ed. Stockholm: Bonniers, 1941.

Brunetière, Ferdinand. *L'évolution des genres dans L'histoire littéraire.* Paris: Librairie Hachette, 1890.

Goethe, J. W. von. *Wilhelm Meisters lehrjahre.* In vol. 16 of *Gesamtausgabe.* Munich: Deutsche Taschenbuch Verein, 1962.

Henderson, Harry B., III. *Versions of the Past—The Historical Imagination in American Fiction.* New York: Oxford University Press, 1974.

Holderness, Graham. 'Agincourt 1944: Readings in the Shakespeare Myth.' In *Popular Fictions: Essays in Literature and History.* Ed. by Peter Humm, Paul Stigant, and Peter Widdowson. London: Methuen, 1986: 173–95.

Holquist, Michael, and Katerina Clark. *Mikhail Bakhtin.* Cambridge, Mass.: Harvard UP, 1984.

Hörnström, Erik. *Anders Odel: En studie i frihetstidens litteratur- och kulturhistoria.* Stockholm: Lundekvistska, 1941.

James, Henry. *Literary Reviews and Essays.* Ed. by Albert Mordell. New York: Grove Press, 1957.

Johnson, Walter. *Strindberg and the Historical Drama.* Seattle: University of Washington Press. 1963.

Lindenberger, Herbert. *The Historical Drama: The Relation of Literature and Reality.* Chicago: University of Chicago Press, 1975.

Lukács, Georg. *Die seele und die formen.* Berlin: Fleischel, 1911.

—. *Die theorie des romans.* 1916. Neuwied: Luchterhand, 1963.

—. *The Historical Novel.* Trans. by H. and S. Mitchell. (Orig., 1937) Boston: Beacon Press, 1963.

—. *Entwicklungsgeschichte des modernen dramas*. 1908. In vol. 15 of *Werke*. Neuwied: Luchterhand, 1981.

—. 'The Heroic Age: From Hebbel to Ibsen.' Trans. by Stanley Mitchell. *Comparative Criticism* 9 (1987): 193–235.

Myrdal, Jan. *Strindberg och Balzac*. Stockholm: Norstedts, 1981.

Nicolovius [Nils Lovén]. *Folklifvet i skytts Härad vid början av 1800-talet*. 3rd ed. Lund: Gleerup, 1908.

Pascal, Roy. *The German Novel*. London: Methuen, 1965.

Poe, Edgar Allan. *Essays and Reviews*. New York: Library of America; Viking, 1984.

Printz-Påhlson, Göran. 'Allegories of Trivialization: Strindberg's View of History.' *Comparative Criticism* 3 (1981): 221–36.

—. 'Det Episka och Diskursiva i Harry Martinsons Poesi.' *Svenska dagbladet* 13 Dec. 1987.

Propp, Vladimir. *La morphologie du conte*. Paris: Gallimard, 1970.

Ricoeur, Paul. *Temps et récit II: La configuration dans le récit de diction*. Paris: Seuil, 1984.

Rivière, Jacques. *Nouvelles études*. Paris: Gallimard, 1947.

Steene, Birgitta. 'Shakespearean Elements in the Historical Plays of Strindberg.' *Comparative Literature* 11.3 (1959): 209–20. Reprinted in Otto Reinert, ed. *Strindberg: A Collection of Critical Essays*. Englewood Cliffs: Prentice Hall, 1971.

Strindberg, August. *Samlade Skrifter*. Vols. 11 and 12 (*Svenska öden och äventyr*), 42 (*Historiska miniatyrer*), 43 (*Hövdingaminnen*), and 38 (*Sagor*) Stockholm: Bonnier, 1913, 1917, 1919, 1916. 55 vols. 1912–20.

—. *Samlade otryckta skrifter*. Ed. W. Carlheim-Gyllensköld. 2 vols. Stockholm: Bonniers, 1918–19.

—. 'The Mysticism of World History.' Trans. by Michael Robinson. *Comparative Criticism* 3 (1981): 237–56.

Szondi, Peter. *Theorie des modernen dramas 1880–1950*. 1965. Frankfurt: Suhrkamp, 1970.

—. 'Friedrich Schlegel's Theory of Poetical Genres.' In *On Textual Understanding and Other Essays*. Trans. by Harry Mendelsohn. Manchester: Manchester University Press, 1986: 75–94.

Tillyard, E. M. W. *Shakespeare's History Plays*. London: Macmillan, 1944.

Törnqvist, Egil. *Strindbergian Drama*. Stockholm/Atlantic Highlands: Aimquist & Wicksell International, 1982.

—. 'Strindbergs Bitext.' *Strindbergiana*. 3 Strindbergssällskapet. Ed. by Ekman, Persson, and Ståhle-Sjönell. Stockholm: Atlantis, 1988: 15–33.

Vernant, Jean-Pierre. 'Le Moment Historique de la Tragédie en Grèce: Quelques Conditions Sociales et Psychologiques.' In vol. 1 of *Mythe et tragédie en Grèce ancienne*. By J.-P. Vernant and P. Vidal-Naquet. Paris: Maspéro, 1972. 11–17. 2 vols. 1972–86.

Part Eight: The Canon of Literary Modernism: A Note on Abstraction in the Poetry of Erik Lindegren

1

In 1943 the Swedish poet Erik Lindegren—at that time still comparatively unknown—published a long essay, in the Swedish journal *Ord och bild* (*Words and Images*), on the poetry of W. H. Auden. It is important not only in that it adds to the bibliography of early Auden criticism and gives an ingenious and sometimes striking interpretation of Auden's poetry and character, mainly based on 'Paid on both Sides' and 'Journal of an Airman' from *The Orators* (1932), but also in view of the light it sheds on Lindegren's own poetics and poetic practice, then in a period of fertile development.

It is known that Auden himself was not very satisfied with 'Journal of an Airman.' In his illuminating preface to *The English Auden*, Edward Mendelson quotes several letters from Auden, who deplores its obscurity and in particular the equivocal nature of its political message. 'It is meant to be a critique of the fascist outlook, but from its reception among some of my contemporaries, and on rereading it myself, I see that it can, most of it, be interpreted as a favorable exposition.' (xv)

Not so Lindegren, who is admirably clear on its political implications and who in addition recognizes the paramount importance of Lawrence for the

96   *Letters of Blood*

psychotherapeutic element running through this work. Auden corroborates this in a letter to a friend: 'In a sense the work is my memorial to Lawrence; i.e., the theme is the failure of the romantic conception of personality.' (xv)

What particularly fascinated Lindegren was what he refers to as Auden's specific perspective, the bird's-eye view: 'Consider this and in our time/As the hawk sees it or the helmeted airman.' (*Collected Poems*, 57)

It is true that the vertical is Auden's favored dimension and that there are many bird images in his poetry; but the Auden who admits, in the 'Letter to Byron,' that his overriding desire as a child had been to become a mining engineer, is always more likely to let the vertical get its proper extension in some gloomy subterranean world. Even when he assumes the persona of a bird, as the seagull in the humorously auto-analytical 'The Month was April,' it is not the soaring so much as the ultimate bringing down of the bird that interests him.

When Lindegren writes: 'The hawk and the airman are among the constant symbols with Auden, the concentrated, detailed observation of the quarry and the extended, always varying panorama regularly recur' (123), it may be partially true as description of Auden but is even more a description of an ever present theme in Lindegren's own poetry, at this time mostly still to be written. 'Old Red Indian' and 'Zero Point' are two splendid instances. An even more apt illustration is found in 'Icarus' (Auden's Icarus poem, 'Museé des Beaux Arts,' had previously been translated by Ekelöf):

> His memories of the labyrinth go numb with sleep.
>
> The single memory: how the calls and the confusion rose
>
> until at last they swung him up from the earth.
>
> And how all cleavings which have cried out always
>
> for their bridges in his breast
>
> slowly shut like eyelids,
>
> and how the birds swept past like shuttles, like arrows,
>
> and finally the last lark brushing his hand,
>
> falling like song.
>
> Then : the winds' labyrinth, with its blind bulls,
>
> cacophonous lights and inclines,

with its dizzying breath which he through arduous
struggle learned how to parry,
until it rose again, his vision and his flight.

Now he is rising alone, in a sky without clouds,
in a space empty of birds in the din of the aircraft...
rising toward a clearer and clearer sun,
turning gradually cooler, turning cold,
and upward towards the spring of his blood, soul's cataract:
a prisoner in a whistling lift,
a seabubble's journey toward the looming magnetic air:
and the vortex of signs, born of the springtide, raging of azure,
crumbling walls, and drunkenly the call of the other side:
Reality fallen
    Without reality born!
(translation by John Matthias and Göran Printz-Påhlson)

The poem is in many ways a reversal of Auden's Icarus poem (or any conventional treatment of the Icarus theme). While Auden is content to follow the Brueghel painting in noticing the surroundings of the fall more than the fall itself, and in particular the indifference of the surroundings, Lindegren boldly concentrates on the protagonist. Auden's language is resolutely discursive and expository:

> ...some untidy spot
> Where the dogs go on with their doggy life and the torturer's horse
> Scratches its innocent behind on a tree. (*Collected Poems*, 179)

Although 'the aged' were 'passionately waiting for the miraculous birth' the fall is for the busy ploughman 'not an important failure.' Life goes on, Auden seems to be saying; even when tragedy occurs 'someone else is eating or opening a window or just walking dully along.' (179)

This sapient moralizing is not for Lindegren. The indifference in his poem is not a property of the surroundings but the exalted ataraxia of the protagonist himself. The very fall is in defiance of the law of gravity: it is a *fall upwards,* toward empty space, leaving the contingent things of this world almost contemptuously behind. 'The miraculous birth,' tentatively dismissed by Auden, here becomes a reality, a bursting of the fetal membrane of the sky, even if the reality born is, although triumphantly proclaimed, syntactically ambiguous (the last line of the poem in the Swedish original contains an untranslatable syntactic ambiguity). The heroic identification of protagonist and poet is never in doubt in the Lindegren poem.

In the aforementioned essay, Lindegren says about the airman: 'It is not unimportant to remember that his genealogy goes back to Icarus, the symbol of the tragedy of setting one's goal too high, or that the mythical aura surrounding him may derive ultimately from popular ideas of the nature of epilepsy.' (125) Epilepsy is, of course, the falling disease (in Swedish, *fallandesjuka*) and altogether this seems to be more a prophetic gloss on the future poem of his own than on Auden's text. One has no difficulty in recognizing this protagonist as the true hero of modernism; Walter Benjamin presented him admirably in relation to the grandeur and squalor of Paris in the Second Empire and called him Baudelaire. 'The hero is the true subject of modernism. In other words it takes a heroic constitution to live modernism.' (74)

The hero is dandy, *flâneur,* suicide, sufferer, social outcast, diseased, in his pursuit of the absolute. Like Baudelaire's Icarus he has broken his arms in trying to embrace the clouds. This is indeed a far cry from Auden's innocent Icarus, let alone from his crafty airman.

It seems probable that Auden's poem exerted some influence on the rhythm and organization of Lindegren's 'Icarus.' But the real sources of inspiration for the poem have to be sought in other quarters, in a tradition of modernist exemplars that are by and large alien to Anglo-American poetry.

When Icarus-the-Poet soars to greater and greater heights, shedding gradually the encumbrances of things, his flight or fall may be meant to illustrate the pursuit of a pure language or an absolute diction. Clearly, the poem lends itself willingly to an allegorical interpretation on even a merely personal and mundane level. There is the distinct possibility that it can be read as a description of Lindegren's own poetic development.

2

There is perhaps a sense in which it is altogether useless to talk about *the* 'canon of modernism' or even about 'canons of modernism.' 'Modernism' or its *etymon* 'modernity' is clearly, historically and logically, opposed to the formation of the models or measuring rods that infuse the classical mode with rigor and stability. 'Canon formation in literature must always proceed to a selection of classics,' says E. R. Curtius, quoted with approval by Harold Bloom, who writes on canon-formation in relation to his own theory of revisionism: '"Canon" as a word goes back to a Greek word for a measuring rule, which in Latin acquired the additional meaning of "model." Canon-formation or canonization is a richly suggestive word for a process of classic formation in poetic tradition, because it associates notions of music and of standards.' (*Poetry and Repression* 29) Bloom goes on to consider the relationship between religious and secular canon-formation with the hardly surprising result that secular canon-formation is more amenable to 'intruders of genius,' and thus to revisionism. Bloom's now well-known essay, 'The Primal Scene of Instruction' in *A Map of Misreading,* does not, however, seem particularly useful in dealing with either the classical or the modernist mode, owing to his dependence on the Freudian model of nuclear family relations. This may be obscured by his customary brilliance of analysis in writing on some modern-era poets, but for the Anglo-American poetry he is confining himself to almost exclusively, the romantic and historicist mode reigns supreme. 'Modernism' is as militantly anti-historical as it is anti-classical: what is 'modern' is dependent on what models offer themselves for emulation *today*, not at any past or future *illud tempus.*

The dilemma of the modernist is that he will invariably find that this has always been the case. 'When they assert their own modernity, they are bound to discover their dependence on similar assertions made by their literary predecessors; their claim to being a new beginning turns out to be the repetition of a claim that has always already been made.' (de Man, 161) So the only course open to the modernists is to set out on a quest for their lost traditions, their forgotten ancestors. In modernism it is not the oedipal Primal Scene of Instruction sketched by Bloom which is invoked; the modernist is not a parricide because he is already an orphan: the mythic figure of his choice must rather be Telemachos, looking for a lost father. Joyce was, of course, very much aware of this when he had his hero of modernism, his Icarus-figure, address the old craftsman and inventor in the well-known lines from the end of *A Portrait of the Artist as a Young Man:* 'Old father, old artificer, stand me now and ever in good stead.' (253) He could then send Stephen Dedalus on a quest for a paternal substitute, donning the disguise of Telemachos, in *Ulysses.*

If the modernist *chef-d'oeuvre* tends in this way to include an allegorical account of the conditions of its own creation, it will also more and more be inviting readings of a flat and abstract character. Lindegren's poem has been read as an allegory of the poetic development of its author (see my own account in *Solen i spegeln* [*The Sun in the Mirror*] 155).

Erik Lindegren did not leave a voluminous poetic *oeuvre* behind him. After a conventional first book of poetry, *Postum ungdom* (*Posthumous Youth*, 1935), he produced his first major opus, *mannen utan väg* (*the man without a way*), a rigidly formalized collection of forty 'broken sonnets,' in a highly personal surrealist style, which has been one of the most influential and normative works in Scandinavian modernism. It was privately printed, in the austere publishing climate of the war years, in 1942. In 1945 it was re-issued commercially and had subsequently an enormous impact in Sweden on the then prevalent style of the forties and the concomitant critical debate on modernism in which Lindegren took part as an eloquent defender of modernism of the more traditional kind. In 1947 he published *Sviter* (*Suites*) in a more lavish and sensuous surrealist manner, which book proved to be, if possible, even more seductive than the previous austerity. A third major collection, *Vinteroffer* (*Winter Sacrifice* 1954) exhibited a more subdued and reflective mood developing alongside a growing desperation. Both these volumes are, in true modernist fashion, strewn with analogies and parallels with music and the fine arts. For the remainder of his life he wrote some highly praised opera libretti, mainly in collaboration with the composer Karl Birger Blomdahl. He died in 1968. His influence and reputation, although to some extent eclipsed by his friend and near contemporary Gunnar Ekelöf's uncommonly fertile poetic flowering in the late fifties and the sixties, remains strong in Sweden. Lindegren was also a proficient translator, from several languages, of Faulkner, Rilke, St John Perse, and of modern French poetry in general.

It is tempting to read 'Icarus'—which is the introductory poem to the last volume—as a poetic summary of his momentous and short career. The labyrinth can be read as referring to the labyrinthine labours of *mannen utan väg*, the contortionist encompassing of experience in maze-like patterns. 'The wind's labyrinth' is then clearly related to *Suites* with 'its dizzying breath,' the transports of sensuous experience, gradually shedding its objects. And the remaining flight towards a cooling sun associates with the wintry landscapes of the last volume a voice like icicles faintly dripping under a bleak sky. No more poetry can be conceived after the rebirth, which represents the final silence towards which all poetry strives. The poem is thus read as a history of its own language, fugitive of its content.

This represents a paradigm familiar from at least one mainstream of continental modernism (French and German) that can be associated with a line from Hölderlin to Baudelaire, to Mallarmé, to Rilke, to Celan. These are indeed the ancestors claimed by Lindegren in translations and essays (which also led him, mistakenly, to make the same claims for Auden's true ancestors).

3

In 1942, Lindegren claimed another, somewhat more surprising ancestor in an essay on Ibsen's *Brand,* also collected in *Tangenter*. This is indeed another 'vertical' hero, but Lindegren is not interested in psychological analysis. Instead he praises its classical virtues of abstract clarity and, following a hint from Ibsen, syllogistic structure, and says, very characteristically: 'The Idea is put forward in such an objective way that it becomes form rather than content, that it is chilled through by the elevated meaninglessness which for many seems to be immanent in the great shaping energies of history.' (105) The wording is perhaps more revealing of Lindergren's own method than of Ibsen's. He further enlarges on the same theme: 'Central to the nature of objectivity is also the fact that it conceals the truth about the individual. In any case, it transposes truth to an esoteric level. Truth is not to be seen, as little as the works of a watch.' (105)

Abstract, objective: the qualities referred to are more easily assimilated in a classicist poetic than in a modernist one. The amphibological structure of modernism is such, however, that it most readily tends to direct its canon-formation towards models of the classicist mould. The destruction of the past that is a commonplace strategy in modernism since Nietzsche makes it necessary to create a canon outside history: the precursors in time are not so much instructors or mentors as problems of assimilation. For that purpose they have to be deprived of all contingent qualities, to be reduced to abstract formulae applicable to all times and all places. This is in sharp contrast to romanticism, which sees history as an organic succession, a handing down of skills through generations. One could be tempted to say, reductively, that modernism equals romanticism minus its historicism, classicism minus its primitivism.

To put a hasty end to this farrago of -isms, let us be reminded by Walter Benjamin, sometimes so surprisingly down to earth, that this attitude of the modernist is to a large extent created by the 'polemical situation.' (82) This is certainly applicable to Lindegren who attained his status as modernist hero in a harsh polemical climate. It is, in such a situation, of paramount importance to select your right teammates. And that is what canon-formation in modernist practice ultimately comes down to.

The question of abstraction, of objectivity, is no doubt, as almost everything else, in the last analysis a question of language. Hegel asked himself *'Wer denkt abstrakt?'* ('Who Thinks Abstractly?') and came up with an answer that discredited abstract thinking outside the sciences for a long time to come. Modern poetry of the romantic persuasion has been involved in a drawn-out campaign against abstraction, taking its arsenal from various modern, not always correctly understood, philosophies of language. It is good to be reminded, in the book *The Situation of Poetry* by Robert Pinsky, that words are not to be confused with things and that a word is always an abstraction in relation to its referent. (5) Perhaps somewhat misleadingly, he relates the common mistake of thinking otherwise to the conflict between realism and nominalism, a conflict that he sees as a crucial area of dispute in most recent poetry.

Even leaving aside the old question of the arbitrariness of the relation of words to things, familiar from a long tradition of contention, from *Cratylus* to Saussure, we may notice that any possible realist theory of language has been severely undercut by the largely nominalist, positivist and pragmatic accounts of language acquisition of the last hundred years. In their insistence on making usage and naming the basics of linguistic understanding and in their neglect of formal principles, these also favor the position that language is in essence a system of designation of things rather than ideas, of individuals rather than universals, and that the abstractions of language are somehow secondary and supererogatory to its real core of concrete semantics. The reductive and primitivist notions of this kind have been seriously challenged from various most dissimilar positions in more recent years.

Even the simplest first order logic operations involve a great deal of abstraction, and as Bruno Snell very convincingly pointed out in relation to the formation of the Greek mind, even the naming of primitive objects requires some degree of comparison and classification. (191)

Attacks launched against 'vapid generalities' or 'empty abstractions,' whether these occur in poetry or in any other context, are, of course, always valuable, but they are essentially a concern of a legitimate demand for specified information and in no way linked to abstraction as a principle of language. It is not possible to say that a dog is a more abstract animal than, say, an Irish setter, nor is the word 'dog' in any significant way either abstract or concrete (one can regard it as either a token or a type).

In the case of poetry this whole matter has been obscured by the general confusion about what a poem refers to. Can it possibly be linked to reality in some way that insures it against drifting to some misty land of generalities? T. E. Hulme and the imagists believed that this could and should be done through some undefined property of language that constituted an image as 'an intellectual and emotional complex in an instant of time.' (see Pound 336–37)

Imagism is perhaps only an extension of the *Pictura ut poesis* doctrine in modern terms (it is to be noted that the famous *Imagines* of Philostratos may have given rise to the nineteenth-century prose poem, through Goethe's admirable translations, but, far from being imagist 'instants of time,' they are just descriptions of pictures, real or imaginary, and not to be mistaken for substitutes of these pictures).

Representations—whether in words or in pictures, whether of concrete objects or of abstract concepts—always involve abstractions, and in order to be representational a work of art has to be selective. The crucial question comes when a work of art is representational of a representation, when it is two steps removed from what was originally represented. This one can call, in accordance with the usage of Walter Benjamin in particular, *allegory*. Representation as abstraction, in its turn, involves interchangeability.

Lindegren shows himself to be very well aware of the nature of these principles when he stresses the *timelessness* of the representative work of art, in his essay on *Brand*. The warning against historical contingencies should be taken seriously. In particular as regards *mannen utan väg* it has been very tempting to offer specific interpretations or critical translations of its surrealist imagery. The critic Bengt Holmqvist ingeniously specified the meaning of a famous line of the poem (from Sonnet xxvi):[26] 'and the dismal flight of fate in the feathered garb of somersault.' (in Franzén 38) This line, according to Holmqvist, could be 'translated' as referring to the flight of von Ribbentrop, then foreign secretary for Germany, to Moscow in August 1939. No doubt many of the lines of the poem could be translated in a similarly reckless way into the world events of these dramatic years. This does not make the poem a history of World War II.

Paul de Man, in the 'Lyric and Modernity' section of *Blindness and Insight*, has an unusually subtle piece of argumentation in which he attacks the view expressed by Hans Robert Jauss and his colleagues and pupils that modernism can be regarded as a movement in history, with a beginning and a (possible) end. He is particularly concerned with an interpretation of Mallarmé's 'Tombeau de Verlaine' by the German critic Karlheinz Stierle. He quotes from this: 'For Mallarmé the concrete image no longer leads to a clearer vision.' If one considers what makes the object of the poem unreal, one is bound to realize that it is 'a poem of allegorical reification' [*Vergegenständlichung*]. This is in contrast to traditional allegory, the function of which was 'to make the meaning stand out more vividly.' (182)

Although agreeing with Stierle about the importance of allegory (here taken in the sense championed by Walter Benjamin), as opposed to the merely representational, de Man maintains quite convincingly that there is no fixed point where representation ends and allegory takes over: 'Up to a very advanced point, not reached in this poem and perhaps never reached at all, Mallarmé remains a representational poet as he remains in fact a poet of the self, however impersonal...' (182) From what was said above about representation one can draw the conclusion that all the possible readings of the poem exist simultaneously. The allegorical reading does not follow on the representational, or on any other reading. They are interchangeable, but not in an ordered sequence as in the solution of a riddle.

The French critic Georges Périlleux has, in an article bravely and successfully written in Swedish, given a detailed analysis of the rhetorical tropes used in *mannen utan väg* (see Bolckmans). The highly intricate and artificial rhetorical patterns revealed—Périlleux adapts the methods of analysis of *Rhétorique générale* by the semioticians of 'Groupe μ'—point to the rigidly formal organization of the work. But rhetoric in this sense—as a set of linguistic or paralinguistic rules—is, as Harold Bloom has reminded us in *Wallace Stevens: The Poems of our Climate*, defiantly anti-historical. (375) This is rhetoric which has renounced all pedagogical intent, thus keeping company with an allegory which has renounced all representational intent.

Lindegren is clearly realizing this in his frequently invited parallels between his poetry and music or mathematics. 'Poetry as higher calculus' is the formula given in his polemical apologia 'Tal i Egen Sak,' reprinted *Tangenter*. Twenty years ago I suggested—following a hint from William Empson's treatment of George Herbert in *Seven Types of Ambiguity*—that the mathematical analogy could be more than vaguely useful for this kind of poetry, as the elements seem to be freely interchangeable while the structure remains the same (see *Solen i spegeln* [*The Sun in the Mirror*], 162). From his point of view, and from the fact that, in contrast to traditional allegory, the readings or transformations are unordered, it follows that no reading can be regarded as in any way privileged. Is there any sense in calling the reading of the political content in the Lindegren poem representational and the personal reading allegorical, and not vice versa? The significance of the allegory is ultimately that it signifies nothing.

How is this dilemma to be resolved? Lindegren seems to be going even further in some poems in *Vinteroffer* where no hints of representation or allegory remain, and the rhetorical devices seem to provide merely a mechanical inspiration:

> *Meditation*
>
> Feel the throb of spring in the glade of simple hearts
> (in aliens' oblivion we live and we die)
> Mark our shadow there beneath the arch of night
> (for what we never uttered we remember best)
>
> See the desert tracks which evanesce like roses
> (the wild is not astray, but it is fugitive)
> Remember trees like dogs leashed tight in dreams
> (domesticity's not home, but it is ill)
>
> ['Cover with your glance the dying mayfly's gleam
> (like scythes the grass is waving on our grave)
> Contain the arch of spring, and touch the desert trees
> (and yet we all are like the grass)']
> (translated by John Matthias and Göran Printz-Påhlson)

This poem seems to be moving its symbols at random within a confined space where no references to public or personal experiences are possible. It could evidently go on forever. Maybe it is just the anticipated exhaustion of the poet, in realizing that it *could* go on forever, that makes him put an end to it at this early stage.

4

The canon-formation of literary modernism is in quite a profound sense an act of recognition, not of affinities but of identity of content. If Harold Bloom has for our time given a romantic interpretation of a literary theory of succession in saying that the meaning of a poem is always another poem, one is perhaps justified in offering a rival modernist theory of discontinuity in saying that all modernist poems have the same meaning, which the poets try to approximate in stating its essential inaccessibility. As this inaccessibility *is* the meaning of the modernist poem, they have, in the vein of classical paradox, quite literally managed both to express the meaning and fail to do so. The only possible remaining step must be silence.

There is no evidence that when translating Lindegren's poetry Auden approached it with anything but suspicion and misgiving. The vatic stance, the orphic mysticism, the rhetoric of paradox: this is a tradition of modernism he could not make his own. Only in the attraction to the renunciation of poetry could these two poets meet. Auden's revolt against poetry as a high vocation was clear already in his early acceptance of a tradition of light verse, of Carroll, Lear, Chesterton, Belloc, Kipling, as his true ancestry. Perhaps it could be said that he had renounced serious poetry for verse by the time of, say, *The Age of Anxiety*. For Lindegren, adhering to a more exacting canon, there was only one way to go, to silence. The moving last lines of *Winter Sacrifice* give his version of the modernist question:

> Why blow on the candle of life
>
> with all this talk
>
> of life or death…

Works Cited

Auden, W.H. *The English Auden: Poems, Essays and Dramatic Writing 1927–1939*. Ed. by Edward Mendelson. London: Faber, 1977.

Auden, W.H. *Collected Poems*. Ed. by Edward Mendelson. New York: Modern Library, 2007.

Benjamin, Walter. *Charles Baudelaire: A Lyric Poet in the Era of High Capitalism*. London: Verso, 1973.

Bloom, Harold. *Poetry and Repression: Revisionism from Blake to Stevens*. New Haven: Yale University Press, 1976.

—. *Wallace Stevens: The Poems of Our Climate*. Ithaca, New York: Cornell University Press, 1980.

Bolckmans, Alex, ed. *Literature and Reality: Creatio versus Mimesis*. Ghent: Scandinavian Institute, 1977.

Franzén, Lars-Olof, ed. *40-Talsförfattare*. Stockholm: Aldus, 1965.

Joyce, James. *A Portrait of the Artist as a Young Man*. New York: Viking, 1977.

Lindegren, Erik. *Tangenter*. Stockholm: Bonniers, 1974.

Man, Paul de. *Blindness and Insight: Essays in the Rhetoric of Contemporary Criticism*. Minneapolis: University of Minnesota Press, 1983.

Pinsky, Robert. *The Situation of Poetry*. Princeton: Princeton University Press, 1976.

Pound, Ezra. *Make it New*. London: Faber, 1934.

Printz-Påhlson, Göran. *Solen i spegeln*. Stockholm: Bonniers, 1958.

Snell, Bruno. *The Discovery of the Mind*. New York: Dover, 1982.

Part Nine: The Tradition of Contemporary Swedish Poetry

1

'…and what are poets for in a destitute time?' was a question asked by Hölderlin in a famous elegy, a question which prompted one of Heidegger's most penetrating late essays. *Wozu Dichter* ['why poetry?'] is a question of perennial importance. 'What are poets for in an affluent land?' might be suggested as a possible emendation, perhaps more pertinent to our times and our culture, and in particular to a country like Sweden which has for many years suffered from a reputation (albeit largely unearned) for almost inhuman levels of social efficiency. It is somehow easier to accept that good poetry should arise from political upheaval and turbulence or from material privation than from the secure contentment of superb social engineering.

It is nevertheless a commonplace of much longer standing that the most durable tradition of Swedish literature has been a predominantly lyrical one, and that consequently the subtleties of rhythm and imagery inherent in the genius of poetry have fared less well in translation than, let us say, the subtleties of thought and observation illuminating the high points of the literatures of the other Scandinavian countries—in Kierkegaard or Ibsen, for instance. This may come as a surprise to the casual observer who has been exposed in the news media to countless tales of the pragmatic and commonsensical nature of the Swedes.

Whatever level of legitimacy one is willing to grant to national characteristics—and their unreliability is notorious—it is true that the conflict in the tradition of Swedish poetry between the practical and mundane on the one hand and the mystical and rhetorical on the other is as old as it is real—even for the poetry of the last twenty-five years. One is probably justified in tracing its origin back to the eighteenth century, to the paradoxical fusion of enlightenment, rationalism and otherworldly speculation in the religious genius of Emanuel Swedenborg and of empirical scientific observation and restless seeking after the divine order in the taxonomic genius of Linnaeus. The highest attainments in Swedish poetry—by which I do not mean only what is recognized formally as poetry—have always in some sense been achieved through such a fusion, in the romantic poetry of E. J. Stagnelius and C. J. L. Almqvist, in Strindberg or Gustaf Fröding and, in our century, in the poetry of Vilhelm Ekelund, Birger Sjöberg, Gunnar Ekelöf and Erik Lindegren. One must not forget that, in the highest poetic triumphs of all these somehow broken or divided geniuses, there is something paradoxical and perhaps ultimately self-defeating which is very different from the unrelenting logic inherent in the intellectual development of Kierkegaard or Ibsen.

Accepting this fusion as the significant emblem of the genius of Swedish poetry—the mystic and the bureaucrat, the efficient engineers of images of transcendental dejection (internationally fashionable examples of figures cast in this mould are not uncommon: Dag Hammarskjöld and Ingmar Bergman come immediately to mind)—we must remember that the most prominent exponents of its tradition have been its victims rather than its exploiters. The relative poverty of this Swedish tradition merely exhibits an over-determined case; it is as much a result of contradictory impulses within itself, often causing irreparable damage to the cohesive powers of the mind or ego, as it is a reflection of the long economic indigence of the country. Hence also the frequent accusations levelled against Swedish literature (and art and film) for its indiscriminate predilections for gloom, madness and suicide. These result from the Swedish writer's incomplete projection onto a problematic scene of international modernism, and are not to any noticeable degree typical of his image seen from a Swedish viewpoint. There he appears rather to be defending sanity and 'realism' against the onslaught of a world gone mad. Hence also the often-deplored suspiciousness in Sweden of those writers and artists who all too easily adapt themselves to the consumer demands of international art and culture. Quite misleadingly, this is often taken, at best, for insular provincialism, and, at worst, for plain old-fashioned envy (known idiomatically as the 'Royal Swedish disease').

It is no doubt with a genuine feeling of relief that the critic Lars Bäckström remarks on the 'lucky' fact that the Swedes at the moment 'do not yet have an *author* who is so exceedingly 'multinationally' well-adapted and trivially brilliant as Ingmar Bergman appears to be in his films.' The mood of inward-looking self-sufficiency in this quotation may in its extreme wording be a fairly recent sign of disillusionment with the world cultural market, but it is still compatible with tendencies that have existed for a long time. In any case, it is a long cry from the avowed intentions of Strindberg to launch a 'conquest of Paris' and, from that vantage point, of world literature.

2

'Modern'—'contemporary': the choice of terms is not exclusively a question of temporal sequence. Modern poetry and its derivative 'modernist' poetry have been with us since at least the latter half of the last century. In spite of the relatively venerable antiquity of modernism in its worldwide context, the phenomenon as a consolidated mode of experience or style is of fairly recent appearance in Sweden. Modernism on a broad basis came to that country, together with peace, prosperity, existentialism and the incipient cold war, just as 'heresy, hops and beer' to England in the old jingle, in 'the very same year.' This belated arrival of modernism is of the utmost importance for the formation of the Swedish poetry that we now regard as 'contemporary.' The 'modernist breakthrough'—in contrast to Brandes's 'modern breakthrough' in the 1870s and the 1880s—was an intensely compressed cultural event, taking place during a few years after World War II, in a period of auspicious publishing policies and economic optimism. Its coinciding with the social upheaval caused by the Social-Democratic reconstruction of Swedish society gave it a heroic aura and almost official sanction. Modernism became *the* language of poetry and literature: the ties with traditional forms and values were severed in a much more effective way than in countries where modernism had been a continuous process rather than an event.

This may account for some of the peculiar, and to some observers unattractive, aspects of contemporary Swedish poetry. As modernism proved to be not so much a mode of experience as simply a temporal event, soon exhausted and remaining only as a paradigm of bravery and moral fortitude, so it had to be replaced by strategies, often much more ephemeral, borrowed from outside the indigenous traditions. Shifting and fashionable attitudinizing, journalistic glibness and media-oriented trendiness have an undeniable presence in post-war Swedish poetry. 'Modernism' is always in danger of being replaced by 'modernity,' and, as Paul de Man has shrewdly reminded us, it may be that literature (as a self-reflecting activity) and modernity are, in fact, incompatible concepts.

3

Even a reader who has some previous acquaintance with Swedish poetry may have difficulty in establishing points of reference in the flux of ideas and events that constitute its more recent history. The literary scene has been extremely diversified but at the same time more vulnerable to external influences than would be the case in a less self-conscious cultural environment. (One noticeable characteristic of the Swedish writer in recent years has been his professionalism: the organizational practice of the Swedish Writers' Union (*Författarförbundet*) has served as a model for similar activities in other countries.)

During the years from 1950 to 1980, one can discern at least two important shifts in the intellectual awareness of the Swedish poet. The opening up of the world that occurred with the end of the war, gaining increasing impetus during the affluent fifties, ultimately resulted in a disillusion with the very forces that had created it. The more intimate contact with other — and in particular non-European — cultures, facilitated by the increased opportunities for travel and by the ever-growing flow of information in the sophisticated reporting of foreign affairs in Swedish newspapers (tendencies which existed elsewhere in the fifties and sixties, but gained importance earlier in Sweden) established the Swedish author in an often unenviable role as a self-appointed intermediary or spokesman for the Third World. The global conscience of a small and still comparatively isolated nation may easily incur the scorn of countries which have had longer-lasting relations with the more remote parts of the world and may lay it open to accusations of smugness and holier-than-thou moralizing. It cannot be denied that breast-beating and exhibitionist self-lacerations have played their part in some of these manifestations. On the other hand, it created the opportunity not only for some brilliant journalism and painstaking documentaries, but also opened domains of poetry that could have been reached in no other way. Spanish, Latin-American and Francophone African poetry were introduced into Sweden and had an influence on Swedish poetry long before their impact was felt in America and England: the poems of Ingemar Leckius and, to some extent, Tomas Tranströmer bear witness to this.

The Vietnam war and what was known in Sweden as the FNL movement (also known by the more derogatory term 'Vietcong') had, I believe, a deeper impact on intellectual life in Sweden than in some countries more obviously concerned with the war itself. The development of an international political consciousness seemed at the time at least to be a mass movement. The supreme example of the appeal to political conscience is found in Göran Sonnevi's moving and subtle poetry that has had—considering its pure and uncompromising nature—an amazingly large following. His poem on the war in Vietnam created almost overnight a demand for this kind of poetry that has hardly diminished even though the situation has altered. His book of poetry, *Det omöjliga* ('The Impossible,' 1976) which runs to an impressive 431 pages, was chosen as Book of the Month and was printed in an initial edition of 10,000 copies.

The main formal influences of the militancy of the FNL-years are not, however, found in poetry as strongly as in the activities of small independent theatre groups like *Pistolteatern* and many others, and in the hybrids of traditional fighting songs and rock lyrics among various left-wing splinter groups. The major shift of emphasis came with the 1969–70 LKAB miners strike. Interest turned, almost imperceptibly at first, from global injustices to the equally real but more closely observed shortcomings of the capitalist system in the nominally socialist Sweden. Social, environmental and ecological issues in politics have for a long time been a matter of concern to many Swedes. The test case for this second phase of political consciousness in Sweden came during the 1976 elections when the industrial use of nuclear power was one of the most important election issues. Although it apparently resulted in a victory for the abolitionists, die struggle still goes on. As a political movement this 'ecosophical' awareness is riddled with contradictions and internal antagonism: obviously, it is difficult to reconcile the demands for devolution of environmentally detrimental energy sources with equally legitimate demands for full employment.

If this new awareness still seems to be struggling with its political persona, it has certainly proved to be very fertile in poetry. Göran Sonnevi again provided what seems to be the *locus classicus* of the political struggle against nuclear power in his poem 'A mother stands in front...' The more broadly 'ecosophical' issues are found especially in Gösta Friberg's thoughtful and beautifully modulated poetry, for example in the global and interplanetary scenery of 'The Growing.' It is a tendency which is at the time of this writing, 1980, fast gaining in importance.

Part Ten: Kierkegaard the Poet

1

One of the disadvantages with the present-day critical and philosophical climate, fertile and exciting as it undoubtedly is, is not so much the apocalyptic tone that, for instance, Jacques Derrida has observed, but even more a predilection for recursiveness, a certain tendency to retrograde movement, tactical manoeuvres, which set their sight on goals further and further back, nearer to the origins of things and ideas. Although such a delaying strategy is hardly foreign to Kierkegaard's own method, I shall try to start by following hints from Kierkegaard's own practice and begin *in medias res*, with the small but substantial philosophical crumbs that Kierkegaard sprinkled fairly evenly over his entire work. The fragment (which is the standard translation of Kierkegaard's *'smuler'*) was an aesthetic category in its own right for the age of Romanticism, since it had been used by Friedrich Schlegel in his famous *Lycäum* and *Athenäum* fragments at the tail end of the eighteenth century. If one tries to follow the conceptual ramifications of Kierkegaard's thought in any straightforward systematic way, one is very soon overwhelmed by the feeling that one is—perhaps on purpose—being led astray, or lured into *cul-de-sacs*. It's all a little like the haunted house in a contemporary American Gothic novel, which had been built in such a way that every door closed itself after a short while, and the intrepid explorers and psychic researchers would find themselves in a room with a multitude of doors and no recollection of which one they had used to get in.

2

As far as we know, Kierkegaard was never a poet in the sense that he scribbled verses. He quotes poetry now and then, in particular in the letters to Regine Olsen, his young fiancée, the relationship with whom is so crucial for his work, but it is always others peoples' poetry. Even when he is at his most lyrical and high-flown, as indeed in these letters, there is no indication that he wants to abandon prose for the formal strictness of poetry. From the very beginning, there is in the copious writings in his diaries and journals a reliance on prose, which in itself speaks of strong suspicions of the particular strictures of poetic expression. On the other hand we have always in his prose—in the style, in the care he takes with each word, in the sensuous and concrete presentation—an *intimation* of poetry, if not a critique of the poetic values prevalent in his day and age (that is, the poetry of Romanticism). The activity he finds himself engaged in is, characteristically, *at digte*, to create poetry: the *Digter* or poet being the representative of the creative genius who, according to Kierkegaard, or rather his first pseudonymous *alter ego* A. in *Either/Or*, creates beauty out of his own suffering. The best-known definition of the poet in the whole *oeuvre* is no doubt the passage in *Either/Or* that is sometimes known as 'The Victims of Phalaris':

> What is a poet? An unhappy man who in his heart harbors a deep anguish, but whose lips are so fashioned that the moans and cries which pass over them are transformed into ravishing music. His fate is like that of the unfortunate victims whom the tyrant Phalaris imprisoned in a brazen bull, and slowly tortured over a steady fire; their cries could not reach the tyrant's ears so as to strike terror into his heart; when they reached his ears they sounded like sweet music. And men crowd about the poet and say to him, 'Sing for us soon again'—which is as much as to say, 'May new sufferings torment your soul, but may your lips be fashioned as before; for the cries would only distress us, but the music, the music, is deligthful.' And the critics come forward and say, 'That is perfectly done—just as it should be, according to the rules of aesthetics.' Now it is understood that a critic resembles a poet to a hair; he only lacks the anguish in his heart and the music upon his lips. I tell you, I would rather be a swineherd, understood by the swine, than a poet understood by men. (43)

We here have a typical Kierkegaardian nuclear myth, or parable (both terms have been used but are to a large extent inadequate) where the partial identification of the real-life author with his pseudonymous voice is briefly brandished only to be teasingly withdrawn or sheathed. It is not so much a question of separating the 'man who suffers' from 'the mind which creates,' as it was for Eliot (31), as it is of disavowing any formal acknowledgement of identity, and so casting suspicion on the obvious interpretaton before it is attempted. In the text, the *caveats*, or warnings, far outnumber the *placets*, or go-ahead signs. If Kierkegaard's anonymous role here is to be the poet, he is precluded, by the harsh rules of expression aesthetics, from any say on how the message is organized. On the other hand, if his role is to be, or simulate, the critic, he is denied both the suffering and the glory. But to the extent that the allegory is invited (and being a swineherd understood by swine may be a minimalist hermeneutic inducement not to be sneered at) it finds itself circumscribed by various rhetorical devices of simple or double ironies. Being a swineherd *mis*understood by swine is perhaps how Kierkegaard fantasised about his own role in his most desperate circumstances. As a paradigm for indirect communication (*den indirekte Meddelelse*), 'The Victims of Phalaris' is as treacherous as any text by Kierkegaard.

Moreover, the very term 'poet' is in itself treacherous, as it clearly has a wider span in English than in Danish, where a distinction between *Poet* and *Digter* is not only feasible but necessary. Kierkegaard's preferred term, when treating his own work, whether pseudonymous or authorized, was *author*: *Forfatter*, and the generic term for his literary production, introduced in a short article published in 1851, and used again in its longer version in 1859, after his death, is *Forfatter-Virksomhed*, 'Authorial Activity.' In this context, Kierkegaard makes the distinction between the pseudonymous works and the authorized works and argues, with great force and ingenuity as always, that the duplicity is a willed duplicity and that the aesthetic works are written, pseudonymously, with one purpose only, to enhance and underpin the religious message, or *kerygma*, directly expressed in the (authorized) religious works. With due reliance on indirect communication, *all* the works are edifying discourses ('*opbyggelige taler*').

3

Kierkegaard's entire work, written in great haste between 1838 and 1855, historically belongs to the end period of the Danish Golden Age, and cannot be properly understood outside this context. It was a period of unmatched creativity and the literary and cultural life in Copenhagen was at its peak. Johan Ludvig Heiberg, the philosophical playwright, Grundtvig, the religious reformer, Oersted the scientist, Hans Christian Andersen (whom Kierkegaard loathed), and many other, now forgotten, names gave a rare glow to the intellectual atmosphere, and Kierkegaard moved, with comfort, wit and intelligence, in this *milieu*. His every text is steeped in references to the contemporary scene, where German Romanticism permeated the air. Hegelianism and other brands of philosophy spiced the conversations and cultural feuds. Still, his work—and in this we are forced to accept his own insistence on reading the entire work as one *oeuvre*—has had, after an incipient period of neglect, an enormous appeal far outside both Denmark and Scandinavia. This appeal is philosophically, theologically and, I would say, poetically, far greater than that of any other Scandinavian author, with the possible exceptions of two Swedish geniuses of the previous century, Linnaeus and Swedenborg. How can this be? To what genre can we assign his writings in this international perspective? He despised theology, he despaired of systematic philosophy, and he took every opportunity to disclaim the poetic existence. What can be the appeal for the reader who is ignorant of the finer points of Hegel's logic, who does not claim to know Grundtvig, for whom H.C. Andersen is just a name on a half forgotten book of fairy tales?

It seems to me that Kierkegaard belongs to a tradition of edifying but secular literature, which, defying formal categorisation or generic labelling, cultivates self-discovery and self-examination of a ruthlessly naturalistic, but nevertheless ultimately religious, nature. The antecedents of this tradition include works on such variegated intellectual levels as John Bunyan's allegories, Montaigne's essays and Pascal's *Pensées*. Among Kierkegaard's contemporaries only Ralph Waldo Emerson (ten years his senior) has a similar position. In our time, there may or may not be many candidates fulfilling the conditions for this line of secular pastoral care: I would offer only two names: Franz Kafka and Samuel Beckett. I am not maintaining that Kierkegaard was, in any profound way, following in the footsteps of his illustrious precursors: in that sense there is no tradition or store of wisdom handed down the ages, outside the evangelical message. In Kierkegaard's works, Montaigne and Pascal get one (perfunctory) reference each. Bunyan and Emerson are not mentioned. Bunyan, Montaigne and Pascal have become, for many people of many generations and many nations, secret friends, life companions. So have, of course, many other writers of religious persuasion, in particular the great mystics. But these writers are not mystics. They, like Kierkegaard, are always the sworn enemies of all mysticism.

Kierkegaard's scepticism always provides a philosophical point of departure, as does his down-to-earth humour, his shield and protection against the mists and miasmas of philosophising Copenhagen of his day.

He wrote in his journal an undated entry from 1848:

> ...my every day has been embittering and nasty, and there is this new misunderstanding where people dare not laugh along with me because they are suspicious and unable to get it into their heads that in all this nonsense I might still have an eye for the comic. Poetically it is of no interest at all, indeed poetically it is too bad that this drama has been put on every single day, year in and year out; poetically it needs cutting down. And that it will be for my reader. On the other hand, it is inside and with the everyday that the religious begins, and this is how I understand my life; for me this, the immensely comic drama, is a martyrdom. But certainly, were I not aware of being under infinite religious obligations, I could wish to go away to some solitary spot and sit down and laugh and laugh—even though it would pain me that this *Krähwinckel* [Dullsville—G.P-P.] is my beloved native land, this residence of a prostituted petty bourgeoisie my beloved Copenhagen. (*Papers and Journals* 345–46)

This dismissal of 'wonderful Copenhagen' at its most scintillating moment in history is not only a sign of unease at being a genius in a provincial town—this phrase often applied to Kierkegaard, and had in fact been used by him about (and to) the culturally alert monarch Christian VIII—but a very shrewd appeal to future readers to appreciate his martyrdom. He is of course fully aware of the duplicity of this word in meaning 'witness' as well as 'victim,' both poetically and humorously.

4

Kierkegaard's main pseudonymous works were written and published at breakneck speed in the years 1843–46. They make up a complex, sophisticated, interrelated web of thoughts and ideas, comprising the works everyone knows: *Either/Or* in two volumes, early 1843, *Fear and Trembling*, the dialectical lyric, and *Repetition*, a strange psychological novella, both also 1843, and as a culmination *Stages on Life's Way* in 1845. These copious books contain the three fictions or novels, where Kierkegaard's literary art achieves its mastery: 'The Diary of a Seducer' from *Either/Or*, *Repetition*, and 'Guilty/Not Guilty' from *Stages:* they are true to, but also transcend, the narrative art and conventions of their day. Their complications and richness are such that I cannot more than mention them here. The best account of these novels is still Aage Henriksen's book of 1954, *Kierkegaards romaner*, still not available in English, for some unaccountable reason. Kierkegaard's pseudo-fictional books wonderfully circumscribe and annotate two nuclear narratives that are central to the whole pseudonymous work: 'The Old Man and His Son' and 'The Betrothal and The Break': these have been the mainstay for every biographical interpretation of Sören Kierkegaard.

The main fictional and semi-fictional works are interspersed with other no less weighty treatises: a penetrating psychological investigation *The Concept of Dread* 1844, and *Historical Fragments* in the same year. In 1846 he published for the first time with a semi-acknowledgement of his authorship ('Published by S.K.') the main confrontation with Hegel and contemporary philosophy *Concluding Unscientific Postscript to Philosophical Fragments* in 1846. During this period he had also concurrently published his more conventionally religious *Edifying Discourses* under his own name. From before the period in question, he also had printed his master's dissertation in Philosophy (virtually a doctoral thesis) *On the Concept of Irony*, and further, an attack on Hans Christian Andersen: 'From the Papers of One Still Living.' From the late period when his copious publications were more focussed on internal criticism of the Church of Denmark and Danish received religion, we can notice two epi-pseudonymou works: *The Sickness unto Death* and *Training in Christianity*, where Sören Kierkegaard is parading as editor, but the author is given ass 'Anti-Climacus.'

It is to the dissertation on irony we have to go if we want to be illuminated on Kierkegaard's true views of aesthetics and poetry. In the pseudonymous works, the dialectical machinery has been put in motion in such a way that it is impossible to understand aesthetic categories unless in relation to some higher category of ultimately religious import. Such is the force of the 'Governance,' the *Styrelse*, he notices in his self-exposé in *The Point of View*. In 1843 he writes, when working on 'Guilty/Not Guilty': 'I am experiencing in myself more poetry in a year and a half than all novels put together. But that I cannot and will not. My relation to her must not become poetically difuse; it has a reality that is quite different.' (*Papers and Journals*, 158) This is an entry in his journal that is emotionally highly charged and difficult to interpret, even syntactically quaint, about his real life relationship with Regine Olsen, whom he had left with seeming cruelty two years before.

Before that, in the dissertation, apprentice work as it undoubtedly was, we find the clearest statements of his views on poetry. The reflectiveness of the age had liberated irony from being just a trope of rhetoric. Kierkegaard writes when discussing Schlegel's *Lucinde*:

> If we ask what poetry is, we may say in general that it is victory over the world; it is through a negation of the imperfect actuality that poetry opens up a higher actuality, expands and transfigures the imperfect into the perfect and thereby assuages the deep pain that wants to make everything dark. To that extent, poetry is a kind of reconciliation, but it is not the true reconciliation, for it does not reconcile me with the actuality in which I am living... (297)

The shortcomings of *Lucinde* (a work that no doubt had a very important part to play for Kierkegaard's formal ideas of fiction), its negation of morality through sensuousness, highlight the general deficiencies of Romanticism:

> The tragedy of romanticism is that what it ceases upon is not actuality. Poetry awakens; the powerful longings, the mysterious intimations, the inspiring feelings awaken; nature awakens; the enchanted princess awakens—the romanticist falls asleep. (304)

This romantic somnolence is just the opposite of what true (as opposed to romantic) irony—the negativity that was Socrates: 'Irony as a controlled element manifests itself in its truth precisely by teaching how to actualise actuality, by placing the appropriate emphasis on actuality.' (265)

To imagine such a propedeutic role for irony does not leave much room for poetry in the actual world. For Kierkegaard, in contrast to the romantics and their followers like Carlyle or Emerson, the poet has no elevated role to play—Kierkegaard is dismissive of that archetype of the poet, Orpheus, whom he calls 'a sentimental zither player.' (*Concluding Unscientific Postscript* 248) Still, the poet remains an exemplar of a very special relationship to actuality. This is eloquently expressed in a later text, *A Literary Review*, from 1846, which contains Kierkegaard's most incisive social criticism:

> What proves to be the law regarding poetic production is the same, on a smaller scale, as that for every person's life in social interchange and education. Anyone who experiences something originally also experiences, through ideality, the possibilities of the same and the possibility of the opposite. These possibilities are his literary legal property. But his own, private actuality is not. His speaking, his producing, are thus borne by silence. (87–88)

It is the loquaciousness of actuality with which Kierkegaard, *qua* poet, is desperate to come to terms.

5

This relationship can be variously described and defined, as it relays immediacy in experience to the category of the interesting, which Kierkegaard had taken over from a youthful dissertation by Friedrich Schlegel, *Über das studium der Griechischen poësie*.

Let us, before we move to a closing comparison of Kierkegaard with his present-day counterparts, examine a text from his journal of 1846, which as far as I know has not found its way, like so many of the anecdotes recorded there, to the published works:

> One day Professor Molbech came to visit with me. He praised my peculiarities, and my peculiar way of living, inasmuch as they favoured my work. 'I would like to do the same,' he said. Thereupon he told me that he the same day was dining out. And 'there I have to drink wine and it does not agree with me; but one can't get away, for then it will just begin: so, so, have a little glass, Professor, will do you good!' I replied: 'It's easy to put a stop to it. You don't say a word about not being able to take wine, because that is to incite their blathering sympathy. You sit down at the table, when the wine is served, you sniff it and say or indicate with your face that it is bad. Then the host will be angry and stop pestering you.' Molbech replied to this: 'No, I cannot do it, why should I anger people?' I replied: 'In order to have your own way. Isn't that reason enough?' But so it goes: First prattle for an hour about it with me and make a fool of one with such twaddle; then go to dinner and prate about it—and drink; and go home and suffer for it—and prattle again the whole night with his wife: that is to live and be *interesting*. (my italics—G. P.-P.)

Is this farcical and very accurately recorded conversation to be regarded as just the tired philosophers irascible response to a boring situation? Perhaps. In that case, the irony is tropical and simple, as the entry is topical and simple. But the warnings of Kierkegaard regarding the double irony, or controlled irony as he terms it in the dissertation, make another possibility appear. Is poor Molbech in fact a poet *volens nolens*? According to the deeper definition of irony as truth he may very well be. But in that case everybody is a poet. The anti-romantic program, hinted at in the end of *The Concept of Irony*, sounds suspiciously close to some form of realism: not a poetry of lofty ideas or feelings, but a poetry feeding on what Merleau-Ponty called, in the title of a 1969 book, *La prose du monde* (*The Prose of the World*). We can now recognize the lowly, earthy tone of the Kierkegaardian anecdote. The self is given full access to its sources of energy and information in snippets of reality that are not interpreted, but rather obscured or occulted. In that sense, Kierkegaard has made of perception the opposite of apocalypse, or revelation. Hence his quarrel with mysticism. This is rather like Montaigne in his last great essay 'Expérience,' or, to go to our contemporaries, the irascible, stoic, triumphant voices of Samuel Beckett's novels: Molloy counting his sucking stones, or the protagonist of *The Unnamable* mustering his troops of representative characters, almost pseudonyms: 'all these Murphys, Molloys or Morans do not fool me.' (237) Time wasted is time won.

Kierkegaard became the great discoverer of the individual: that is, in Danish, as he always puts it: *hin enkelte*. But finding complications in the individual did not deter him from his campaign against all kinds of holism, also in ethics. He annotated in 1850 on his youthful dissertation:

> Influenced as I was by Hegel and by everything modern, lacking the maturity really to comprehend greatness, I was unable to resist pointing out somewhere in my disputation that it was a shortcoming in Socrates that he had no eye for the totality but only looked, numerically, to individuals. Oh, what a Hegelian fool I was! It is precisely the big proof of how a great ethicist Socrates was. (*Papers and Journals* 506)

This can also be read as a gloss on the motto to *Concluding Unscientific Postscript*, which shows what his facetious title to the previous book really signifies: *Philosophical Fragments* (we may care remember that the Danish title meant 'philosophical crumbs'). The motto is derived from 'Hippias Major,' one of the lesser Platonic dialogues (perhaps not authenticated): 'the shavings and parings' to which the hapless Hippias objects represent the very core of Socrates' method of cutting up, *diairesis*, which he elegantly encapsulates in the last words of the dialogue: 'Beautiful things are difficult.' (423) The poet in Kierkegaard might be tempted to try the inversion: 'difficult things are beautiful.'

Works Cited

Beckett, Samuel. *Three Novels*. New York: Grove, 1965.

Eliot, T.S. 'Tradition and the Individual Talent.' *The Sacred Wood and Major Early Essays*. New York: Dover, 1997: 27–33.

Kierkegaard, Søren. *The Concept of Irony, with Continual Reference to Socrates*. Trans. by Howard V. Hong and Edna H. Hong. Princeton: Princeton University Press, 1989.

—. *Concluding Unscientific Postscript to Philosophical Fragments*. Trans. by Howard V. Hong and Edna H. Hong. Princeton: Princeton University Press, 1992.

—. *Either/Or: A Fragment of a Life*. Trans. by Alastair Hannay. Harmondsworth: Penguin, 1992.

—. *A Literary Review*. Trans. by Alastair Hannay. Harmondsworth: Penguin, 2002.

—. *Papers and Journals: A Selection*. Ed. and trans. by Alastair Hannay. Harmondsworth: Penguin, 1996.

Plato, 'Lesser Hippias.' *Cratylus, Parmenides, Greater Hippias, Lesser Hippias*. Trans. by H.N. Fowler. Cambridge, Massachusetts: Harvard University Press, 1996: 333–424.

Part Eleven: Surface and Accident: John Ashbery

John Ashbery's position in modern poetry (or modernist poetry or, indeed, postmodernist poetry) is now so secure, but also so peculiar that it seems more difficult than ever to bring it into focus, relating it to the American poets of his own or a slightly younger generation. Critics like Harold Bloom and Helen Vendler have worked hard at rounding it up in a more traditional fold of American poetic development, but for every new departure taken in his later books there seem to be more and more stray mavericks among his poems, which quite definitely refuse to let themselves be classified in those terms. It is some time since the heyday of the New York poets, and it might be difficult to remember how Ashbery could be seen to have anything in common with Ted Berrigan or Frank O'Hara. There is, however, in his latest books—and perhaps more so in *A Wave*—enough to remind habitual Ashbery-readers of the time when he was considered *l'enfant terrible* of the American poetry scene.

Whereas quite a lot of ingenious and sometimes brilliant criticism has been directed to important areas of Ashbery's activities, in poetry—and one should perhaps add, fiction and drama—the main territory they are addressing themselves to and, in a way, the very rationale behind those activities, have remained in need of elucidation and confrontation with the poetic practices espoused by his rivals and peers. This is, let me reiterate, a peculiar situation, in view of his undisputed importance, but it is also eminently understandable. The acceptance of Ashbery has to a large extent been a matter of trust, as it must have been for the very early modernists. There have been no popular introductions to Ashbery's works—many have attested to the difficulty involved in teaching his poetry to undergraduates. For those who have accepted the trust, or contract, matters of elucidation are thoroughly irrelevant; as for the poetics of undermining reference which can be seen at the core of his style, questions of meaning become irrelevant. For those who cannot accept the contract, the poetry itself becomes irrelevant, meaningless, and critical elucidation just a part of a strategy of obfuscation. What has appeared is a critical void, similar to the one Ashbery himself mentions with regard to one of his early heroes, the French pre-surrealist Raymond Roussel. Roussel made the principles for organizing his work—fantastic as they were—explicit in painstaking and pedantic detail. The principles immanent in innovatory work of this kind—however eccentric or alien to accepted literary conventions—have to be taken at face value or not at all.

It is of paramount importance to bear in mind that this situation is radically different from the one pertaining to the acceptance of modernism in the 1920s or 1930s, both in England and in the United States—it may of course be much more similar to the slower acceptance of surrealism in France. The principles of modernism were here inculcated with expository and explicatory zeal by a whole generation of scholars and poets, and related in great detail to various cultural and moral and educational schemes that had it as their rationale to make these principles plausible. One only has to think of Leavis and Richards, of New Criticism in America as expressed in simple terms in the egregious Brooks and Warren; but one should remember as well that the main protagonists of this struggle for acceptance were directly involved. The very considerable critical work of Eliot or Pound constitutes—apart from its critical worth *per se*—a concerted pedagogical effort that has changed the sensibility of this century to a remarkable degree.

It is easy to see that these conditions do not apply today. The turn taken by critical practices—and it is a moot point whether we call it 'linguistic' or 'philosophical'—has perhaps irrevocably gone in a different direction, and the kind of instructive and interpretive sensibility which went into a document like Pound's *ABC of Reading* would seem today very naïve in its assumptions, and anyhow out of place. The preconditions underlying this somewhat artisan-like belief in the substantiality of the images invading our minds has been obliterated very thoroughly, likewise any faith in a cultural unity where these images can find a natural home.

Some of the problems have been fairly and squarely faced by Charles Altieri, most recently in his comprehensive critical volume *Self and Sensibility in Contemporary American Poetry*. For Altieri, Ashbery appears as a cultural anti-hero, and his quest is intimated on the very first page where he cites the opening lines from Don Juan: 'I want a hero: an uncommon want.' (11) It might be doubtful that it is such an uncommon want, even in these times of anti-heroic agons. But Altieri is certainly correct in associating Ashbery and Byron as cultural phenomena, at the same time catering to needs of novelty and profundity and to the virtues and conventions of popular culture.

The kind of rhetoric we associate with Byron and Ashbery has always had a self-perpetuating quality that does not easily subordinate itself to the constraints of narrative or description. I think that Altieri is justified in describing Ashbery's concern with the muddledness of language as fundamental, as an area where he finds grounds for the recovery of the philosophical ambitions of High Modernism. 'Concern for rhetoric,' he writes, 'becomes a meditation on rhetoricity, on what is involved in being thrown into a language which corrupts all it touches and on the other hand keeps promising to take it beyond its corruptions to some still point...' (150) There seems to be more Derrida than Ashbery in this, and the formula Altieri has devised for his poetry—'Discursive rhetoric within a poetics of thinking' (150)—appears ultimately misleading, in that the kind of mental activity referred to seems very different from what we normally call 'thinking,' e.g. problem-solving or evocation of past events. Furthermore, 'discursive' is never defined in a satisfactory way, but in relation to poets of very different outlook, Pinsky and Creeley for example.

Altieri is quite unabashed in his attempts to accommodate Ashbery's poetry within the perimeter of modern Mandarin culture, but he has to admit—which is quite damaging to his argument—that remaining on an abstract level entails missing the true emotional drama in the poetry. And it is similarly difficult to see that Daffy Duck—in one of the most famous or infamous of Ashbery's pop poems—as a dramatic persona can live up to the expectations of highly abstract discourse, not because the poem does not deserve to be taken seriously, but because that discourse is obviously part of the things it mocks and undermines. Ashbery's infatuation with popular culture has to be taken more seriously, in fact, than either cultural analysis or ideological criticism can begin to intimate, as a very thoroughgoing identification with or loyalty to that culture with all its debunking force. I discern the same loyalty in some of his younger American contemporaries, like Robert Hass or Robert Pinsky, who have found completely opposed, or at least very different means for the restructuring of their poetic territory.

I might be excused for advocating a more relaxed and less intimidating (or intimidated) approach to John Ashbery's poetry than is nowadays most often the case, as my preoccupation with his poetry has not been in the main as a critic but as a translator. I have been engaged in translating Ashbery into Swedish, off and on, since the mid-1960s, and I have been much cheered and sometimes utterly baffled by the process. Most of my translations were collected in a volume, with the perhaps inescapable and at least easily recognizable title *Självporträtt i en konvex spegel* (*Self Portrait in a Convex Mirror*), although it contains poems from all his major volumes with the exception of *Three Poems*—up to and including *Shadow Train*.

The difficulties facing the translator of poetry of this type—and I can only speak from my own experience—seems to me to lie less in the cultural, popular or literary references ingrained in all modern poetry, as in finding and maintaining a tone which seems right and convincing, including the registers Ashbery might have used had he been writing in Swedish. This clearly is an intuitive undertaking, where actual interpretation of the cultural ambiance plays a fairly minor role. It is no doubt important to be able to place these references when they occur in crucial contexts: as, for instance, recognizing—to take a perhaps uncharacteristically simple and straightforward example—the anonymous ballad 'Tom o'Bedlam' behind the poem 'Loving Mad Tom' (from *Houseboat Days*). But the reference occurs, apart from the title, only in one line: 'A spear of fire, a horse of air,' (17) and there has been enormous care taken in not letting the rhythmic magnificence of the old poem shine through in any line:

> With a host of furious fancies
>
> Whereof I am Commaunder,
>
> With a burning Spear and a horse of Air
>
> To the wilderness I wander. (See Logan 180)

It would be futile to expect a rendering of this poem in a version where the Swedish reader could sense that magnificence. But it would be more than futile: it would be wrong, if it could be done. For such are the rules of Ashbery's poetic universe that references are allowed only as negations.

On the other hand, some more mundane references tend to create worse problems. How do you convey to the Swedish reader what it is like to be in Warren, Ohio? 'Are place names central?' Ashbery asks in a poem from *Self*

Portrait in a Convex Mirror, 'One thing that can save America,' immediately, and characteristically, preceded by the obvious retort 'Is anything central?' (44-45)

The makeshift nature of poetic translation can certainly be felt almost painfully when working with somebody like Ashbery, but it might also serve to re-interpret the whole question of reference in poetry and the fact that no reader, ideal or real, can be expected to be familiar with the frame of reference as part of an incontestable body of shared knowledge. This makes the whole business of poetic translation somewhat haphazard, but not necessarily any more so than other forms of cultural dissemination, the point being that the Swedish reader may know nothing of Warren, Ohio, but the same may apply to the British reader, not to speak of readers in Canberra or Saskatoon, who can partake of the original in their native language. The indeterminacy of the text is clearly a case in evidence; but the word 'indeterminacy' gives a false impression as far as the negative principle so often invoked in Ashbery's pronouncements goes: i.e. that if a text of Ashbery's is called 'The Tennis Court Oath' or 'Civilization and its Discontent,' they are in fact determined by their titles in so far as they cannot possibly be about the Tennis Court Oath or our civilization and its discontent. There are of course some exceptions to this: most notably that most famous and quite unusual excursion into ekphrasis, 'Self-Portait in a Convex Mirror.'

Summarizing the experience of translating Ashbery, I can just say that it feels very different from what one would expect when faced with the philosophizing of some of his critics. Literal translation was in most cases out of the question: one had to find the conversational flow of the language and make adjustments as one went along. Some recalcitrant clichés had to be abandoned, metaphors and similes substituted. I inserted a nice quotation from a seventeenth century Swedish poet in the middle of Section III of 'The Skaters.' Other similar allusions had to come out. A line from the Swedish translation of 'The Internationale' about pursuit of happiness (indeed not in the original!) gave me the title for the poem of that name from *Shadow Train*. In short, very much what one is normally forced to do in poetry translation (or allows oneself to do, as the case may be).

What one is made to realize, however, is that the self-reflexiveness of the kind of poetry Ashbery represents, which is always contending with its own creation, is able to supply amazingly straightforward and down-to-earth descriptions of this very process (I am thinking of Ponge as a parallel case)

And when the poem pauses, which does not happen too often, in order to give a notation to its own progress, it is very much an occasion for serious reflection, as in 'The Skaters':

> This, thus is a portion of the subject of this poem
>
> Which is in the form of falling snow:
>
> That is, the individual flakes are not essential to the importance of the whole
>
> > becoming so much of a truism
>
> That their importance is again called in question, to be denied further out, and
>
> > again and again, like this. (*The Mooring of Starting Out* 199)

When, however, it encapsulates a statement on poetics, as it does in 'And Ut Pictura Poesis is her name,' it is with an uninhibited gleeful matter-of-factness that it parodies its antecedents in the high Modernist tradition:

> So much for self-analysis. Now,
>
> About what to put in your poem-painting:
>
> Flowers are always nice, particularly delphinium.
>
> Names of boys you once knew and their sleds,
>
> Skyrockets are good—do they still exist?
>
> There are a lot of other things of the same quality
>
> As those I've mentioned. Now one must
>
> Find a few important words, a lot of low-keyed,
>
> Dull-sounding ones. (*Houseboat Days* 45)

'The extreme austerity of an almost empty mind' (45) being presented as the fertility principle of poetic creativity, does not allow many inroads for sweeping philosophical generalizations. In a way, it both confirms and erases the artisan-like naïveté of Poundian poetics.

In 'A Wave' we are very much back in familiar Ashbery surroundings, presented almost with contempt: 'In the haunted house no quarter is given: in that respect/ It's very much business as usual. The reductive principle/ No longer there, or isn't enforced as much as before.' (*A Wave* 69) The wave seems a perfect embodiment of his austere emptiness. It is insubstantial and still well formed, individual, but collectively placed, as are indeed the flakes of falling snow on 'The Skaters.' Never before have so many themes been combined and fully orchestrated in Ashbery's work. This is not the place to attempt a fuller consideration of what is new and what is familiar in this masterful summation. Some of the lesser poems in the book show new departures, although in not unfamiliar territory, in particular in the exacting form of the prose poem. Others, like 'The Songs We Know Best' seem to be moving towards a painfully gruff idiom, unmistakably American, cracker-barrel.

It is perhaps in this direction one can feel that John Ashbery wants to move in the future. But the programmatically unpredictable has always been his forte. His dream world America may be escapism or nightmare: it shows both the smooth surface 'and the accidents/ Scarring that surface, yet it too only contains/ As a book on Sweden only contains the pages of that book.' (*Self-Portrait*, 55) This reading from Sweden can only try to contain the images shaped by such surface, such accidents.

Works Cited

Altieri, Charles. *Self and Sensibility in Contemporary American Poetry*. Cambridge: Cambridge University Press, 1984.

Ashbery, John. *Houseboat Days*. New York: Viking, 1977.

—. *The Mooring of Starting Out: The First Five Books of Poetry*. New York: Ecco, 1997.

—. *Self Portrait in a Convex Mirror*. Harmondsworth: Penguin, 1976.

—. *A Wave*. New York: Viking, 1984.

Byron, Baron George Gordon. *The Works of Lord Byron: Poetry, vol. 6*. Ed. by Ernest Hartley Coleridge. London: Murray, 1903.

Logan, W.H., ed. *A Pedlar's Pack of Ballads and Songs*. Edinburgh: Paterson, 1869.

Part Twelve: The Voyages of John Matthias

In August 1974, when the Watergate scandal was moving into its last phase, the American poet John Matthias returned to his home, in South Bend, Indiana, after a year's stay in England, traveling on the Polish ocean-liner *Stefan Bathory*. In June of 1976 he set out to sea again, this time on a Russian ship, the *Mikhail Lermontov,* in order to spend another year in England, as a Visiting Fellow in Poetry in Clare Hall, Cambridge. The voyages took approximately nine days each, and on both ships he was accompanied by his wife Diana, who is English by birth, and his daughters Cynouai and Laura. Prompted by the now comparative rareness of such expeditions, he decided to record his experiences in poetic form, allowing one poem for each day at sea plus introductory poems covering each departure. The *Stefan Bathory Poems* were printed in *TriQuarterly,* Winter 1976, and both sequences are included in the volume *Crossing* published by Anvil Press Poetry, London, and Swallow Press in the United States.

Matthias' recording of his sea-faring activities is evidently not to be taken as a simple day-by-day account of maritime pleasures and calamities, no more than Coleridge's *Ancient Mariner,* Baudelaire's *Voyage,* Hopkins' *The Wreck of the Deutschland* or Hart Crane's *Voyages* — to name only four antecedents in nautical poetry which are patently unlike the *Bathory & Lermontov Poems*. The log-book of comic-heroic experience is systematically and sometimes willfully expanded to embrace both personal and public phases of historical understanding, as regards the actual adventures of the four protagonists and their commingling with superimposed information of real of imagined historical events. On the Bathory journey (homward), a typical passage occurs in part 5, 'The Library.'

> The weather improves. Serious now,
> I attend to correspondence.
> Here they read the news and study
> Not Mickiewicz or the other unread
> Poets on these shelves
> But ups and downs of stocks
> And the extraordinary language
> Of my president reported in the
> Daily Polish/English mimeo gazette.
> The banalities and rhetoric of power
> Dovetail with the mathematics
> Of the market: Soon the brokers,
> As in 1929, will sail nicely
> From the upper stories
> Of the highest buildings in New York,
> Their sons will pluck the feathers
> From their hair and look for jobs
> A thousand miles from the ethnic
> Bonfires of their dreams, the poor
> Will stand in bread lines,
> And I, a curio from 1959, will find
> My clientele reduced to nuns
> And priestly neophytes. I return
> To Indiana—the only place
> Save Utah where the Sixties,
> Though Peter Michelson was waiting,
> Failed to arrive.

In confronting his growing feeling of disorientation and rootlessness in the modern world, in a decade that had been less accessible to grandiose generalizations than the previous one, Matthias consistently invokes the life and times of the eminent eponyms which provided his means of transport across the Atlantic. Stefan Bathory (or Batory) was King of Poland 1576–86 and renowned for his battles with Ivan the Terrible. Of Transylvanian origin, he was the uncle of the infamous Elizabeth Bathory and married into the Jagellon family, like the Swedish Vasa family whose heir Sigismund succeeded him. Mikhail Lermontov was the author of *A Hero of Our Time* (1839), and in many ways, along with Pushkin and Gogol, the creator of modern Russia prose. Indeed, Lermontov, along with his antihero Pechorin, refined and modernized the psychological picture of the Byronic elegant sufferer with a subtlety which has only Kierkegaard's Seducer as its equal.

Further presences which let themselves be felt in the poems are: Adam Mickiewicz, whose rhetorical epic of the Lithuanian nobility of 1812 is quoted extensively in Bathory Section Two (from the beginning of Book IV, 'Diplomacy and Hunting'), Ernest Sandeen, American poet of Swedish descent and former Head of the English Department at the University of Notre Dame, Peter Michelson, author of *The Aesthetics of Pornography*, Jessie Harris, appreciated former nanny in the Matthias family, Olga 'our commissar,' George Learmont, Scottish mercenary and supposed ancestor of the Russian Lermontov family, Andrew Jackson, known affectionately as 'Old Hickory,' Thomas Jefferson, Richard Nixon, Gerald Ford and Jimmy Carter, Natty Bumppo, better known by his sobriquet 'Leatherstocking,' plus a great host of Polish noblemen, Russian soldiers, Indian chiefs, British politicians and American poets, pamphleteers and *pasticheurs*. A full expository roster would no doubt run to as many pages as the poems themselves. May it just be added that the 'wise Printz-Påhlson' is identical with the present writer, whose very decision of undertaking a translation of Matthias' poems into Swedish—a work of some magnitude and difficulty—might call in doubt the appropriateness of the complimentary modifier generously bestowed on him by the poet.

Other presences are equally important, albeit unnamed. Two American poets who in the early years of this century undertook the voyage of no return to Europe, T.S. Eliot and Ezra Pound, and one British poet, W.H. Auden, who went, like the *Stefan Bathory*, in the opposite direction, are constantly in evidence in the quirky pastiches and parodic homages which time and again insinuate themselves into the diction of these poems. The libretto at the end of *Lermontov* Part Four has its point of reference and model in a similar one in Canto LXXXI of the *Pisan Cantos*; the 'Weialala leia, Wallala leialala' of the Conclusion (somewhat perversely rendered into sonorous Don Cossack warbling in the Swedish translation) comes straight out of the Fire Sermon section of *The Waste Land* ('Past the Isle of Dogs'), and the thickly atmospheric ending of the same Conclusion, with its customs agents, clerks, porters and symbolic strangers in furtive and probably nefarious pursuits on foggy quays and in seedy hotel rooms of some minor British port are so reminiscent of the early Auden that one could very well place them in *The Dog Beneath the Skin* or *Letter from Iceland*.

> Standing on the promenade
>
> In attitudes
>
> Of suspicion, attention, or anticipation
>
> Hoping for some fine
>
> Benign surprise
>
> Each of us looks at the land
>
> Thinking still of the sea.
>
> Each contrives
>
> To be abstracted one last time in sea-thoughts
>
> Or in dreams
>
> Before the symbolical stranger
>
> Posing as a customs agent
>
> Or a clerk or porter in a small hotel or pension
>
> Asks the questions symbolical strangers ask
>
> Which only actions answer . . . .

The pastiches and parodies, the knockabout farce of diction and events, should not be allowed to conceal the very serious concerns eloquently expressed in these poems: concerns with permanence of character and conditions, as well as with change of habitat and heart; concerns with seeking roots and facing exile, and with politics and personal experience, which are what finally give importance to these poems. Nor should the erudition and wit, which illuminate and sharpen the slapstick and facetious language, be permitted to obscure the good humor and fun that provide the basic mood for this sagacious and graceful poetry.

For my time, too, impinges oddly,

Painlessly, obscurely—this kind of inbetween—

Impinges surely

This time of jokes & parodies, pastiches.

An inbetween

When I don't know precisely what I want to do in time

But only where I want to go

Again—

And so we're here and waiting

For a berth

To park a ship in—

Waiting in a time of waiting

A time of waiting for—

For semi-retired former semi-active veteran-volunteers

Of oh our still belovéd

Dear and hopeful

Sixties

To arise again arise

Again arise

For some kind fool to build the equestrian statues
And compose the elegiac songs.

Letters of Blood: Poems

Letters of Blood

For Jesper Svenbro

'Here I am, an old man, being bled by a nun'
would be one way of starting this poem,
unless it didn't sound too much like a quotation.
But in this a poem, or a book, or the parabola
of the arrow, is at one: it doesn't matter overmuch
how it starts, it is the end, although
predictable, which is at stake, the founding
of the monastery, the killing of the fallow deer,
the blowing of the horn, and all heroic antics.
And where that arrow falls there is a
legend: 'Everyone is entitled to have
one puzzle waiting, if he is
arrogant enough.' Phlebotomy
was for a long time the only
regiment of the *pharmakoi*:
scapegoats stochastic at their checkered sports.
History has many canny spoors.

Nowhere else is syntax so close
to the angry syllabics of the track,
patterning the snow with countless decks
of playing cards, first black, then red.
This is the patience, the true game of patience
of the wolves…

One

My Interview with I.A. Richards

For Constance Horton Greenleaf
In Memory of Ivor Richards and Robert Gessner

I

Inversion is a counterfeit experience
there is but one irreversibility.
Chestnuts, rabid squirrels, slosh and sleet,
the sullen, birdstained wisdom of John Harvard.
O Fyffes bananas, obscene planks,
the flexes bared to vision like the sinews
in Vessalius. I grope my way
through the intestines of heuristic house.

II

Last night we heard in Kresge Hall
a lion-vested English poet fulminate
like an under-paid volcano against Science,
applauded by a host of boffins.
Afterwards, a girl called Shirley took my hand
and wished to lead me through the maze
toward the magus posing there as Tannhäuser,
fettered with electric wires in a great maidenform

III

'I never liked the man.'—'Grotesque...'
His face (a breakfast fruitjuice of a face
—like Santa's after years of seven daily shaves)
frowns towards the window. I try
another angle—Oxford, Cambridge, the sad
dignified silence of his friend,
the poise of Perry Miller as a demon.
He floats like Peter Pan towards his country.

IV

Suddenly, the telephone in boredom
jumps from the cluttered table, spelling
its coincidence of quick relief:
the establishing of friends of future
forfeits the nodding present, and we drift
through mists of April with the sleepy
drone of summer knocking at the door.
Time leaves us breathless at its wake.

V

The evenings walk together, and we flee,
convened, rebuffed, solidified and sad.
Memory whistles round that cataleptic hour,
wasted to the world but not to me.
The silent voice behind that black receiver
will speak and ask and read a poem
about the mountaineers of mind (if mind has
mountains) with verses streaming from their rucksacks.

VI

One evening in the future we shall meet
and speak of music, indigestion and delight,
and Connie, lovely Connie, will comply
to show her knickers on request. The night
is full of eyes, and trees, and bushes
bristle with the flat twang of summer.
We finish our drinks and walk away.
My wife and I walk home in silence.

VII

Friend, there is a carrot-farm in heaven
providing food for rabbits, remedies
for nightblindness. In your preferment
of the second-rate, Battersea Park amusements,
walks at night through warm, protective darkness,
tarry awhile, and first consider
those who dwell in darkness through the night
with electronic eyes, blistered by insights.

VIII

Drinking soda pop and smoking
innumerable cheap cigarettes. They
are the Kierkegaards of their own destruction,
breathing hatred on their bellies. Pity them.
But think also of the truly innocent,
the lonely typists in their immaculate rooms
with a small fridge and biscuits on the mantelpiece
where nobody except the caretaker has ever entered.

IX

Friend, poet, the unterminated interview,
unwritten poem, unmade bed, or girl,
call out for completion. Do not
heed them. Learn how to revere
the unfinished, generating moments from its teeth
of happiness, hysteria and love
as useless, beautiful, incongruous and light
as sparks from high-heeled shoes against the flagstones outside
M.I.T.

Generation

I

We children of the thirties got daubed with melancholy.

We were not lucky like the sons and daughters
Of the twenties, christened in jazz fumes
And the colored clothes of their first cries,
Nor free and desperate like the newborn
Of the forties, soothed by blackouts,
Liberated by flak bursts and search lights in the sky.

We became late sleepers, mind readers,
Violent and autocratic statues in
The sea, skin divers in our amniotic juices.

II

The streets were longer in those days,
    The trams made noises in the nights.
In the small room a young girl with a child,
    Waiting at dawn for darkness to
    Be sucked out into the sky,
And the hours of low-paid work
    Like scabs you cannot leave alone.

The hours were smaller, the winters
    Longer, with more wet snow on the window-sill.

Bananas were coming in, and silver hydroplanes
Descended on the dead wet sea. The pilot
Waved and thought he looked like Charles Lindbergh.

We had our games. The soldiers were
Italians and Abyssinians. It seemed the
Abyssinians always lost their feet and heads.
Their Jesus robes turned into moldy grey.

III

My uncle who came to America
Before I was born,
In the sly and wincing first year of the depression,
Went into a barbershop in Buffalo.
Shaved by a Negro he saw, against the
Grayish palm the later white and jolly
And heard the thick black lips say:
Du e la svensk. The black man was a Swede, too,
From Gothenburg.
My uncle became a carpenter in Quincy, Mass.
But remembered the lather in the hand,
Snow on squatting slagheaps like some unwritten
                        Dylan Thomas story.

IV

I wake before dawn
With a night's small poems swarming in my head:
'Now when I am forty-five and almost dead
I'll let my hair grow long and wild
And I'll be stalking flowers in the parks
And by observing learn to pick them.'

Televisiondreamroutines

Galvanizing, I would think, said Peter rabidly.

Their son, called Justin, had invented a new game.

The three men hanging from the chandelier broke the fall of the fourth clinging

To the flex and ripping the stuccoed ceiling of the Moroccan Room.

Charles fingered his brocaded necktie nervously.

Now we have to face the *most unreasonable* man on earth, presumably a *hotelier*.

Meanwhile at the Zoo, Melchisedec the Cow.

The crew, mostly dressed in rather momentous black, except for Celia who was un-

Accountably naked, were cheered on by the vicar himself.

There the victuals precede the auditorium.

Meanwhile back at the Zoo, Celia dressed in rather demure black, was naked, cheering

The cow and the vicar.

Now we have erased from this earth *l'homme moyen sensual*, presumably an ostler,

    Charles

Said, fingering his Moroccan necktie with remorse.

Well, at last, their son invented a new game. They were just in time.

Patronizing, I would think, said Peter Rabbit avidly.

Note: The phrase Well, at last *is taken from the MGM 1949 version of Dostoevsky's* The Gambler, *starring Gregory Peck and Ava Gardner.*

The Longest-Running Show on Television

The longest-running show on television
Is the one in which the moderator is also the chairman of
                        The board of your company.
He is half-asleep most of the time, and you can never understand
His jokes. Surely he has gone mad.
Most of the discussion seems to be about the proper way
Of conducting the proceedings, but it is hard to know for sure
As the languages used are Tamil, Basque or Arawak,
But never a language you can understand. Prizes
Are given out, sometimes for the dumbest answers.
People nobody has ever heard of are constantly being invited
To give speeches. References are made
To the fat reports littering the tables, but only to the pages
Which have gone missing. In the lobby
Of the hotel where you are all staying,
The bellhops are unspeakably rude. They always demand
Money of unknown denominations, in particular small
Octagonal coins, almost as fat as they are large.
In the creaking of steel-tubing of stylish rusty armchairs
Sleepers are snoring, hecklers heckling, most people bored…
Nobody knows whether he is spectator or participant. The program
Is entitled 'Life before Death,' or sometimes, simply
'Goings-on.'

The Enormous Comics

I. Superman, or: How to Succeed as a Failure

The simple silent feat is first; the bridge
Collapsing needs a steadying hand;
The masked and hook-nosed robbers, on the average,
Fall to abject poses at his harsh command.

Then the retreat: how cleverly, how smart and smooth
He beats the lightning as a transvestite
In that conveniently empty booth
Before a man has time to whisper *kryptonite*.

The drag is next (and tiresome it proves to be)
The girl reporter gloating in her mad pursuit
Of her Man of Steel; loved at a distance and myopically
By the owl-like clerk for whom she doesn't care a hoot.

And history: from noisy quasar, distant star
A dying world expels a fotus-rocket with a roar
To impregnate our helpless planet from afar
With the surreptitious virus of a dedicated bore.

The hidden meaning of this farce no doubt
Will find itself reduced to something cute:
The analyst will see the writing on the wall spelled out:
SUPERMAN LOVES CLARK KENT. He is a fruit!

The moral of the fairy-tale is clear:
We love our failures, fondle our distress
And cling to our coward selves in fervid fear
Lest we shall lose them to the lover dumb success.

II. Bringing up Father: or, The Unending Revolution

When I consider how the monstrous years were spent,
The years that man has called this star his home,
I see enormous heaps of human excrement
In growing piles beneath the starry dome.

We often contemplate our forbears down below
And treasure recollections of the primal horde.
This serves to gratify the impulses to go
Down to the mucky depths we can't afford.

What could induce our youthful minds to dwell
On the adventures of this hen-pecked immigrant,
A ne'er-do-well who inadvertently did well
And had to pay the price in cultured cant?

Remember how the rolling-pin was swung
By hefty arms; how crockery was hurled
To force the husband to ascend another rung
In the social structure of his conquered world.

The impact of this stubborn downward urge
Which made him real where his wife was not
Gave us excuses in our mind to splurge
All operatic tantrums in a shower of snot.

Think of the tale of the Icelandic priest
Who promised to become a Christian instead,
If seats be promptly booked at the Eternal Feast
For all his relatives who were already dead.

We can forgive our ancestors the mere
Deception of their ruthless living lie
But hardly the brutality to leave us here
And rot away and stink and simply die.

This goes to show that feeling is without pretence,
Construing the unbearable (as our pun gets slyer)
In bringing up our fathers in the awful sense
Of exhumation of a dreaded sire.

III. Recollection of Innocence in Experience: Or, the Katzenjammer Kids, Middle-Aged, Remembering their Happy Childhood in Africa

Remembering the golden days, the door
That's shut forever on the toy-shaped scandals,
The pop-art palm-trees and the muffled roar
Of the bright red bombs, like Christmas candles,

We can still feel the paper breeze that tries
To rock the cornflower billows, still
Smell the artificial fragrance of the pies
Forever left to cool upon the window-sill.

The obscene innocence of the childish pranks
Was just a weapon in our constant strife
To give the bug-eyed, absent-minded cranks
Their smarting lessons in the School of Life.

Our childhood was all childhoods, for
In adult tranquillity we let go the grip

Of the secure exposure of the secret core
In the spasmodic movements of the comic strip.

In this two-dimensional Eden of repose
We dwell for ages, weakening by degrees,
Stalking the obscure powers that disclose
The subdued rage of fitful memories.

Poem Unnamed

So, at least, there is one thing we have in common,
The habit of assuaging the country mist:
Because there is one thing you must not allow,
In particular in the autumn when the
Pastures are trivial, leaves playful.
This is how I figure: a disruption
Of any kind of narrative (as I a daughter
Asleep from drinking, left alone)
This is the time I don't come from
But rather the opposite, like St. Augustine,
Another installment in my debt to you
My darling Janet: Negation NEGATION
At least I can speak now and not
At that omen (I was a poet once and
Then) miraculously (read an old
Acquaintance: is that first-order logic is
Consensually agreed on, or words to that effect.
That is why this poem is called 'The
Decline of the Supernatural,' although its
Title is 'On what was as near to

Happiness,' but dedicated to Henry Mayhew
and the memory of Clive Jenkins.

   I do only countenance arithmetical order
Which is the stark nonsequitur of most
Vengeful fathers.
   Forgive me, as vulgar as a poem mentioning Chomsky (incognito
There), or whales, or wage demands.

Botchuana

When I molested your plaits I was
reminded, inadvertently, of Alameda County,
doctrinal. Period. Useful. Insolence.
Substitute <u>solitude</u>. Hitler made sin and me. Quote.
Bristols. As little poetry comes out of
Dialectics as out of South Africa: That is,
Svegdir, a way to cut open.

We gleaned one thing, from G.M.
Hopkins at least: not to waste time on explanantion.

   Whatever it may seem like.
   He was a big man: eighteen stone.
   I never carried the coffin.
   I cried when my father's workmates spoke.
   I remember that line
  'Master bridges
   Dirty breeches .'
      This is a love poem.

Two

Aelius Lamia: Tankas for Robert Hass

Autumn: Stapleford.
The fine badge of air between
the branches of trees:
a squirrel jumping from one
to the other one, bending,

reminded me at once
of other squirrels in the parks
of my own childhood
in the cold winters of war.
They were red, like foxes tails,

Not grey, American,
silver-speckled tanderfoots.
Memories are eggs,
spotted, in colours, numbers
as in poems by John Clare.

But this is their true
significance: transience
in the permanent;
when blown, enduring as shell:
The man Aelius Lamia

(vide Suetonius
who loved idle gossip)
was put to death by
the Emperor Domitian
'on account of certain jests'

of which the one is self-
explanatory, but not
particularly
funny, the other—of his
silence when exhorted to sing:
heu taceo:—has
to this day never been
explained nor understood.
There is, as you so well know,
comfort in silence, sadness.

Odradek

for Bo Cavefors

Es klingt etwa so wie das Rascheln in gefallenen Blattern

Their cases are locative or instrumental.
Here, in this place, I see the leaves falling
on the fabulously stayed crosses and inscriptions,
as they fell on the Homeric simile of generations.
You have heard them, the little dissuaders,
whispering in the attics, or from behind the creaking stairs,
with their busy spools and laughter, seemingly
from no human lungs. You proceed to ask:
What's your name? Answers: Odradek.
Where do you live? Unbestimmter Wohnsitz.
They cannot die but cease to exist
when you do not listen. In another place,
in Paris, a car is stopped: a little dog
in the lap of a young girl exploding
like a ripe autumnal fruit in her hands. Her
lover is already carved in half by bullets.
There are cleaner cases, more winsome
uses for the accusative. Do not heed them anymore.
Here we all die, in bits and pieces.

Turing Machine

It's their humility we can never imitate,
obsequious servants of more durable material:
    Unassuming
they live in complex relays of electric circuits.

Rapidity, docility is their advantage.
You may ask: *What is 2 x 2?* Or *Are you a machine?*
    They answer or
refuse to answer, all according to demand.

It's however true that other kinds of machines exist,
more abstract automata, stolidly intrepid and
    inaccessible,
eating their tape in mathematical formulae.

They imitate within the language. In infinite
paragraph loops, further and further back in their retreat
    towards more subtle
algorithms, in pursuit of more recursive functions.

They appear consistent and yet auto-descriptive.
As when a man, pressing a hand-mirror straight to his nose,
    facing the mirror,
sees in due succession the same picture repeated

in a sad, shrinking, darkening corridor of glass.
That's a Gödel-theorem fully as good as any.
    Looking at in-
finity, but never getting to see his own face.

Broendal

Raining no longer. (Water like a mirror)
The words are all bright in your mouth.
White light on the wet pavement. Language a mirror
Or another way of breathing outside your mouth?

We are speaking and the words are all white.
The wind speaks to the rain and the rain to the sea
And the wind is blowing, though just a bit.
Do you think language is anything like the sea?

The rain is wholly adequate and one can see
That the wind is precise. Words rain into the sea
And no words are drowning.
We gather here in groups. In the blowing
Wind words whistle pure and tender:
The sea forgets what everyone cannot remember.

Note: Viggo Broendal was a Danish speculative linguist of the early twentieth century.

Two Prose Poems

I

In what way is the stone a world? Not in the same way as dandelions are canaries which do not fly or waves are knives scraping across the beach. The stone is a world: note the wolf-like spider stalking lambs, the small tired flies which leave the edge of seaweed at closing time and listlessly drift homewards, in swarms. Can anyone endure that much? The stone in your hand is one thing, incredible and grotesque with large holes and its ridiculous appendix of dry seaweed; it leaves the hand and flies in its partial ellipse, like a comet, out and down towards the waiting splash, with its tail waving wearily as the last we handkerchief at the stern of an emigrant ship.

II

On sunny days the sea is divided into differently colored areas, partly according to the nature of the bottom, partly according to the direction of the wind. But today the sea is gray as the sky and without any visible boundary between air and water, between the bluish milk and the porridge. No sharp boundaries: even the shoreline is ugly and rugged today. It annoys me. By keeping constantly on the move, constantly changing my vantage points and by alternately closing and opening my eyes, by using piers and jutting headlands and by covering the parts that don't fit with my hand, I try to produce increasingly pure configurations. Is that of no use? In fact I know it is in here (*indicates his breast*) where all the theorems are found, not only the solution of the equation but the equation itself. Once I may have believed that I would be able to find a form beneath this wet licentiousness, this criminal indifference to our laws.

Sir Charles Babbage Returns to Trinity College

After having commissioned the Swedish mechanic Scheutz to build a difference engine. On the bank of the River Cam he gazes at the Bridge of Sighs and contemplates the life of the dragonfly.

No man can add an inch to his height, says the Bible. Yet once I saw the detective Vidocq change his height by circa an inch and a half. It has always been my experience that one ought to maintain the greatest accuracy even in small things.

No one has taught me more than my machine. I know that a law of nature is a miracle. When I see the dragonfly, I see its nymph contained in its glittering flight. How much more probable is it that any one law will prove to be invalid than it will prove to be sound. It must happen in the end: that wheels and levers move accurately but that the *other* number will appear, the unexpected, the incalculable, when the nymph bursts into a dragonfly. I see a hand in life, the unchanging hand of The Great Effacer.

Therefore be scrupulous and guard your reason, in order that you may recognize the miracle when it occurs. I wrote to Tennyson that his information was incorrect when he sang 'Every minute dies a man,/ Every minute one is born. 'In fact every minute one and one-sixteenth of a man is born. I refuse to abandon this one-sixteenth of a man.

Man-Made Monster Surreptitiously Regarding Idyllic Scene

...*in Swiss hermitage, a copy of Goethe's* Werther *resting in his lap.*

It is sometimes considered to be an advantage to start from scratch. I myself would be the first to admit that my maker did a good job when he constructed my brain, although it must be said that he was unsuccessful with my outer appearance: my ongoing program of self-education has provided me with many a happy hour of intellectual satisfaction. Spying on these touching family tableaux unobserved makes me nevertheless both excited and dejected. I suspect that only with the greatest of difficulties shall I myself be able to establish meaningful relationships with other beings. It is not so much my disfigured countenance which distresses me—I have accustomed myself to *that* by gazing at it in a nearby tarn and now find it, if not immediately attractive, then, at least, captivating: in particular the big screws just under my ears which my maker insisted on putting there for God knows what purpose, accentuate my expression of virile gravity and ennui—as rather a certain lack of elegance and animal charm. It seems for instance to be almost impossible for me to find a suit that fits as it should. One of my more casual acquaintances, a certain Count Dracula, whom I vaguely remember having encountered in some circumstances or other—regrettably I cannot remember where or when—is in this respect much more fortunate: I envy him his relaxed manner of deporting himself in evening dress, but I have to admit that I cannot understand the reason for his negative (and extremely selfish) attitude to his environment. For myself, it seems as if my background and construction limit the possibilities for the successful development of my personality in socially acceptable forms. Evidently, I must choose between two possible careers: either to seek self-expression in the pursuit of crime—within which vast and varied field of activity sexual murder ought to offer unsurpassed opportunities for a creature of my disposition—or during my remaining years quietly to warm my hands at the not altogether fantastically blazing but nonetheless never entirely extinguished fires of scholarship.

Joe Hill in Prison

Memory: slapping sails in the harbor.
Skipper in calfskin gloves, his spyglass
pressed against a watery eye. Haze over Gävle's port.
Winter-gray days of refusal to thaw.
Then cannonades of ice-breaking and jubilation.
Spring with a song in its arms.

Work heavy as sodden clothes.
Tramping the Dust Bowl toward the Rockies.
Tramping with pocketfuls of borrowed years
over territory where only the water leaves tracks,
where the heat is a faded gold-brown in color
and the birds speak with leathery tongues.

Looking through the bars (like a brother
from other centuries he never heard of
transported far off into the Finnish mountains) Writing a song.
Waiting and thinking, while the time idles along
like a night shift, over that which never happened,
the futility in these methods

of taking, hating, and giving. Once life was
hard and clean as a handshake. Then
it became a mask with a stiffened grimace.
Waiting in the morning chill for the bolt to be
drawn from the door. Deadly fear blinking sleepily even now
in the bright lair of freedom. It is done.

Translated by Richard B. Vowles

Note: Joe Hill was a Swedish-American song-writer and labor organizer, executed in Salt Lake City in 1916.

Remember the Rosenbergs

They have almost disappeared in the near-history.

Theirs are no substantial ghosts—
Wraiths like half-forgotten memories—
No palpable phantoms like the children of Hiroshima,
The contortionist dolls of our blackened dreams.

They lived for a short while in something that approximated reality,
Before others' fears blotted out their fate.

It has been said that they lost their identity.
So we deprived them of even this.

How could they ever haunt their dreary cells
With all emotions spent as dialectic smallchange,
Stripped as spirits to their bonewhite cores?
Even their children know them from a brief.

So this we did to them before and after
They sang their treacley songs and lost their lives.

Still their poverty, as our guilt, was real.

When Beaumont and Tocqueville First Visited Sing-Sing

When Beaumont and Tocqueville first visited Sing-Sing
To gather material for a treatise on American penitentiaries,
They saw something like a vision of a future world.

The convicts who, unfettered, labored side by side
In dour silence, united in hatred,
The guards, as if on the brink of a crater,
Propping their panic with perfunctory brutality,
The dark houses, halfway finished cellblocks.

* * *

So was corrupted before their eyes throughout the decades of the American Dream,
Hot-dog stands mushroomed like tracks on a dirtroad,
Billboards crowded in admiration among the scenic views,
The Indian sold his smirking souvenirs from Woolworth's.

And Natty Bumppo, returning at night from the office,
In vague desperation that he has no more vistas to conquer,
Checks that no trespassers have stepped in on his property,
Looks in the closet for Russians or Jews and flicks on the TV,
Opens a flip-top can and drafts a letter of hate to the paper.

* * *

The silent unfettered convicts: this is a dream
That will haunt Europeans in nameless nights,
Worse than the horror of chaos, more real.

Three Baroque Arias from Gradiva

I. Gradiva: Hanold Sings

Such milky mildness shines forth only from the mouth of an archaic goddess
Such living limbs can, stonebound, shimmer only in the telescope of history reversed
Such eloquent temples can be taciturn only in terracotta colored face against a freer
    firmament.
Freer than Medea of Pompeii in motherpain, in motherpride against
    sirocco-mutilated skies triumphant,
Her sorcerer's wand pressed against an empty uterus,
Prouder than Prospero who gelded his own weapon of desire, denying
All his children the common act of freedom, the killing of the old king.

Seen against more sacred skies, in more limpid light, rather like Greek Helen,
Reflected not in language but in old men's bursting eyeballs
In convex catatonia preserved through snowing centuries in the apocryphal
    times of conception,
Even in Teutonic Tannhäuser-woods, in the glimpse of shadow in the mirror of the
    study...

Such pride in her pace can only a goddess display, with perpendicular uplifted foot,
Arrested in her movement, immovable and traveling through the whirling fall
    of centuries.

II. Hanold's Last Dream

She sat in the sun, with a snare

of grass, in the door of waiting.

Still, observe fluttering

              floundering things,

hold to the dream which tosses in your hand.

A bird fell to the deceitful

floor of the dream. The lizard fled.

Colleague, hunter, who then hunts?

III. Vertumnus: His Sestina

When I am changed the young bud turns to leaf.

When I am changed the bare hills turn to vale

And when I breathe I turn to cotton cloud

The heavens which are mirrored in my eye,

And when I wander, I wander deep in woods

And when I close my eyes there is no sun.

At one time on the world there was no sun

And every soul was an unwritten leaf

In the middle of the dark Unchanging Woods.

On the Tiber's banks and in the Tuscan vale

I flew in every downy seed for I

Was born of wind and wind-begotten cloud.

A Warrior who went prancing round the cloud,

A sower with his basket in the sun:

So was born this metamorphosis, this I;
Along the sunburned thighs there grew green leaves
And toes flowed like water in a vale
To take quick root in some vast wonderous woods.

There went an apple-selling lady in the woods
Whose ancient features were as fuzzy as a cloud.
She reached the boundaries of fair Pomona's vale
And smiled at Beauty there as at a gallant sun.
She wished to kiss each green and dew-fresh leaf
Among the fruit. She loved and she was I.

A frightened girl—and also she was I—
Ran panting and pursued through darkening woods.
She stumbled and observed among the leaves
A black and curly head against the cloud—
Beneath the god surrendered to a violent sun
And then bark covered up her chaste womb's vale.

I remember once in a Thessalian vale
How straying lost in that strange province I
Perceived a glimpse as from a naked sun:
It was a crowd of women in the woods
Who in a panic clustered like a cloud—
Pale waiting chrysalis beneath the leaf.

On mountains, in the vale, at sea and in the woods,
There consumed am I as when a summer cloud
Annihilates a sun and closes all the leaves.

Note: **Gradiva** *is a novella by Wilhelm Jensen, analyzed by Freud in a celebrated essay. Vertumnus was a Roman deity, referred to by Ovid and Propertius.*

Three

Comedians

for Kenneth Koch

Before it had become fashionable to write poetry
about writing poetry, it was considered
so exceedingly difficult that it was next
to impossible, or perhaps it was considered impossible.
How can one possibly do this, one thought,
surely one must lose one's concentration,
or the flow of rhythm, or metaphors, or *something*
(or, perhaps one didn't think of it at all)
But consider instead a little girl in, say, 1937
who has come down to the seaside with her parents
and nanny (she is that sort of girl) and has
after some token resistance been enrolled
with the private swimming instructor, and walks
every morning with her inflatable yellow-
patterned little wings (how the thirties loved yellow)
down to the beach, with the cold washboard clay
and small brown dried starfish, and pink shells. She
thinks: OK, I'll go along so far, but I shall never <u>really</u>
learn to swim, learn to float like a boat in the water.
And she goes on, irritated with her elder sister
who is carrying on a flirtation with the handsome
swimming instructor in his baggy blue trunks,
and being teased by her kid brother as
she struggles on top of her wings, her body,

arched backwards, her eyes closed and mouth
puckered as for a kiss. She dreams every
night that she is floating through cool, green
water, saying hello to the sea-horses and the fish,
and sometimes she paints in her dream an
oil-painting, something along the lines of Géricault,
where she and two friends are cowering
clutched in each other's arms on the gaudy
stripers, of the inflatable mattress while
breakers of incredible size are washing the
jetty protecting the little harbour. But one day
when the summer is close to its end and the
morning as crisp as green September hazel-nuts,
she forgets everything and—hey presto—she is friends
with the water. 'Soon I can swim without wings,'
she thinks by herself, 'soon I can fly without air,
without rhythm, without metaphors… Wait a minute,'
she says to herself, indignant (she is that kind of girl),
'I am being used as a metaphor now. Well I never…'
But there she is wrong. The poem, if it is any good at all
is never about writing poetry: but rather about
making jokes, or love; or deceit; once again she (in
spite of her perky independence of mind) and the reader
have together been lead up that proverbial old
garden path. But, in that case, consider a boy
on the first day of spring when the rain has just stopped,
playing (with) marbles up that old garden path,
water-logged still by the rains…

Songs of Dock Boggs

There are gridiron reverberations

in the hills, sourmash

blandishments bleating

from the sheriff's office.

Ah, the *gavroche* innocence of a barnyard rape!

He offers a smile, mild

as pick-axe handles a

mile wide which kindles

the hide of rutabaga;

their red necks swabbed

by cool, pale blue grass

in the abstracted stare of poverty

Bushwhacking the melodies of God

for the breakdown of bushfires

he nurtures illustrious health

with the grating pap

of pink indigence,

plucking the lure of life

from the audible *mouchoir* moment

when distant authority suppurates

the blueridge landscapes of childhood.

Raw death: a clodhopper shovel

smack in the kisser.

In the Style of Scott Skinner

The kelp is not enough. Two hundred
thousand wet sea-birds every
minute serve the mind with constraints
in pizzicato dancehalls all over
the moody crags. A lonely kipper
is seen to flounder in the volatile traffic
leaving his ladder, embarking
for France, land of cotillon and plenty,
prognathous and proud in the strathspey
prattle of little Jacobite girls in terror.
Far, far away, *o domine*, from
glamour-grammar grit and the sweet
mountain smell of mossy socks in Allenvale!

Acrobats on the Radio: Letter to Newcomb

For Newcomb Greenleaf, Naropa Institute, Easter 1980

I

The idea of privacy is perhaps not really germane to Eastern thought.
How can you perform your secret rites when the air is swarming with demons?
Or else you are crowded by all these planes of existence, all twenty-five of them
(twenty-four, if you count them non-Boolean)?
How can you perform anything on hoary mountain-tops under such circumstances?
And I assure you and Mme David-Neel, I was ready for it, tantricly, and then in
comes this *tulpa* and disturbs my concentration.
I do confess I find it tiresome. It is all a question of excess of willpower,
and I was never given enough of that stuff in the first place.

I much prefer the letter you once wrote; from Rochester,
when you had taken the boys to a circus and seen some acrobats
who were absolutely tremendous. Your enthusiasm was so great
that you started to describe their acts in detail. It
reminded me of an old Stan Freberg routine (remember
Stan Freberg? The fifties? Jokes about television?)
about 'Acrobats on the Radio.' How great they are
& etc. Oooh!! Aaahhh! Look at THAT! Sorry it's RADIO.
It occurs to me that description is perhaps more loving
than interpretation. It is not that I am knocking
Eastern modes of hermeneutics, it is just that sometimes I think
we might both have got it wrong. When Naropa

was looking for his guru-to-be, Tilopa, in the mountains of the eastern border
He met up with a number of strange characters who mainly seemed
concerned with having his help slaughtering their relatives.
That he refused to do so was promptly taken on his part
as a sign of lack of sincerity or dedication.
A saga for the businesslike and glib. For Americans, alas.

II

    The years go by. In that they much & oh so much
resemble the planets, turning in their orbits like an old
    scratched record of Ewan McColl or A.L.Lloyd, bestowing
that past dignity of tiresome toil that we have lost, or never had,
    on the commonwealth of aimless thinking (or drinking). Are we then
slumming like the demons, sucking satisfactions from
    the lives of others, making what's past a prologue?
I know you're not a Platonist. Your constructions suffer
    the scapegrace mind to build it's harum-scarum
world willy-nilly, free from clanking, cumbrous
    forms, like the vast *vers-libre* epic which is
the American prairie. That is a place for acrobatics, in
    some lonely pylon, performed unseen, unheard-of,
in the violence of thunderstorms. When I met you & Connie
    I was ambitious, crisp, refractory, European. You & America
taught me to flatten my desire onto the untoward topology
    of the ingenuous. This is the freedom of Ariel, the pensioner & pardoner.
We all want to save what there is, appearances, the phenomena.
    Happiness doesn't enter into it at all. We learned that Ditty's

with child. Last spring we heard & saw here in this craven city
    Ginsberg & Orlovsky sing about the lamb, debonair
& sacrificial in their clean, white shirts, repatriated.
    We wish for you, your boys, your unborn child
('The man i' th' Moon's too slow — till new-born chins
    be rough & razorable') the tardiness of the lamb's-wool-white
sheet lightning of the plains, tough as yoghurt, the two-
    dimensional liberty of tenderness, of saving (σώξειν)
without the customary Osimander preface to your Revolutions
    τά φαινόμενα (yours & theirs)

The planets turn in their eccentric orbits. We are the demons
    of electric privacy, in our broadcast dereliction.

To John at the Summer Solstice, Before His Return

Verba nitent phaleris: at nullas verba medullas
Intus habent, sola exterius spectatur imago
Marcellus Palingenius, *Zodiacus Vitae*
Liber Sextus: Virgo
Digenes Akrites, Liber Quartus, 1028–9

I

There is one stanza, and one stanza only
Which is worth our ordering, John:
The names of days and months and years;
For this is measurement of the unique,
Of the abominable recantation,
The palinode that is our lives.

II

'Five years have passed, five summers,' or
'Sixty times the moon has wandered round the heavens':
The ancient poets knew the score:
How day is laid by side
Of day, like stars: rescinding
The spiking of a fulsome calendar.

III

We dined in splendor on the lawn,
Sunlight refracting greenish wormwood
Akvavit in glasses, on Baltic herrings.
The verdant sadness of the height

Of plangent summer: sylvan days beleaguered
In the *pankarpia* of souls.

IV

Now (five years later) I have put
My books in order. There always is a vaster
Section, spurning clarity, the keen division;
As in Robert Fludd, the teeming theatre
Of demons, thrones and powers is perched
On the dark Aleph where divisions are cast out.

V

Seated on this dark column, naming
Whatever creature raised at random,
We expunge ourselves, like the spry seed.
Obsequially bedded under ground,
It shocks our tardy minds with parables
Of reason, exiled, risen in the vastness.

VI

'As each new stage succeeds,
The older festivals are not abolished,'
Whispers another voice from Cambridge.
There is a perdu day in Sweden of St. Matthew
When youths with bears did wrestle, apposite
To our long *lack-lustre*, or quinquennial of want.

VII

You write of games and voyages and friends,
Turnings and crossings, to contain the void
That lies between the dreams and waking.
You write your cunning engram on the trail
Of time, to rout the beasts of history
With full sagacity and justice.

VIII

John, it is indeed your feast today,
St. Jean—the fete of hapless magic,
When language can be fashioned out of silence.
You write about your daughter's want and naming.
You name a house. I call it *economics*:
Your large, fair dreams of sharing and of roots.

IX

Do then the planets roam and turn
In your exorbing geocentric circles?
(Perhaps when demons rode them.)
They are the wanderers, strangers
To every house there is,
In all twelve houses of the zodiac.

X

You name a house. You name your honorable longings.
(Or, what Bob talked about—like Keats—
the staleness of the poet's life.)

There is in every haunted house in Suffolk
A spot which is so bitter cold because
it once drank thwarted love or murder.

XI

This is the true mouth of the Aleph.
In Britain now the jealous autochthonous gods
Have risen, fragging their *Themis* of the land,
Sacrificing for the sake of trite Boudiccas
The splendid loyalties of base mechanicals,
The distributive dreams and universal style.

XII

'Words have inside them no marrow!'
The re-born Wanderer sang,
'Although with ornaments resplendent!'
The Twice-born Borderer had answered:
'And when they came together to the house,
They ate and drank and day by day rejoiced.'

XIII

Words have no roots, nor proper names.
They are called up to fill the slots,
Insubstantial and gauche, as are the dead
With their orectic tongues, scratching at the table,
Galavanized and twitching like the frogs,
Wired to the work-bench of the sage.

XIV

Resist the stillness. Command

The darkness of our motor fantasies,

The listless whispering of inner voices.

Save the phenomena with demon festivals.

I order now this stanza to return to

Graves; there are no others.

XV: Threnos

There are so many stars and only twelve signs

There are so many days and only five feasts

Somebody remarked that the nights have no names, but nor have days,

only cyclical ciphers.

There is so little order.

It is not the loss of reality which is grieved for, it is

the sparseness of order.

The few named ones are just hostages of order.

Besides, they had no proper names, nor numbers, sitting round

the table, jury-fashion

Unclaimed signs, or star-ciphers, open like days? and cyclical…

Only, voyager, do not presume to think that

short-cuts are in any way privileged.

Only, fellow-traveller, do not think that *we* are.

Four

The Green-Ey'd Monster

> **i.** *She lov'd me for the dangers I had pass'd,*
> *and I lov'd her that she did pity them.*
>
> **ii.** *As if our hands, our sides, voices, and minds,*
> *had been incorporate.*
>
> **iii.** *In thy dumb action will I be as perfect*
> *As begging hermits in their holy prayers.*

I. The Mezzotint

Imagine a picture.

In an English countryhouse, Salop. or Derbyshire, Essex or Sussex possibly, upstairs in the gallery, to the left, between hunting engravings by Weenix and a sketch by Gainsbourough, 'Lady in the wood with two Pomeranians,' a mezzotint, of negligible artistic merit. You pass through the darkening galleries, at dusk, past modest rows of arms and armor, whispering *sallet, greaves, ambrace, gauntlet, quarrel, snaphance*. The print is there but impinged upon, by the house, by the windy park outside, the cawing of the rooks, it is a mezzotint, 15 by 10 inches, black frame, *(illegible) sculpsit*, scoured, harrowed by the hand, *manière noire* or English manner. It is the picture of a house, a manor-house, Salop. or Derbyshire possibly, not *this* manor-house, but similar. The pseudo-
> Grecian porticos, the mansard-windows closed.
>> But one casement-window stands, to the left, in the moonlight,
> slightly open.

> But this is not the picture. The picture was
> painted by the dark-eyed interloper, vendor of plaster figurines,

wares of Autolycos, free ladrone/improvisatore who, after having inveigled into the arms and favors of a hapless (downstairs) maid, having access to the kitchens and the larder, just had escaped though that window, facing woods and

    dark oblivion.

The picture is of an Italian villa on the bleak Dalmatian shore, a woman (his sister)

in the foreground, vacantly regarding

the iron billows of the Adriatic waters,

leaning on the gray granite, hands clasped

behind her, dreaming

of the handsome *giaour* corsair,

mustachioed, with cone-tipped hat and puttees

who killed her parents, raped her, abducted

her young brother for a ransom and left him

on an islet, for dead (shades of Böcklin!). She does not know

her brother has recovered, discovered and abandoned

painting, in Germany, Westphalia, where now

his masterpiece is housed in Folkwang, Hagen, and

at this very moment (when? time is indeterminate)

escaping through a window in Salop. (or Essex) with

four shillings sixpence and a half-eaten

leg of mutton, buttoning up his trouser flap.

But this is not the picture.
The picture is being painted far inside
the gray granite at a time indeterminate, by a
magician, some poor relation of Sarastro,
who in peaked turban and wide, star-spangled cloak (some soup stains)
is called to Frederick Barbarossa in the mountain.
He is now preparing, for the Eighth Centenary of Old Redbeard, a mandala

of Oriental opulence and splendor

straddling the world.

But this is not the picture.

The hardly perceptible spot (minestrone?) on the golden

Turtle's shell, just beneath the Eastern

foot of the blue elephant:

a speck:

this is the starship U.S.S. Enterprise bringing a suspect

mimeobionic, infraquarcine, microplane android artist to Starfleet Headquarters for questioning

by the Galactic Council.

His crime is Re-Creation of the Past,

and palinpoietic activities are, as every callow space cadet will know, punishable

by Eternal Life.

In six days he divided

light and darkness, sky and water,

named the turtle and the elephant,

built the granite, cooked the soup and spilled it

and raped the maiden,

spending the seventh wandering down the dusky galleries, whispering *intercalary*,

astrolabe, Sidereal, diapason, equinox, in that manor-house in Essex (or Salop.)
But this is still not the picture.

* * *

O precise pleasures of pedantry, ineluctable

routines of the imagination! It is the

sensuousness of the commonplace that breeds

philately, curling, Culbertson bridge

rather than ghosts;
yarrows talk auguries
ouija confidences
and orifices.
Indeed, this has nothing whatsoever to do with
the picture.
Imagine a child, lying in bed wide awake in the whey-
coloured light, looking
at the rustic tapestry, counting
the tines of the antlers of the heraldic stag emerging from the
woods, surrounded by does and fawns,
or seeing faces of people, to be met in life or not
in the russet damp-stains
on the ceiling, or thinking of
the frightening figure who has just disappeared from
the mezzotint, leaving the window ajar
with a dead child in its fleshless arms,
or of the little boy who decided to
stay in the walled in, wainscoted bed of the old, old
grandparents while the house
crackles with fire,
going behind the fusty draperies, into the pickled air of old age
as if into an upstairs gallery,
whispering *soup, sun, morning, prayer, breakfast, embrace;*
Or imagine two lovers who have long since ceased
to talk
to one another, or who will go on talking to them-
selves, whispering *quarrel, gauntlet, equinox, soon, same, graves.*

This is the same picture, the same

treasure-filled *Spelunca,*

darkness scratched from the dry copper plate.

Every conversation is inbetween these two,

not between the maiden and her ravisher, nor the child

and God, nor the artist and his shrunken world.

II. A. The Conversation: An Ode

1

So she says: 'The lambent disguise
of my future employer
is the case in point .'
And he would say: 'The cruellest
enemy
And I wander. endlessly forlorn,
evading
The obvious recompense
of the peat turf of my childhood.
Then I was an Irishman of the mind
relaying quarrelsome

2

murders in contumaciam.
Remember?
And I revere actors like John
Qualen, Andy Devine,
and pity poets (like the imitators of
Frank
O'Hara who invariably refer to The
Cinema. Which is, after all but a poor
substitute for Nature) Where
Wordsworth
would have hissed along the
polished ice,
or else, 'cut across the reflex of a star,'
benignly to forfeit the movements
of the ruse,

1

*A magician and a sorceress
vie in single combat. The
transformations begin. He
tests his weapon. (IIBc)*

3

naturally, she goes, where existence,

a mandible, belatedly, of Science,

chewing the fat with who knows how

numinous and tuberous a crowd,

laughs, uproariously, at an

opportunity of health

and variously dastard mulch,

foresworn

in innumerably wicked ways

to what I call in lucid moments

despicably voracious happiness.

4

That is how we have it plastered,

friend;

(and do not spurn that sobriquet!)

Maranatha admen split our world

in twain,

and for two short years I skated

down the wold,

sequacious to reason and to my eye;

how much I loved you and how

much

foray I rapaciously bestowed upon

myself

is quite beyond the point and

ludicrously connected with other

questions.'

5

'May this aduncity suffice; let
foregone conclusions
in antres vast beteach the
adumbrations
of the bizarre bananas of
intelligence,' he says,
'(indeed, as was observed by
Pantagruel:
'Que diable de langage est cecy?')
thus, harnessing clandestine
strategies,
in this world of blanc-mange,
I am looking for the crookedness,
the corners, in language and in
love.'

6	**6**
Then he says: 'I like to tell you	*He resorts to anamnesis. (IIBb)*
of Iamblichos, how he twice	
stepped into a spring and twice	
summoned a youth thereafter.	
One with golden hair called Eros,	
the other, darker, Anteros.	
They clung to him like children,	
like right and left. —'Better,' she	
says,	

       'Eunapius, he told that.

7

(Or else, of the leaping hare,
how she springs unto the fire,
and through it, singeing her back,
through crackling may and
brambles,
emerges as she goes, with one
enormous bound, homing
to her *form*, or home-hollow,
as does the poem, facing
its self-destruction, find its form,

8

'or, for that matter, any life or force –)'
So she adds: 'The curls of his
beard are wet, Glaucus, and white
as gushing fountains to the sight,
but the little god Palaemon,
sleeping
on a dolphin, is beardless
and suckling. The isthmus
is a recumbent demon. On the right
it has a youth, on the left are girls.

9

These are two seas, fair
and quite calm. The sacrifice
is in progress. Life seems a joke,
a cruel, grim joke. You are
a laughable incident, or a terrifying
one, as you happen to be

less powerful or more powerful
than some other form.
You are a comic little figure
hopping from the cradle to the
grave.'

10

And: 'Furthermore, I don't like
irony,'
she says, 'it indicates a small soul.'
'But metaphor,' he intervenes,
'however
politic, never slaked a dry throat?
To enjoy Caprona's romantic
suggestions
we must have water,'
'Succotash! Cumquats! 'he suddenly
ejaculates,
as W.C. Fields was, with some
justification, wont to remark.

11

The gravedigger with the gravelly
voice, yes,
in stronger moments I do identify
with the sage and his rage;
who, I say, is willing to look after
(all things being equal as they most
decidedly are)
the casualties of verandah,
or jacaranda, elmtrees dying

in the West Country, old men
flimflammed
out of their lingering lingam.

12

Hey, you (and naturally I mean
you)
greatgranddaughter to forfeits,
beldam of advice and underwear,
so you merchandised me
out of my life, inspiring
petty murders in the better circles
(how gracefully: you once
gobbled it up,
not the splinter, but the whole
bloody
ice-cold mirror)

13

For this poor right hand of mine
is left to tyrannise upon my breast
—farouche memento of its spiel!
simulating mascara-like *evoe*
(Yeux glauques: green stalagmites
of ocean floor,
verdant pools of peevish massacres)
in decking, speleologically,
with labyrinthine favors
any growth of fur one might
suspect,

13

*Political solutions are tested
and abandoned. (IIBd)*

14
as when *Dolomedes,* the intrepid fisherman and skater, with coal-black cuticle, majestically is striding cross the pond,
pushing his shadow like a wheelbarrow.
Often did I see him when a boy, on Scanian peat-pits,
contemplate his picture in acidulous dark waters,
which is a picture of some kind of quietism, no doubt,
part of my life, telling me half-truths,
      which are, after all, true, too.

15
How can you love a mirror-image?
How can you love anything else?
Such is the emptiness of enantiomorphs.
Is anybody happier, scanning,
radiant with sleep, time and time again,
    the same hand, like a zodiac
with equal emphasis to all twelve fingers,
spelling out the alphabet of simulacra
to the biosphere? O romance

16

of the gravity-defying leap when in

exalted *Stimmung* belabours with

might *fa belle baleine*

the oil-stained ocean and, emerging

al fresco and full length to view

above the eldritch image of its

taunting paramour,

meets the refracting spectral

gleanings of its

colloid hue; confirming thus its

habit of

mating not a tergo but,

like Narcissus, frontally.

17

'Jealousy is the delirium of signs,

at least according to Gilles Deleuze,'

he says,

'how much more debris then in the

other green-eyed

vituperative blandishments which

have learned

to eat, Catullus-fashion, their own

organs.

Left-handed electron meet right-

handed amino-acid: is called life,

an extension of the right hand,

like the Nuer spear.'

18

'I am sorry to interrupt your masturbatory
fantasies:
Nuer spears indeed!' she retorts.
'May I remind you that Deleuze speaks of
aggression against the self
answer to Evans-Pritchard's allegations)
    which ensures, fastidiously
and blandly, the mere refusal of
    everything. But the blunt
    feeling of irreparable

19

loss, the yearning for one's lost loved ones,
the numbness of social injustice,
the irrevocable pain of past happiness
in the present; those are the real
transmigrations and not this
paltry transmogrifactioning;
for solace please reflect on how Loki
in venom-induced convulsions,
    remembered the feeling

18

She enters into eschatological detail. (IIBa)

20

of how to be salmon, and,
sequestered
in some icy cataract,
endure the slackening of mighty
muscles, the dimming of his eye,
the loss of teeth, the shaping of his
jaw
into that humiliating hook of age,
knowing that he never would reach
the looming estuary. So you never
    shall, or could, catch me.'

21

'It is not so much,' he says, 'in
personal terms
that I believe in vampires
(I'd rather believe in the pelican
whose blood siphons off to its
nearest)
but the fantasies of colonialism are
rife with creatures
winging the night with streaks
of darkness; an aide-mémoire
in how to use the fustian
in writing: sparingly.

22

Yes, magic is equity, necromancy
national independence,
autochthonomy.
My wife not a vampire, not a poor
harassed creature doomed
to terrible woe, but a splendid
woman, brave beyond belief,
patriotic in a way which has
but few peers even in the
wide history of bravery!

23

No wonder that she could find
   a way to the battlements
mysterious to everybody else!
   As she is a real woman, she is
in greater danger then ever in the
   hands of Turkish ruffians.
Life-long misery and despair
   must be the lot of a Christian
   woman.
   She must be rescued – and
quickly!"

23

*Political solutions are
once more abandoned for
scatological detail. (IIBe)*

24

"Consider instead," she muses
dreamily,

"the pallor of the ptarmigan, or of

the streaking cotton-tail of the hare,

running errands for the shrivelled

crone. Magic is equity, yes, but
milk-wise,

white as her talented hair or

the stolen sticks in her apron,
insurance

against the tabernacle weight of

humdrum charity.

25

"No," she resumes, "I do not like it,
    this studied innocence, this
    wearing

of an 'I was a teenage werewolf' —
badge

    on the sleeve of a mouldy shroud.

That innocence smacks of
insouciance.

    Ah, this is what the poem tells
    you:

Can't we get a laugh out of shroud?

    She came shivering, looking for
    a fire

and found a dressing-gown.

26

Instead of food, what is sent to stangers is

pictures of food, XENIA.

The hare in his cage is the prey

of the net, and he sits on his haunches

moving his forelegs a little and slowly

lifting his ears, but he also

keeps looking with both his eyes

and tries to see behind him as well,

so suspicious

27

is he, and always cowering with fear;

the second hare hangs

on the bare oak tree, his belly

laid wide open and his skin

stripped off over his hind feet.

In a bed in her cottage the old woman

is dead, from hypothermia, or abdominal

cancer, or hunger: she has tried to chew

the white whittles off her firewood."

26

She deflects from her time loop.
(IIBf)

28

First now he says: "Lansdale,
CIA Intelligence officer of the
Philippines,
most ingeniously used psywar
methods
against the Huk insurgency:
he had his men catch a *guerrillero,*
puncture him and drain him,
hanging from a tree. The blame
was then
on a local vampire, an *asuang.*
Like a dank breadfruit from a tree."

29

And a little further on: 'My friend
who had been a naval petty officer,
told me a better story: once in
the Philippines he had done a band
of Huks
a good turn. They came to him, in
the evening,
saying in soft Tagalog lisp: 'Hey,
senor,'
you done us big *favor.* Is there
anything we possibly
could do for you,

28

First now he says: 'Lansdale,
CIA Intelligence officer of
the Philippines,
most ingeniously used
psywar methods
against the Huk insurgency:
he had his men catch a
guerrillero,
puncture him and drain
him,
hanging from a tree. The
blame was then
on a local vampire, an
asuang.
Like a dank breadfruit from
a tree.'

30

mister? Anybody we could kill
for you, a superior or sweetheart,
no?'
And that really puts the lid on the
question:
is not every true poem reading
like the ruined phrases of
endearment
at the end of a relationship or life:
'You are killing me, lady,'
'My heart bleeds for you,'
and 'Thanks for nothing, lover boy!'

30

*Cycle completed. Hostilities
resumed almost immediately.
(IIBg)*

II. B. A Dream, A Memory, A Text
Translated From Memory, Another Dream, Two Recursive Devices. Concluding Anecdote

a. A Dream

In Southern Sweden where the sky is wider but the day is smaller (than in pretty parklike England) I found myself one morning at that chill hour when the owls have stopped their hooting and the birds not yet commenced their singing on a huge estate walking with my (then) love past the derelict cottages of tenant-farmers in the back of parks and gardens. A younger woman in an apron, hands akimbo looked out through the door almost rotten hanging on one hinge; over her shoulder we could see an older woman, an immensely old and shrivelled creature, born before the Flood it seemed in the absolutely bare room sitting motionless on a high stool. Her eyes were closed. A voice, belonging to neither of them, was saying:

Gack till de nidhra tecknen

och kallom opp de undre vecken!

which means in slightly ancient Swedish more or less: 'Go to the lower signs, and let us call up the subterranean undulations. 'My companion went past the younger woman and, almost gracefully, pushed the old crone over. I tried to stop her. We went out: the morning was as crisp as glass. I looked into her green eyes: the world had ended.

b. A Memory

When my granduncle was a boy, also in Southern Sweden, he was working as a sheepherder. His dog was called Pædo. One evening, when on his way home, he met with two very small men standing by the roadside. They looked at him and said, with utmost seriousness: 'Dagen är förliden oeh natten tillstundar,' translated: 'The day has gone by, the night is nigh.' They wore peaked helmets, like Bismarck, slighty frayed. Faintly, they smelled of pickled herrings; their eyes were invisible.

c

Fulle exerptis ot the Tryal, examinynge & Executionn of ane Johanne Andirsdother, a Witch, at the Forum Judiciarum Malmogiensis, *or the Assizes there, in the yere of Our Savior* **MDLXXXVIII,** *in Inglis transl.*

—ITem, *ye saide giudwyfe Johanne, bein arraignit at the Assizes on various Testimonies forasmuch as schee tuke in hand tae helpynge those sairelie aggreivid & sufferyng with Sicknesse and Infirmitie & prepairynge Potions & Ffiltres for thos panit by Lufe vnrequitet, wars accuseth by ane Mogins, a youngcarle, ane orra lad and a Tinkler, og maleficia, quaha wars unco inamourit of ain Judith Hansdotr, a queanie of Alberta parishe quha nae abidith him. Ye Saide Guidwyffe Johanne had gefan himm a Locke of haire in Pretense it came of the heid of saim queenie Judith, ilkamorn to mixit inta hiss bros or Denner, But (quodh hee) qervpon hee hadde Lost his Powre of Manhuid. Said mogens thervpon seekit advyce & Succor of ye Weelkennit Boye of N. Aasum, a cannie man & auld, frae quha he learnit he bee beglaumit and For spake.*

—ITem, *the saide Johanne quod I was ganging furth frae markit in urbe Malmogiae in simmer at Whytesunnetide ooten East Tolbothies shee met aforesaide Mogens acomin ore a Style hee caim vp tae her an liftit her Kirtel & sark. I wars nae afered thoo he lukit ferefui an Sweety. I thocht he was oer keisty & wishedh his wille wyghed mee, awthocgh me bee ane auld carline an mawkinhaunchit. He anelie pluckit twa hairies frae me Priuadys, neer tooching mee quihim lippis afore he slenkit awa.*

—ITem, *Ye Saide guidewiffe was examynid as to quaar her Maistere, war, an wyth Pilli Winkies vpon her fingers quid is greevous tortvre, an schee tolde her guidman was deid and her bairn ill an her kyne deid, & she was make and hevye sair dule wyth hirself qhen shee met ane honest, wele, elderlie man, gray bairdit, and had ane gray Coitt with Lumbart slevis of ye auld fassoun; ane pair of gray brekis and quhyte schankis gartanit abone the kne ane blak bonet on his heid cloise behind and plane befoire, with silkin laissis drawin throw the lippiis thairof; and ane quhyte wand in his hand, and ane blak buik. He said he wars the Archebiscoppe Absolon and hadde come frae his Antres or Spelunkerhame on Yvey in the loch queher he hadde bee brocht by the Elphis levande neathe the Muckle Stane near Liungby. With him hee bracht iij Servant Spiriti or Familiares, a Merle blacke wyth quhite wingis ane Mawkin, and a Blacke Puddie quho weren to serue hir ilka quhim & licke ye Priuy Parties of Her bodie. Aforesaid Johannem confessit & fylit she was* conuicta et combusta fuit in Anno Dominie 1588 *feftane ochtye ocht on the Mounte of Executioun at Kiersebierghedh in cruelle paine quhill she gaiv hir ghaist leafande her the iij Familiares, l:mo ye blak Merle, secondo ye Toade, Third and laist the Maukin aspringande outen the Pyre.*

Synchronicity, the memory-trace engulfs everything, annals of suffering and effluence, focus on two discrete points of geography. Desk-memories of Mogens Madsen's Ciceronian periods: names of Rutger MacLean, Malcolm Sinclair, frigidaire nighmares of three mercenaries burning and lost on Swedish ice; Bothwell's trace of pacing length of table in Eric of Pomerania's fortress: he could have seen the reek of his desire: the burning of the witch. North-facing City, sequestered like any northern town between gasworks and canals, tethered to the cemetery: child watching sky-written letter of blood across the wake of père Ubu escaping, Hamlet haggling over the price of drugs with pirates or William Burroughs. Reich, the other Wilhelm, in his *Wanderjahre* commuting for nine months, before rebirth. As she said, in the sweet transport of burning on Cherry Mountain, haunted by the prevenant wraith of Anita Ekberg returning to nativity, echoing the fortunate fall of Melville's ghostly sailor, from the tallest tree of the sea:

Oh ffilme... that bluidy ffilm before me eyen.

d. Another Dream

I was dreaming of Robben Island
that the inhabitants were,
somewhat like centaurs
half man, half sheep,
expertly stitched together
with South African skills
in grafting and immunology.
One man showed me with pride
his honorable scars
his record collection
(mostly bad)
and the little anus
in his left side.
Naturally, he was pissed off
with being forced
to give up the dietary
habits of sheep.
Due to the shortness
of the alimentary canal,
he was now training
to become a predator and insectivore.
I hate bugs, he confided,
and in particular the crunching
sounds they make, between molars.

e

The Lyndon Baines Johnson Lavatory Seat Refurbishing Rightwinding Leftbranching Recursive Selfperpetuating Paradox Memorial

Here I sit thinking: Aw, shit, think how great our country is.

Here I sit, scratching my ass, thinking: Aw, shit, think how great our country is.

Here I sit, smoking some grass, scratching my ass, thinking: Aw, shit, think how great our country is.

Here I sit, sticking my middle in, smoking some grass, scratching my ass, thinking: Aw, shit, think how great our country is.

Here I sit, farting through my ring, sticking my middle in, smoking some grass, scratching my ass, thinking: Aw, shit, think how great our country is.

Here I sit, flexing my prick, farting through my ring, sticking my middle in, smoking some grass, scratching my ass, thinking: Aw, shit, think how great our country is.

Here I sit, sucking my stick, flexing my prick, farting through my ring, sticking my middle in, smoking some grass, scratching my ass, thinking, Aw, shit, think how great our country is.

Here I sit, blowing my horn, sucking my stick, flexing my prick, farting through my ring, sticking my middle in, smoking some grass, scratching my ass, thinking: Aw, shit, think how great our country is.

Here I sit, bridging a loan, blowing my horn, sucking my stick, flexing my prick, farting through my ring, sticking my middle in, smoking some grass, scratching my ass, thinking: Aw, shit, think how great our country is.

Here I sit, entertaining a friend, bridging a loan, blowing my horn, sucking my stick, flexing my prick, farting through my ring, sticking my middle in, smoking some grass, scratching my ass, thinking: Aw, shit, think how great our country is.

Here I sit, waiting for the end, entertaining a friend, bridging a loan, blowing my horn, sucking my stick, flexing my prick, farting through my ring, sticking my middle in, smoking some grass, scratching my ass, thinking: Aw, shit, think how great our country is.

f. In Freedonia

with apologies to Professor Quine

In Freedonia all men are free. Rarely is a capital sentence being pronounced, more rarely still is the punishment ever carried out. The reason for this is as follows.

It is deemed inequitous to inform the prisoner of the exact time of his impending demise. But it is considered equally unjust to let the poor wretch sweat it out for an unspecified number of days. Therefore, when pronouncing sentence, it behooves the judge to give a fixed terminal date for the period within which the culprit can be executed, e.g. -given sentence is pronounced on a Monday—'before next Sunday.' The prisoner then knows that he cannot be executed on that Sunday. But he can also rest assured that the execution cannot take place on the preceding Saturday, as he then would not be ignorant of its date, having survived all the preceding days of the week. When he realizes, however, that this is the case, it is equally impossible to carry out the sentence on the preceding Friday. Come Thursday he is already alerted to the fact that any execution is out of the question for Friday, Saturday or Sunday: he can spend that day in happy contemplation of his safety. If it is further taken into consideration that he on Wednesday must fully realize the impossibility of using any of the days Thursday, Friday, Saturday or Sunday as day of execution, he is clearly in no danger on that day. Again, considering his awareness of the necessary exclusion, for purposes of hanging, beheading, strangulation, garotting etc., of the entire week from Wednesday on, the omitting of Tuesday from the list of possible dates is already a matter of routine. He then knows that he must be executed on the Monday itself, but this knowledge is evidently contravening the intention of the law. Consequently, the prisoner is safe.

When last sojourning on the bench of the accused, I conveyed this argument in identical or similar terms, to the judge. The result was unexpected. 'Then, by all means, let's have it over with right now, while you still think you are safe,' he said, carefully refraining from looking into my eyes.

g. That's All, Folks!

with apologies to Myles na Gopaleen

When falling on bad times financially, which frequently happened, Keats and Chapman were wont to help out in the kitchen of a well-known Tottenham Court Road inn, called 'The House of the Rising Sun.' One day, when arriving at the establishment just before tea-time they were surprised to find the chef, a sturdy German lad in a terribly agitated state over his dinner preparations. 'Look here, fellows,' he hailed them, 'I have mislaid yesterday's remains of *nasi goreng*; be sports and try and find them for me: I cannot leave the parboiling of the rollmops unattended, as you doubtless perceive, 'They gladly complied, looking everywhere for the missing victuals. Finally, in despair, Keats exclaimed, not without emotion: 'Indeed, I know where the "House of the Rising Sun" is situated, but where, oh where, is the Rice of the Sousing Hun? 'Overcome by the enormity of this utterance, Chapman reeled backwards and fell into a trough of Friesian coleslaw, where he was granted a speedy and merciful release from the shackles of human existence. Thus ended a beautiful friendship.

III. The Zodiac Of Life

'Lord Saturn is a dry, cold and dexterous king
only fit for hanging or burying alive,
or, perhaps, for dancing. Old
age is elaborate and dumb.

A *carmen saliarum* hurts my head;
feet and hands drumming, stamping:
'Round and around and around
we go. Sow your seed under ground.
We are raking the fallow…'

The cruellest thing you did,
Hartgrepa, was throwing a strangled
cockerel over the wall.
I could hear it crowing…:
'The little animals follow me
everywhere: they importune me,
they enter through my eyes, my skull
and bring with them of their anxiety. Close
your eyes, O soul! let us absent ourselves
from all things, so that we are seen
no more, nor can see them.'

* * *

Inside the mountain dwell the paladins
of pain: Ogier le Danois, Frederick Barbarossa,
Arthur, Charles XII, Durandarte…
all of them seated round the table,
beards and hair growing like tendrils.

I saw royal children playing,
armies clash, and clearly heard
from the other side of the enormous
wall a wasted cockerel crow.
They all seemed to be saying:
'We were here long before you,
we are not awakened yet!'
The hebephrenic girl, barefoot,
with grimy legs and glittering eye,
the paranoid mutterers, the stony-faced
depressives, the catatonic old man,
contriving his own crucifixion,
they are all there, in silence,
but yet saying: there is pain here,
but more pain in being wakened
and remembering. They are the
houses, the little animals of cunning
wherein our lives, the wandering
planets, move, interpreting signs
which are not their own. These dragomans
inculcate, unwillingly, like the
dead trapper in the hut, the devious
truths of time and all times. They
court the *sparagmos* when round-
faced Titans, their features stiff with
gypsum, tear them limb from limb.
They are the emblems of their
own silence, of the thoughts that never
were, and never can be, uttered.

* * *

The woman who rose from the hearth,
was it you, Hartgrepa, fostermother,
nurse, more to me than lover?
Enveloping me in your cloak, as
you had borne me many times as a child
on giant arms, binding me here in the
earth, my skull shaven and tarred
to mimic the stones of the turf.
Do you remember the time when
we came to the deserted house
—no food, no furniture, just
the skins of small animals—
where we found the body
of a man long since dead?

You sang your sullen runes,
dancing in the rank smell of furs,
stuffing herbs under his rotting tongue.
Slowly it rose, stiffly prophesying
the end of all things, us in particular,
Were you prepared for the monstrous
hand that you held while I
hacked it off with my sword?
Were you prepared for the
invisible hands of your nearest...?

The little animals are posted
in my head, an antonymic sphere,
charred island in the green sward.
It is an orrery of stealthy

motion, like a nesting-place
under a bullock's hide,
a head concealed in the Trappist
monastery of the mind.
The cave of Montesinos,
the head of Madame de Montbason.
It was your head, Hartgrepa,
torn from your shoulders by the
invisible hands of your kinfolk,
as the limbs were torn from the soft
body of the child watching its face
in the mirror. It was your cloak
enveloping the child in the fire,
like a bullock's hide covering
the two dead bodies, shining,
and between them the child,
their grandchild, with only one
finger charred, having said:
'I want to be with my grandparents!'
while the clasp of the cloak is
wrought in solid brass, not an
ouroboros, the scaly serpent
biting its own tail, but a snake
with two fierce heads, an *amphisbaina*
signifying the openness and pain
at both end and beginning (although
it's hard to know which is which)
This clasp is fastened to a torque
with plates where the golden eagle

spreads its wings, of jasper, and of
pale selenite (the fading stone,
geared to the phases of the moon)

Where the two brazen heads
of the serpent come together
—mouths yawning wide over
the eagle—peering with ruby eyes
unto a sea of grass-green
emerald containing all the
denizens of the deep: dolphins,
fish, whales and crustaceans:
not least crustaceans, like
the trusty crab, the lively shrimp,
prim prawns and the majestic lobster.
This is the necklace of Harmonia.

* * *

Both brazen heads will say, in turn:
'I claim divining space and hallow ground
where I have duly named them with meet tongue.
Whichever tree is good and true which I
declare to have pronounced, to the right
divining space and ground belong to me'; and the other:
'I claim divining space and hallow ground
where I have duly named them with meet tongue.
Whichever tree is good and true which I
declare to have pronounced, to the left
divining space and ground belong to me.' I asked
the heads to read my thoughts and future.
The Left replied: 'Of thoughts I have no knowledge.'

The Right: 'Thou knowest who thou art.'
I knew that one of them was lying,
so I said: 'Answer me truly this:
is it the other head which is lying?'
They both said: Yes. And next:

'Is the right head lying?' Left
said: Yes, and Right said: No. 'Is
the Left Head lying?' Right: Yes
and Left: 'No, I mean… No!'
Again: 'Do both heads lie?' The
Right said No, Left: 'No, Yes… I am sorry.'
I looked at my hands, they had been
chopped off, and I had no more questions.
There were no tines of antlers to be
counted: no harts, and leaping does,
nor rust-coloured spotted fawns. The woods
were like the tapestry, two empty hands
clutching each other, writhing worms.
As I walked away, the heads were saying:
'Fare-thee-well, *hidalgo*. We know who thou art,
from thy sorrowful contenance. Thy fate
is writ in a book whereof we know the ending.'
I wish they had been more forthcoming,
especially the lying head
who is the more sincere.

* * *

The *ekphrasis* is, as always,
pertinent. It is comforting to talk
of the sea when one is born to be hanged,

as it is to wash the gypsum off one's face,
or to be buried in cool earth, or fall.
The *phalarae,* or little reckless monuments
of words are shining bright, but words have
no *medulla.* Or, to misquote Dr.
Samuel Johnson, to be hanged elongates
one's spine most wonderfully. Inside words

there are dwarfs within our Giants cloaths,
but no Degree is vizarded, no little animals,
just a monster mocking the meat it feeds on,
green-eyed, or whey-faced like a corpse.
Everything else is in your head, just like
the crab inside its shell, the dead
in the earth, time in its moment.

* * *

There is something right down
sexually attractive in the Jungian
way of confronting one's own
anima (which should be you,
and also, through you, me)
but the experience is a little
like the feeling a cynical
poet might be subjected to
after having concluded a bio-
graphy of one of the lesser saints,
or, when a comedian has
so perfected a double act
that he knows it can survive
entirely on the strength of

the straight man and doesn't need
the funny man (i.e. himself)
Yes, perhaps more like the comedian.
The poet may be more ardently content
with homilies. My song is
soon to end, but don't mistake
my placid tone for equanimity.
Most of all it is itself
a metaphor, in which the
vehicle is missing but the
tenor, in wonderful belcanto warblings
goes on and on and on. *Encore, da capo:*
'The little animals follow me
everywhere: they importune me,
they enter through my eyes, my skull
and bring with them of their anxiety. Close
your eyes, o soul! let us absent ourselves
from all things, so that we are seen
no more, nor can see them.'

The voice stops. The earth continues to fall
like the first snow of winter, filling the space
filling his mouth, his eyes, silently
save for the faint sound of dancing feet
growing stronger and stronger as in a film
exposing its rhythm and gaining momentum
in this new rhythm, thousands of feet
tapping, finally to lose itself
in the scream of a falling woman...
Sleep tight, baby...

Select Bibliography of Works by Göran Printz-Påhlson

Books of Criticism

Solen i spegeln [*The Sun in the Mirror*]. Stockholm: Bonniers, 1958.
Appendix till Solen i spegeln [*Appendix to The Sun in the Mirror*]. Lund: Cavefors, 1960.
Förtroendekrisen [*Crisis of Confidence*]. Stockholm: Cavefors, 1971.
Slutna världar öppen rymd [*Closed Worlds Open Space*]. Stockholm: Cavefors, 1971.

Books of Poetry

Resan mellan poesi och poesi [*The Journey Between Poetry and Poetry*]. Malmö: Image, 1955.
Dikter för ett barn i vår tid [*Poems for a Child of our Time*]. Stockholm, Bonniers: 1956.
Gradiva och andra dikter [*Gradiva and Other Poems*]. Stockholm: Bonniers, 1966.
The Green-Ey'd Monster. New York: Bryn Mawr—Kivik: CCRI, 1981.
Säg minns du skeppet Refanut? [*Remember the Ship Refanut?*] Stockholm: Bonniers, 1984.

Major Articles

'Krukan och bitarna I: Strindberg och 1800-talets romantradition' ['The Pitcher and the Pieces I: Strindberg and the Tradition of the Nineteenth-Century Novel']. *Bonniers litterära magasin* 33:10 (1964): 740–55.
'The Liar: The Paradox of Fictional Communication in Martin A. Hansen.' *Scandinavian Studies* 36:4 (1964): 263–80.
'Krukan och bitarna II: vad händer i *Röda rummet?*' ['The Pitcher and the Pieces II: What Happens in *Röda Rummet?*']. *Bonniers litterära magasin* 34:1 (1965): 12–27.

'Concepts of Criticism in Scandinavia, 1960–1966.' *Scandinavica* 6:1 (May 1967): 1–15.
'Concepts of Criticism in Scandinavia 1966–1967.' *Scandinavica* 7:1 (May 1968): 1–15
'Tankens genvägar om Strindbergs antropologi' ['The Short-cuts of Thought: On Strindberg's Anthropology']. *Bonniers litterära magasin* 38: 4 (1969): 594–610.
'Strindberg och totemism' ['Strindberg and Totemism']. *Konstrevy* 4 (1969): 154–160.
'Realism as Negation.' *Literature and Reality: Creatio vs. Mimesis*, Ed. by Alex Bolckmans. Ghent: Seminarie voor Skandinavistiek, 1977: 133–47.
'The Canon of Literary Modernism: A Note on Abstraction in the Poetry of Erik Lindegren.' *Comparative Criticism: A Yearbook* vol. 1. Ed. by Elinor Shaffer. Cambridge: Cambridge University Press, 1979: 155–66.
'Tranströmer and Tradition.' *Ironwood* 13:7 (1979): 62–80.
'Allegories of Trivialization: Strindberg's View of History.' *Comparative Criticism: A Yearbook* vol. 3. Ed. by Elinor Shaffer. Cambridge: Cambridge University Press, 1981: 221–56.
'The Scandinavian Ideology: Towards a Mythology of Modernism.' *Facets of European Modernism*. Ed. by Janet Garton. Norwich: University of East Anglia Press, 1985: 219–41.
'Surface and Accident: The Poetry of John Ashbery.' *PN Review* 12:2 (November–December, 1985): 34–36.
'The Invention of Scandinavia.' *Scandinavian Literature in a Transcultural Context*. Ed. by Sven H. Rossel and Birgitta Steene. Seattle: University of Washington Press, 1986: 10–18.
'Historical Drama and Historical Fiction: The Example of Strindberg.' *Scandinavian Studies* 62:1 (Winter 1990): 24–38
'Passions and Interests: Anthropological Observation in the Short Story.' *Strindberg and Genre*. Ed. by Michael Robinson. Norwich: Norvik Press, 1991: 61–81.
'Rosmersholm as Novel, as Film: Passion as Action.' *Contemporary Approaches to Ibsen* vol. 7. Ed. by Bjørn Hemmer and Vigdis Ystad. Oslo: Norwegian University Press, 1991: 185–203.

Major Translations into Swedish

Åtta engelska poeter [*Eight English Poets*]. With Petter Bergman. Stockholm: FIB:s Lyrikklubb, 1957.

Räkna ditt hjärtas slag [*Count Your Heartbeats*]. With Göran Bengtson. Lund: Cavefors, 1959.

Självporträtt i en konvex spegel [*Self Portrait in a Convex Mirror*]. By John Ashbery. Stockholm: Bonniers, 1983.

Bathory & Lermontov [*Batory & Lermontov*]. By John Matthias. With Jan Östergren. Ahus: Kalejdoskop, 1980.

Färdväg [*Itinerary*]. With Jan Östergren. Stockholm: Fib:s Lyrikklub, 1990.

Major Translations into English

Contemporary Swedish Poetry. With John Matthias. London: Anvil, 1980.

Rainmaker. By Jan Östergren. With John Matthias. Athens, Ohio: Ohio University Press, 1983.

A Note on the Text

The essays of 'The Words of the Tribe' have never before been published, and are based on a series of lectures presented at the University of Notre Dame in 1984. Printz-Påhlson's manuscripts for the lectures contained some irregularities of style and punctuation that have here been corrected. The alert reader may notice some anachronisms in the list of works cited appended to each essay: editions of some works come from a period after the lectures were given. No bibliographic information appeared in the manuscripts, and I have chosen to cite editions readily available to the contemporary reader where they are consistent with the versions of texts quoted by Printz-Påhlson.

This book does not end here...

At Open Book Publishers, we are changing the nature of the traditional academic book. The title you have just read will not be left on a library shelf, but will be accessed online by hundreds of readers each month across the globe. We make all our books free to read online so that students, researchers and members of the public who can't afford a printed edition can still have access to the same ideas as you.

Our digital publishing model also allows us to produce online supplementary material, including extra chapters, reviews, links and other digital resources. Find *Letters of Blood* on our website to access its online extras. Please check this page regularly for ongoing updates, and join the conversation by leaving your own comments:

http://www.openbookpublishers.com/product.php/86

If you enjoyed the book you have just read, and feel that research like this should be available to all readers, regardless of their income, please think about donating to us. Our company is run entirely by academics, and our publishing decisions are based on intellectual merit and public value rather than on commercial viability. We do not operate for profit and all donations, as with all other revenue we generate, will be used to finance new Open Access publications.

For further information about what we do, how to donate to OBP, additional digital material related to our titles or to order our books, please visit our website.

OpenBook Publishers

Knowledge is for sharing